THE HEDONIST

BOOK I
Second edition, revised and augmented

JP GOFFINGS

The Hedonist

ISBN - 1456338641
ISBN13 – 9781456338640

You can purchase or comment on this work at the author's email: goffings@hotmail.com

Hedonism: Theory which makes the pursuit of pleasure
the main goal of life.
Hedonist: Adept of this philosophy
Merriam Webster´s Dictionary

" I cannot do anything for those
who do not ask questions "
Confucius

"I have an irresistible natural tendency
to give into the things I like"
Don Juan

The immortality of the soul exists
Because millions of people believe in it.
These are the same people who believed
That the earth was flat
Mark Twain

Science is capable of unforeseeable improvement
A religious concept of the world is not
If these concepts are wrong
They will remain wrong forever
S. Freud

The man who is going to tell the truth
Should have his fastest horse saddled and close by
Arabian proverb

Homage to Michel Onfray and Eduardo del Rio

Thanks to: Paule, lifetime companion, organizer, source of encouragement, provider.
Marisela: who had the good idea to push me to write, which I would never have done without her.
Annie; source of encouragement and provider.
My good friends and pre-readers: José, Patricia, Evelyne, Angel, Enna, Luis, Clothilde, Dany, Pamela, Gabriela, Juan, George, Carlos, Mariana, Patrick, Sally, Victoria, Guadalupe, Jorge, Adrian (and his whole family), Hervé and Sébastien (sons), Stefania, Jermina, Denise (sister), Mia (also sister), Dave, Alex, Eduardo, Sergio, Rosario, Patricia, Silvia, Dacha, Philippe, Sylvie, Chanona, Edelio, Jean-Louis, Manuel, Alvaro.
Special thanks to Marcela Reyley.

NOTE FROM THE AUTHOR

Belgium, Upper Volta, Nigeria, Ivory Coast, the United States, France, Mali, Cuba, Chile, Chad, the Congo and Mexico are some of the places I am going to take you to... you'll meet people and civilizations different from yours and from you. You will experience that it is not the geography that is covered which liberates, but the voyage in your values and beliefs.

Hedonism is made up of values and ideas which question all other ways of behavior and beliefs. Great - since without questioning we'd go back to nothingness, where we come from, only having been another social security number.

Supporter of pleasure, all pleasures that life and our body can procure, here and now, Hedonism is as old as awareness is. It always was and always will be, because it embraces nature, regardless of all the obstacles and killjoys along the way, since Plato and Paul to Benedict XVI, passing through Rah, Mohamed and many more. Hedonism is a way of living which does not prosper on the unhappiness of the others.

Campeche, Peninsula of Yucatan, fall 2010.

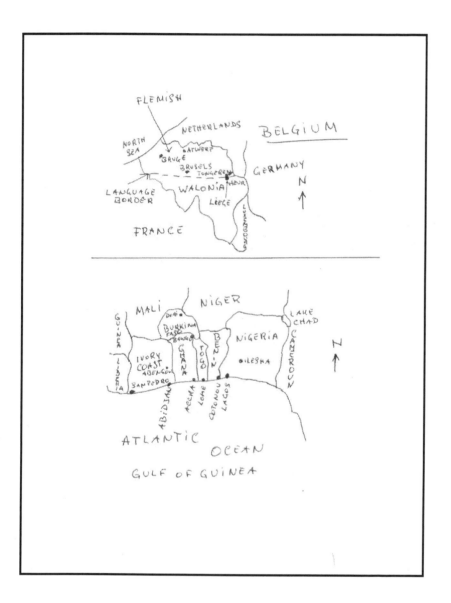

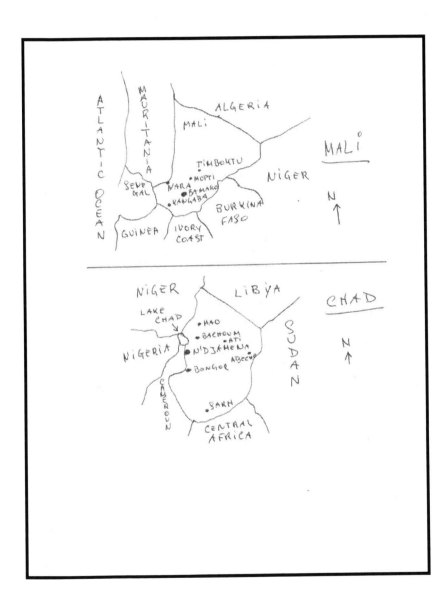

The Hedonist

THE HEDONIST
BOOK I

INTRODUCTION

Jean Pierre Louis Marie Goffings was born in the night of "Saint John of the summer", the night when witches and marlins jamboree and party, in the year 1943. I know so: I was there, because that's me. The place which witnessed this biological accident was a small village of just 180 human voting elements. Of which two were teachers, four bartenders, one priest and one blacksmith who, in those days, mainly fixed horseshoes. This blacksmith, a tall man wearing large moustaches like the Gallic chiefs, occasionally was our dentist, managing clove oil and pincers with mastership, while whispering some...who knows what. He also played the big bourdon in the village band. I am telling you that because this village was a real village, with medical services, a mayor, a town council, a football team, a band and even a theatre group. Who every winter made us weep with the same story: A farmer sold his soul to the devil for a bigger barn and ended up, with the help of the priest and his wife, regaining his soul but losing his life in the process. We all wept for weeks.

The people from Diets-Heur belong to the Flemish ethnic group of the country which is still called the Kingdom of Belgium. But tomorrow it could be named anything. Since, for cultural and money reasons, the place is disintegrating.

Years after it happened, they told me that I was born in a cave. It's not a big deal, since in this village there are plenty of them. Excavated in the soft chalky rock that runs along the only village street on the left side, the peasants used them as refrigerators before there were refrigerators, to store milk, potatoes, apples, butter and even the Sunday afternoon pie. They said that my mother, like all the people in the village, used to hide in the caves seeking protection from the bombs the Allies dropped there every time that the Nazi flak was too active on the other side of the river Meuse, which was also the German border, just two dozen miles away. So, for not having to fly back to England with a plane full of bombs, the pilots preferred to drop them there. If I had been a Word War Two bomber pilot, I might have done the same thing, probably.

So, I was born in a cave. I can imagine it: among apples and pears, potatoes and milk jars. Many years later, after having lived in places like the Sahel, Ivory Coast, Congo and the Nigerian rain forests, close to the Escambray mountains in Cuba, in Bowling green Virginia, amongst the Mapuches in Chile, in Paris, Washington, Berkeley, Cannes, Havana and even in Carmen city in the Yucatan Peninsula, Diets-Heur is not a bad place to be born, even if my parents were among the poorest people of a village where not everybody was poor.

Today I live and write in the Mexican Spanish colonial town of Campeche, on the shores of the Gulf of Mexico and I am sixty five years old. Psychologically and socially speaking, Campeche and Heur (as we call it) have many things in common. So, Campeche is not too much of a culture shock.

Completely new to the art of writing I do have to tell this story in the first person form before my last neurons have washed away. I am just not good enough to invent personalities to hide behind in a novelistic way. I could have written in other languages but I am writing in English because I like that tongue.

Why am I doing this, since I am convinced that everything has already been written, who knows? Maybe for my children, so that they discover how this all happened. Maybe so that my friends have a good time, although I suppose this is somewhat presumptuous. Maybe just because it is life, a piece of eternity we spend together.

It is probably true that, as in all stories written by the winners (and we all are winners since once we were the fasted spermatozoid of the whole gang), I am giving myself the beautiful role and what follows looks better than it really was? What I do know, is that I am going to be honest with you. By Jove, I will.

CHAPTER I
FROM HEUR TO OUAGADOUGOU

Through the bathroom window, which is just a moveable board in this wooden cabin, soaped from hair to toes, I watch how "the muchachos" anchor our small 25 feet boat on the beach, prow seawards. It's not an easy maneuver. One needs some experience to get as close as possible to the shore so as not to sink to the waist in the mud and an always somewhat dirty water. Because of the current, passing Punta Xen, which deposits all kind of dirt composed of who knows what bacteria in the Ensenada Bay, it's not easy to throw the anchor at the right distance. I admire their seamanship and experience. Great.

For all the time I have been a sea farmer entrepreneur, I have always been reluctant to call the people I am working with "employees". To me the connotation of "employees" is pejorative, too close to: servant, domestic and slave. That's why I call them "muchachos". Nothing but our age difference would justify that. Besides, I have to call them something. When I address them I use "Caballeros". For knowing them every day more and more, that is what they are: gentlemen

For not having paid enough attention when they explained to me that a well is paid for by the meter - and the deeper the well the more money the driller makes - today I am showering with half sweet and half salted water coming from a well that is seventeen meters deep and should only be eight. Drying my ears and beard I take a last look out of the window, the boat is anchored, just where it is supposed to be at about two meters from the shore. Offshore, just two fingers below the horizon, I admire the floating cages, full of fish of all sizes.

Yes, I am proud of owning the only integrated (that means that we have our own lab to produce larvae) offshore fish farm in Mexico. But that's another story you'll hear about later.

Because memory and thoughts have their own reasons that we don't completely control, my brain was not concentrating on sunsets, or on boats, or on half–Maya gentlemen. I just remembered the day I received the news that my mother had died, way back in Diets-Heur.

I wept and just walked around in this wooden cabin, of six meters by four, made of pine boards and a zinc roof. I was ashamed not to be able to be there because I didn't have the money and

13

besides I couldn't make it in time for the funeral. Even more so, since apart from my sisters, I no longer knew anyone anymore in that village, which I had left forty years ago. Anyway it would not do anything for my mother. Funerals are for the living, the dead don't care anymore. These were the things, among others, that I was telling myself.

My mother was a fervent catholic who invented many rules, inquisition type rules, in order to adjust her life, and ours, to the conquest of heaven and the way she thought one should live to deserve paradise. Later on, when I was able to think, I understood that she was prepared to forego happiness in life down here in order to gain a better life up there. Katharine was her name. Like her namesake, she was convinced that she was a martyr and that heaven was won with privation, suffering and holy fathers, although my sisters, born after me with big age differences, let me know over the years, that with age she became more tolerant and less fanatic. This is a period which I did not experience.

How much hardship was generously distributed in her surroundings for not being able to divorce or get a separation because it is a sin and gets you to the burning hell? She just was not aware that she was making hell in her own house.

One example of rules initiated by my mother: Going to mass gives right to breakfast. So, during my childhood, the 365 days of the year started at seven in the morning with mass. Even better; before I got to the age of two digits I was appointed to ring the church bells at six thirty. Whether it rained or snowed, even if the unpaved street was covered with a thick ice cap, I ran the one kilometer long muddy street in the dark, solicited and pursued by all the devils and monsters of hell who wanted to take me away. They were hidden behind every tree or wall. My not even ten year old legs broke Olympic records of that distance. Just making a stop now and then under the seven streetlights that illuminated the road. Because we all know that monsters and devils don't operate in the light. The rest was deep darkness, not a single window lit, which was normal, since they waited for me ringing the bells to wake up. The church key was behind a loosened brick.

After mass, which lasted about half an hour, the priest kept us for another half hour of catechism. Filled up with all the spiritual food available and running again, I returned home where a pile of pancakes and toasted bread with marmalade were waiting for me. Roman Catholic education with an unmovable timetable scheduled my boyhood: Mass, catechism, school.

Salvation was on the street or as a refugee in one or the other houses of my four aunts. In total, I had eleven aunts and uncles, only on my mother's side. All of them the consequences of the village priest recommendations according to which: women are created for reproduction and the good catholic education of their offspring.

All of us knew that village like our pockets: no barn, house, field, tree or path had secrets. We knew where the first ripe cherries appeared and against which wall the first ripe pears would inaugurate the season. In which barns were the best hideouts and whose hay was the best stocked.

As I said, Heur only had 180 adult souls. This does not prevent that it was divided in a "high" and a "low". The "low" goes from the highway (Tongeren to Liege) to the church, which stands about in the middle. The "high" from the church to the last houses close to the Hamal forest. The Hamal forest separates Heur from Godogne in Walloon territory, the other ethnic group of which Belgium is made up. That is foreign country. Heur is the last bastion of the Flemish ethnic group, who speak some sort of Dutch-related language with some German in it. Just a mile farther south, one falls in territory where only French is spoken: to us, the "enemies". We don't mix.

This cultural-linguistic antagonism does not prevent the Flemish working class from making a living in Walloon territory where the coal mines, the Belgian steel factories and the very powerful Herstal arms makers are located. All these were the destiny of the Flemish, blue collar, overall-wearing, working class and of course our future. Like all my friends, I was destined by my parents, my teachers, the holy priest and all the adults who interfere in the future of Flemish youth, to integrate these contingents. That's what my father did and that's what I was supposed to do. But something did not work out and the plan went off the road.

When I got to a two digit age, my mother took me to the school of the Marists in Tongeren, our nearby city founded by no less than Julius Cesar himself. The tribe that occupied the territory when Cesar's legions invaded were called "the Eburons". Their chief, Ambiorix, has his statue on the market place: short axe in his right hand, a long sword in his belt, winged helm, a who knows what hide over his athletic shoulders, big mustache falling to his chest, left hand over his heart and a very furious look towards the church towers in front. The story is that when Julius Cesar went to conquer Great Britain he left a small cohort behind to occupy Tongeren. Ambiorix united some tribes and defeated them.The year was 57 BC. Of course when Cesar came back from England he got very upset, did not like that at all and smashed the rebellion. Ambiorix was taken to Rome and, with some other Gallic tribal heads, died in the circus. To justify the lost of his cohorts, Cesar wrote to the Senate that "The Belgians are the bravest among all the Gallic tribes". All Belgians, Flemish and Walloons alike, are still very proud of it. Even though probably 2.100 years later there is not a single Eburon left, apart from a basket ball team that bears the name.

This is why Tongeren is a Gallo-Roman town. It's possible that with the death of Ambiorix the resistance remained active, since the Romans had to build huge walls to protect the town, the remains of which can still be seen.

For us, "village kids", the Town was synonymous with vice, perdition and sin: we were convinced that all the "city women" were "hoeren". There was always an aunt or an uncle to take us along to the Thursday market just to help them carry the products they wanted to sell: fruit, vegetables, rabbits, chicken and more. For us it was feast. Tongeren city of doom, but how much envied.

Many years later in Africa, mingling with Arabic speaking populations I learned that the "houri" is women of the harems. Could it be that the word filtrated to the Flemish language through the three centuries of Spanish rule, who at their turn got it from the Arab occupation of Spain?

Before reaching the status of student with the Marist fathers, where physical punishments and humiliations were part of the teaching process, I learned the humiliating lesson of my social status and how to stay in my place. Previously, there had been four years of primary at the village school where the two teachers tried to hammer into our peasant brains: reading and writing, the first elements of history, geography, mathematics and religion, of course. This was done in two rooms. Each teacher managed three levels at the same time.

She was an angel, even better: a princess. Pure, good, and intelligent. With her long, blond like wheat in august hair falling on her shoulders, always dressed with beautiful and always clean garments. I was sure she smelled of soap even if it never occurred to me to go that close as to smell her. I loved her to the point of stomach pains. I ran all over the village just to see her going by, when she came back from school or after mass. Just to see her made my whole body itch and prickle, and dried up my throat. She was the daughter of one of the rich farmers from the "low". I was from the "upper" where there were no farmers with more than one horse. My father was a metallurgist and only owned some chicken and rabbits.

One of my aunts was employed in her house, which gave me the pretext to stay for hours just across the street, waiting for my aunt Geraldine, just hoping to see her through a window. This Aunt Geraldine was the sugar aunt for all the offspring of her brothers and sisters, the one who defended us against the anger of our parents and protected us when they were looking for us, broom in hand. She must have noted something of my loving fervor for Josephina. One winter afternoon when I was sitting close to the coal stove to heat my frozen bones (we all wore short pants until twelve) in her living-kitchen-dining room, this common sensed, loving, much appreciated second mother, said:

- Pierre, Josephina is no bacon for your beak.

She did not look at me and I did not lift my head. I just kept staring at the stove as if wanting to be part of the burning coal. Something happened to me. I got my head deeper into my shoulders, pretending that I didn't hear and that I had no idea what she was talking about. Someone had discovered my secret love. I started to feel miserable.

- Pierre, Josephina is no bacon for your beak, let her alone. She repeated.

I wanted to enter a rat hole and never come back.

It was not the end of this love, but from then on I felt humiliated and discovered. I believe that in this kitchen-dining-and living room of my sugar aunt, sitting on a chair with the stove between my legs and my hands stretched over it, pretending I had not heard anything, at that very moment I started my long rebellion against the social order.

*

Since I am writing in Mexico, I should tell you something about my country. But then what? The news: always the same old stories of how politicians, union presidents, civil servants are stealing, plundering the national treasure. Overlooking and just not bothering about: rules, democracy, justice and other concepts like these. Of course, this fills me with anger and shame. Shame is a concept that has no value for any politician. I could tell you a thousand detailed stories. But it will be boring to you. Just be aware that here on the other side of the border, justice is a merchandise like any other merchandise and up for negotiations. Exactly like buying socks in the store, a cow in the market, a car, a house or whatever. At one end of this country: 52 % of the population lives with less than two (2) dollars a day per family. At the other, a senator pays himself eight hundred dollars a day. We have the richest man in the world as fellow citizen (the one who received the only phone-communications company from the hands of his buddy, a former president). Of course we pay the highest rates in the world. Every time I pick up the phone I can't help thinking of that poor man, who owes the national treasury around 34 billion pesos in unpaid taxes – so a national newspaper said – he must be thinking that with just 20% of this amount he can buy the whole government including the secretary of the treasury, the supreme court and the whole congress and senate. Even the rich in Mexico are of secondhand. Of course all their offspring went through the very conservative, fanatic catholic private schools belonging to the "Christ's legionnaires", a congregation founded and headed by "Father Maciel" who, yes indeed was a real father of great productivity and also one of the world's most horrendous pederast. Of course, all that does not keep them one minute from sleeping. Neither does the misery of so many. Here, the words that are thought and quoted are "If you don't cheat, you don't advance", "A politician who is poor, is a poor politician ". "No one can withstand a 50,000 pesos cannonball", "The form is the essence", and many more. The politicians of this country just behave as their ancestors, the Spanish conquerors sent by their very catholic kings of Spain to plunder America.

Priests and politicians are ruling Mexico. Both these categories of people got rich with words without having to bother about where dinner was going to come from, their children's shoes or their education fees. The first ones play on the register of our fear of having to disappear one day: dying - one thing that for some reason we just do not accept- the second ones play with our hopes to get to the grave in good shape, without doing a thing about it.

Latin America entered modern history with acts of plundering, violence, war, corruption, theft and treason by the agents of their very catholic kings of Spain. The Spanish conquerors left the place to the politicians who keep doing more or less the same things. This became with the ages a lifestyle and part of the culture. Want an example? The second wife of the former President, Martha is her name, trafficking with her position, in no time made her sons multimillionaires. An opinion poll showed that 85 % of Mexican women

18

said that they would have done the same thing, if they had had the occasion to do so, using the usual pretext that you have to favor and protect "the family". Doesn't that mean that corruption is part of Mexican culture? It could be. One more: A study in my state of Campeche showed that all the public works – schools, hospitals, roads – over the last twenty years - have been paid three times their real value. Which means that the money spent was enough to build three times as many schools, hospitals and roads. Where did the two missing parts go to? Straight into the politicians and friends´ pockets. If this is not "plundering" it looks very much like it. Does anybody bother to bother them? No Sir, no one will do such an uncivilized and unfriendly deed. This is Mexico, by today's standards underdeveloped in almost all ways.

Bad luck, for Latin America and specially Mexico, having been colonized by the very catholic kings and queens of Spain and the Vatican. If it had been the other way around and colonization would have been in the hands of some fanatic protestants, it is possible that my fellow citizens of today would be as well off as their counterparts from across the border and they would not have to expel a quarter of the population as migrants to keep alive half of the other part staying here. On the other hand, the United States colonized by the Vatican and the kings of Spain most likely would be sending migrants to "Las Americas". But this is a fantastic, pessimistic speculation, isn't it?

Today is Wednesday, the sky is charged with heavy grey and black clouds. Like those inside my head. Nothing moves, not even a leaf on the trees on one side of the cabin, nor a ripple on the sea on the other side. Everybody and everything is waiting for the lifting of the curtain for the tropical storm spectacle. The first lightning hits the horizon, now completely black. We are in the playhouse and this is the third call.

*

There were two amusements in Heur. I could say even three, but the third one only lasted one week: the feast of our holy patron Saint Donatus whom we have to pray to protect us from lightning, thunder and storms. He has his statue in the church, dressed up as a roman legionnaire. Nobody ever could tell me why this legionnaire had something to do with lightning and thunder, but that's how it is. One day every year, together with the Holy Sacrament, Donatus is walked around the village, up and down. On this occasion the street is dressed up with banners of saints and holy virgins. The more banners, the bigger your property and the higher your social status. Flower petals are strewn all over the dusty dirt street. Almost everybody takes part in the procession. As a mass-servant, I marched, with half a dozen more servants, just behind the Saint Cecilia band and behind the holy sacrament which was carried by the sweating priest in his heavy garment sewn with gold thread.

We marched with our pockets full of incense which, secretly, we put on the burning coals to produce a maximum of smelling clouds. This had to be done out of the priest's sight. Since he was asthmatic, he never put much incense on the burning coals. That was our revenge for all the ear tearing, cheek slapping, bottom kicking we had been treated to in the year: trying to suffocate him.

That day, lunch was special in company of several aunts and uncles who lived in other villages. Plates and cutlery, which only were used three or four times a year, were displayed. Invariably the dish was "rabbit cooked in brown beer and herbs, Katrina style" served with boiled vegetables and potato puree balls wrapped in breadcrumbs. In the afternoon, there was a bicycle race in which I was good in my category and a donkey race, in which I was no good. I felt pity for the poor animal and in these conditions one cannot win.

The most horrendous was the "goose throat pulling": A goose was hanged with her legs tied up from a tree branch, beak down. The competitors sitting on a donkey, without leaving a circle and in a certain time had to pull off the neck of the animal. The winner took the goose home. Fifty years later, I saw the same game played with a rooster in a village in Oaxaca, Mexico. Could it be that this sport originated in Spain? Both of them, the Indian tribes of Oaxaca and the Flemish peasants experienced centuries of Spanish occupation. Some peasants isolated themselves in a barn or a field to bet on rooster fights, which is prohibited by law and enforced by the only police element of the village. Often we saw the sheriff – to call him something- his stick up in the air running after the criminals, but more often by five o'clock in the afternoon he was too drunk to run after anyone. Around three, the first drunks made their appearance. It was not rare to see them being carried home on a wheelbarrow by their wife or sons.

In the evening, there was a dance party at the community hall. That's where I learned my first dance steps. This art, I learned many years later, is an introduction to love making. I learned; fox-trots, waltz, tango, mazurkas, boleros, cha-cha-cha, and paso doble, dancing with my aunts and cousins.

*

Thinking it over again, these dance occasions, under the eyes of the whole village, are the only official and admitted sexual education I received. Sure, neither a fanatic catholic mother, nor the Marists, nor the village priest Eyskens nor, later on, the Jesuits from the seminar, are the best teachers to teach us about our body or the mechanics of sexuality. Even less, of course, about frustration, desire, feelings, pleasure, stimulations and all the things that make that a human being lives in harmony with his body. How much time I lost, which later I had to make up for. In matters of the poorest sexual education, it must be sure that the youth of the Flemish catholic villages of that time, gained the gold medal.

In that time and that place, dancing was a physical exercise for two of opposite genders. It is a sexual approach socially acceptable in our civilization. Culturally, it belongs to the category of the nuptial parade or, if you want, to a battlefield of physical demonstrations with a sexual goal by way of muscular fatigue, perspiration, changing heartbeat and breathing rhythm. Sometimes to the extent of complete exhaustion, even if the postulated fatigue is another one: the fatigue of making love. Dancing is measuring with the eyes, body wrinkling, legs displacements, hands touching and finger mingling, hips moving to the rhythm of the music and desire. It's not a matter of love, it's an erotic matter. Dancing is of bodies, not of souls. It's a desire to spend sexual energies.

For those who dance alone (everybody does it now, since the twist and the post rock-n-roll period) dancing can be read as a solitary pleasure, a showing off of one selves in order to demonstrate how pleased one is with oneself, with the objective to spend and discharge a plenty of energy.

Some churches dedicate themselves to discharge this energy in a collective way, guiding this energy to religious concepts and to the pockets of the preachers. In these churches there is dancing, waist twisting, some gymnastic exercises with hands and legs, singing, screaming, all in order to discharge energies originally sexually oriented. These are the innumerable protestant churches of Anglo Saxon origin: Baptist, Presbyterian, Seventh Day Adventists, Pentecostals and many more. The common background of all those people is sexual oppression, refused and suffocated desires, all prohibited and hidden in a most hypocritical, secret way.

The Hedonist

Whatever, dancing is a demonstration of a body which is consumed by a desire of well being, rhythm, lightness, swiftness, movement and challenge. I don't remember who said it, but it could be Woody Allen: "Dancing is a vertical exercise with a horizontal aspiration."

*

I knew that the rich from "down" seldom came to the village dances, which did not mean that I did not have the door in sight all the time, hoping to see her appear and knowing that I would never have the courage to invite her for a dance and even less, superior happiness, touch her. I never managed to touch a hair of Josephine but kept searching her eyes to see if there was a response. Soon, when she became aware of my circus, she avoided crossing me and if this was impossible, she turned her head away. I don't know how many times I wanted to die.

On Sunday mornings, in the winter, after the early mass – also called the small mass - you could see many people on foot or bicycles going to the pub. Carrying small wooden boxes out of which at one end appeared the tail of a rooster and at the other end its head.

They go to the "cock singing". Between two beers, four gins, laughter and shouting, they register, bet and guess the number of times their rooster is going to sing in fifteen minutes or in half an hour. At the master of ceremonies' – the owner of the pub - signal, everybody goes to the terrace behind the building where some fifty small wooden boxes are aligned about one meter above ground level. Five wooden sides and the sixth closed with a metal screen. About three meters in front of the cock boxes, an alignment of benches behind a board, on which is pinned a label for each cock. The owners don't have the right to register the songs of their own cocks since one of my uncles had taught his champion to stop singing when he put his pencil behind his ear. Behind every five markers there is a controller whose eyes open wide if ones makes a noise, or touches your shoulder if you forgot to register a song. This competition passes in silence. The only time I ever saw these peasants silent. The cock who sings the right number of times forecasted wins, one song below still wins, two too, three pays back the registration money. But one over looses. I've seen some, out of pure outrage, squeezing their rooster's throat right there. The poor animal didn't know how to count.

Many times I went along with my father who was fond of that game. I can't say that he was a man of few words: he never said anything. When he opened his mouth it was to scream at something or someone who was doing the wrong thing, using cursing as a common language. Nevertheless, if his mouth remained closed, his eyes seemed to always be smiling.

I liked the company of these rough and loud people who drank and smoked much, cursed even more, laughed loudly, who heavily slapped each others' backs with big hands of people using shovels and picks. But who were able to handle a one thousand kilo horse with a click of the tongue. Proudly I moved among them like a fish in the water, serving them their glasses of beer or gin, carrying their cock boxes for which they overwhelmed me with Coca Cola or lemonade and chocolate bars. Sometimes too, they sent me to call for their wives to tell her that she should come to the pub with the wheelbarrow.

Many times my father took me along to other villages. We bicycled in rain, mud and wind until my legs were blue, as far as the Walloon villages where betting was higher and the competitors less known. My father chewed a little French but with hand language and signals all aficionados understood themselves. That's how we passed winters; with spring coming cock singing became uncontrollable.

In the summer, the Flemish peasant and working class divert themselves drinking beer and betting their money on pigeon racing. The walls of the kitchen, bedroom and   living room of my uncle Gustav were full of pictures and certificates of his champions. With their names and inscription of their prizes printed on them. In this village an egg of a champion could sell for a month's salary. But what is it all about? Let me explain: Long ago you converted your attics in a pigeon house, and registered your future champions on the national register of racing pigeons. From then on, they carry a metal ring with a number on the right leg. In the running season, every Friday evening you'll select and carry your runners to the pub. Here, – always amongst shouting, laughing and much beer drinking – you register them according to the announced distances they will travel. (As for our Olympic champions, there are sprinters and marathon runners). They get a colored rubber ring put on the left leg. Once that is done, you will receive a register-clock in a wooden box with as many small metal capsules as you have put pigeons in the race.   You also, of course, bet on them but that is off the record. This clock you carry home, late at night and probably "slightly emotional", as they call

23

being right drunk in these parts. Meanwhile, your pigeons are put in big baskets, charged into trucks first, and loaded again on train wagons which take them on a trip to the south, sometimes as far as the centre of France.

On Saturday you always have an ear on the radio reports, from which you learn how far the pigeon convoys have gone, and the estimated time of releasing. According to wind directions and speed, weather conditions, the state of mind of your champions, you calculate the approximate time they will present themselves in your pigeon house on Sunday morning.

Not only you, but all your family and friends are pointing their noses in the air on Sunday morning screening the sky to notice the smallest plumed and flying movement. Normally, the poor animals, without food for three days (you don't feed them so they will not be heavy) let themselves fall right into the pigeon hole as soon as it is in sight. But some of them play around, staying on the rooftops, playing the "difficult to get": even if you are throwing food and calling them with your secret whispers, they just don't come in.

One day my uncle Gustav's champion was the first one to get to the village, but instead of entering the pigeon hole, it played around flying from one rooftop to the other, while the other competing champions were filling the village sky. Outraged, my uncle Gustav shot him. After that he did not speak to anyone for weeks. A champion that does not enter the pigeon hole fast enough is not a good champion.

Ok, suppose your pigeon entered the pigeon hole: here starts a sprint against the seconds. You have to grab him, get the rubber ring off his legs, put it into the metal capsule, put the metal capsule in the clock and turn the register key. Every second counts.

Once all your pigeons are home, and their rings registered, you take the clock to the pub. Always accompanied with loud laughs and louder cursing, your clock is opened and your results registered in a big book with the results of the village. This register is taken to the regional office where time will be discounted according to the distances between villages. Meanwhile, you have gone home with a smiling face or a sad one, but probably "slightly emotional" as is the word used to indicate being stoned. Sunday night or Monday morning through the radio you will learn if you won money, or lost it.

Don't laugh: these things are serious, deadly serious. Up to the point that the mass hour is fixed according to the estimated time of arrival of the doves. Therefore, the priest made us run through the village shouting the hour that the Lord, creator of pigeons and co-

24

regent with one in the Holy Trinity, will be honored. It wouldn't occur to anyone to have the church bells ring when the pigeons are coming. The pastor of the next village, Vreren, had pigeon champions known over the whole province.

Between singing roosters and flying pigeons there was enough, much more than I liked, time left to go to school in the Marist primary school in Tongeren. The Marists hammered the basic notions of Roman Catholic morals, history and mathematics and a few more things, into my brains with their fists, sticks, and bottom kicking boots. The most common however was "being glued". I explain: after the heating of your cheeks with a bare hand, usually they added a fifteen minutes to half an hour standing, your nose almost glued to a wall after class. I believe that the idea was to make you think and meditate about your bad behavior. It did not work very well with me because I was "glued" at least twice a week. This was not without consequences because being "glued" after class meant that I missed the tramway with all the village school goers and that I was left without the pleasure of contemplating Josefina with my cow like eyes .

In that school, and for the only time in my life, I always got the best grades and came out as the best student. This had its importance for what is going to follow. I liked history, geography and even the religion classes - above all the old testament, with its stories about battles, fights, treasons, fornications, about women one day whores and the other heroic warriors. I learned to like reading stories about fearless knights who loved in all honor and saved virgins of incredible beauty, virtues and purity. Who killed the non believers in the crusades, the traitors and the dragons – all of them devil's creatures. The world was opening. I regretted very much not to have been a fearless knight, putting my sword and life at the service of the honor of a beautiful virgin. Which in my case of course was nobody else than: Josephine.

This was where I gave a first demonstration of my acting talents, which years later will put me on a real stage in N'djamena, republic of Chad. One day that going to school was really making me sick –we all have known these days - I feinted a stomach pain. There was no use doing that with my mother, she saw through me. So I played it to the good fathers of the Marist school. I must have been pretty good because they sent me, walking, for a consultation to the town hospital. After briefly touching my stomach, the good doctor decided to lighten my body of its appendix, which was done right away. Hours later; my mother and my aunt Geraldine, panicking, brought me some clothes, just when I woke from the anesthesia. I spent three days in the hospital eating ice cream. I never feigned anything anymore.

These memories just give me the feeling of how fortunate I am to have been educated, even in the rough way, and with many shortcomings, by the good Marist fathers and not by the teachers of the Mexican Unique Syndicate of Teachers, which are a disaster. A national catastrophe, as I am witnessing.

*

Yesterday afternoon, in the light of a splendid sunset with a blood colored calm sea and clouds painted in all the possible tones of blue, red and orange, we had our weekly chat about how things were going on the fish farm. Sometimes there is beer or even a bottle of rum but this time there was only Coca Cola. They were all there, Francisco, or Pancho as we use to call him – I'll talk later about him – Angel, Daniel, Carlito, Efrain, Roberto, Roger, Khalil, Rogelio, Thomas and the French: Patricia, Patrick and Willy. I like to call them all by their name, because so far they are the totality of the intellectual fish farming capital in the whole of Mexico. These moments of near camaraderie between staff and employees are not common in Mexican labor behavior. It costs us patience and time to get to this before they "defreeze" and feel comfortable. After all, they are the ones who decide that we are doing well or doing bad, making or losing money. They are the ones who feed the fish. So if we win, they win. All of us are equally responsible. This co-responsibility has created a pleasant atmosphere and solidarity among us, without, however, falling in displaced familiarities. The relationship is working and works everywhere. Maybe it cost more here, where relations are built on brutal exploitation. Sharing responsibilities and profits is not part of Mexican labor culture.

When everything was said and jokes and laughter started, Thomas- el Flaco- looked at Patricia and simply asked: "Is France farther than Texas? And how much time it takes to go there by car?" Thomas is about 26, he has gone through primary and done some secondary school in   public education. I am not going to expand on public education in Mexico. Just know that the whole system is dominated by the president of the union, Elba Esther Gordillo (who, lives more in San Diego, USA than in Mexico). All her life she has been a civil servant, which has made her a multimillionaire, in dollars of course –. As a good patriarch, she has taken all her family to syndicate and high level positions in the ministry of education: ex husbands, daughters, their husbands, lovers, ex lovers, nieces and nephews, boyfriends and girlfriends: Come along, muchachos, everybody up to high public paychecks. Of course, she knows how to blackmail the governments and the governments just cowardly submit. How to ask about educational quality in these conditions? Eighty seven percent of Mexican teachers did not pass the qualifying exams to be teachers (out of which 6 % were declared perfect illiterates). How did they get there? Ask the teachers union that put them there. Recently, the minister of education found out that 117,000 teachers in Mexico are paid to teach in schools that don't exist and 17,000 more teachers are paid by the government to work for the syndicate. No comment.

Mexico produces this kind of personalities by the dozens. Whole industrial and economic sectors of this country are just high jacked by these kinds of people who take advantage of seven decades of coward, bad and corrupt government. There is nothing wrong with getting rich – on the contrary- the thing that got lost in Mexico is how one got there?

Thomas' question just gives way to the fact that Mexico has one of the lowest rates in educational quality. One thing explains the other: The syndicate recruits the teachers on its own criteria, decides programs, school calendar – which for this year is 115 half days of presence- but it is not held responsible for the fact that Thomas on his 26th year still thinks that you can drive your car from Campeche to Paris. Most probably, in the present state of affairs, his children and grandchildren are going to think the same thing. There is a Mexican saying that is very true. "We are where we are because we are what we are"

*

One day, as I was taking off my mass clothes (white shirt and red robe hanging to the floor) in a room as big as a closet, pastor Eyskens called me. This was the signal to start trembling and begin study the tip of your shoes. He put his enormous hands on my shoulders, which instinctively made me go one step back. Sometimes, when he was in a good mood he did that, but you never knew if it was to put his fingers through your hair or to grab your ear, pull it, with you following the movement, towards him and with his other hand slam you the opposite cheek with such a strength that you felt it down to

your ass and your eyes instantly started producing tears while your cheek turned dark blue. This time, I was lucky, my ears stayed in their natural place and his hands did not get to my face and my cheek kept its natural color. I dared to look up. Eyskens was a wardrobe-like man, tall and wide, with a big red face in which a pair of pool-blue eyes, hidden under very black and big eyebrows, always had an accusing expression. His cassock always was dust clean, ironed and impeccable. Not like the cassocks of the Marists in Tongeren where you could find traces of what they had been eating a week ago and with plenty of elbow patches. He was almost bald, only a few hairs which he tried to hide behind his ears. Even his shoes always were brightly shining, because he lived with a niece who cooked and took care of him, in all honor and good of course. I know so because the village doctor, who every two weeks made a tour of the village on horseback, said so after a few beers in the bar: I overheard that the niece was a virgin. He Father pulled me towards him and whispering in my ear - for which he had to bend deeply - with his heavy voice:
- Tell your mother that I want to see her after Sunday mass.
It took me a few seconds, but I managed to ask:
- After the small or the big mass Pastor?
- The big one.
With that, he just walked away and let me contemplate his enormous back

My mother got the message with a very suspicious look and for the rest of the week she was very nervous. I stayed out of her way, knowing, as she did, that the only reason for such an invitation by the pastor could only be me and for certain, a great sin I committed. It did not even occur to both of us that there could be another reason. All that week I stayed out of reach of her hands.

Sunday morning big mass is the religious but also the social event of the week. There was no new dress, coat, hat, shoes or any other wearing item that was not inaugurated by their proud owners at the occasion of the great mass. Of course, every living soul in the village was there, except the ones that had gone to the small mass. Not being seen in church was to risk to be denounced publicly by the Pastor in his preach from the highs of his preaching chair. Only two families did not come to church. One was a couple of military pensioners, strangers to the village. We never knew why they had come to live here and disturb the social peace. The other one had two sons who even went to the public school – the Athenaeum- where there were no priests and religion classes were optional. Both these families were hated by the rest of the villagers and were treated as the devil's agents, Bolsheviks, communists, and their wives as whores. Secretly they fascinated me.

In front were the children, behind them the youngsters in expectation of "communion" or "confirmation", among whom of course the only one who existed for me in the whole world: Josefina. Behind were the women, and behind them, partly standing, halfway outside, because of lack of chairs and also because they didn't want to appear too devout, the men folks. This converted the church entrance in a talk and business saloon. Eyskens tired himself out, calling the men to respect the house of God, but with little success. The volume of the men's voices was proportional to the volume of the music that came out of the grand organ, played by the teacher Jules. One Sunday, Jules had pulled all the registers of the organ and played at maximum volume. All of a sudden he stopped and we all heard loud and clear a big voice shouting "... and that cow, I sold her for a thousand francs" followed by a long minute of cemetery like silence. After which all the men folk ran from the church laughing, shouting and cursing. This is the only time I ever heard laughing in that church.

The big event of mass was neither consecration, nor the fashion show at communion. The main course was the sermon of Pastor Eyskens known in the whole region for painting the hottest burning hells, the most beautiful paradise and for throwing at the sinners´ heads the most horrendous lightning. Everybody had right to his part of hell: those who did not come to church, the girls who came to their wedding night without being virgins, the bicycle thieves and many more like: the Bolsheviks, the communists, the socialists, the free thinkers, the protestants, the free masons etc.... He particularly did not like the latter, which he treated as the most implacable enemies of the church, who spit on the cross in their secret reunions and made pacts with the devil. What a pity that we could not burn them anymore on the bonfire. Then came: the liberal government, the readers of books prohibited by the church, the readers of the holy bible which is dangerous reading for the vulgar, and so on and so on. Years later, when I was initiated as a free mason I thought of Eyskens, by that time since long dead.

It must have been the end of April or the beginning of May. The day before it had rained all day and it was bitter cold. So, although a wet sun was shining, I was dressed up as for the coldest winter day with a big coat, over a jacket, over a woolen sweater, over a shirt and over an undershirt, with double socks and heavy shoes. In fact, I was sweating like in a sauna standing at the church door waiting for my mother. Probably I was sweating more from anguish than from too

29

many clothes. What could the pastor have to say to my mother that could not wait until her confession?

Every year in these days of April and beginning May, there were three days of winter like weather. As if winter did not want to give up and tried to stop the glorious road to summer. These days are called "The Knights of May" or "the Ice Saints". These days are the great anguish of the peasants, who already have the wheat coming up, the fruit trees in flowers and the potatoes sown. If the Knights of May are too mad, all is lost. The second flowering never is as good as the first one.

Time was getting long. I left the church door to join a soccer play that started in the street between "down" and "above". This could degenerate easily in a street fight because the ones from "down" were cheaters and played dirty.

I came home with my head hanging low, wishing that I was a thousand miles from there. I was expecting the worst. For sure, my mother and Eyskens had made up a plan to give me an exemplary punishment so I watched that the table stayed between me and her, and kept the door in reaching distance to run for the kitchen of my sugar aunt or a secret hideout, to stay there for a while and let the storm pass. But no screaming came. Slowly, I raised my eyes, looking at my mother. Surprisingly, there was no hostility on her face. I decided that there was no more reason to keep the table between us. My mother kept cleaning strawberries which later on would become a strawberry pie with vanilla cream; the classic treat for a spring Sunday. She did not look at me and kept concentrated on the strawberries. When it seemed that my situation was completely secure, I moved to her side. My sister Maria - we called her Mia - sat beside her, her doll in one arm and the thumb of her other hand in her mouth, making sucking sounds. My other two sisters – Denise and Lutgarde – sat on the floor playing with my lead soldiers. Something was going to be said. One does not come out of a chat with the pastor and keep silent. Slowly she got up, I reached to her shoulders, she looked at me with no anger in her eyes, and with some joy in her voice she said:

- You are going to be a priest.

She said that slowly and well articulated. It must have been written on my face that I did not get it, for she repeated:

- Pastor Eyskens wants you to study to become a priest.

I still did not get it, although in the backyard of my brain I understood that I was going to leave the village to go to a boarding school where

boys went to become priests. Little by little, a certain form of excitement was creeping up from my knees to my throat.
- When?
I thought this was going to be the next day.
- In September.
She picked up the strawberry plate and went to the kitchen.
The first thing that came to my mind was that priests don't marry and that will be my vengeance from Josefina who for weeks was giving me the back, she did not even look at me anymore, as was the case this morning at mass. I knew something about vocation and the call of God of which priests, nuns and other holy people are advantaged with. I realized that Pastor Eyskens and my mother just decided that very morning that I had the vocation and that God just called me. Up to there I hadn't realized or heard anything. Sure I was very devout; I prayed very much, I went to mass every day. But these things had a straight relation with my breakfast and the pile of fifteen pancakes which I got as compensation.

When my mother came back from the kitchen, with the pile of plates to set the table, helped in that by my sister Mia, she looked very satisfied and happy. No doubt that she was seeing herself as a Saint, the only woman in the village to give her only son to the Lord.

Later on, Pastor Eyskens told me that he was sort of complying with a promise. He said that; kneeled before the bishop of Liège, he had sworn to give the church a priest from the village. A condition the holy bishop had put forward in order to keep a priest in the parish. As to the matter of being called by God the thing looked somewhat short to me.

But who cares? Already I saw myself as a missionary in Africa, converting Negroes to the Christian religion and making them members of the holy Roman Catholic Apostolic Church.

*

Seven years later when I put foot on African soil, I met the people I wanted to convert in these days. I found out that different religions already had taken possession of their brains, their means and ways, but that there was still virgin ground to be covered. I found peaceful people, genteel, caring for their children and each other, helpful, kind and with a great sense of humor and pleasure. They lived and died for thousands of years without ever having heard the words: sin, hell or original fault. Sure they had in their values what is right and what is wrong but the idea of being born already blackened by an

31

original fault that someone else had committed, never occurred to them.

*

Let's go back to Heur in the fifties.

In the following months, my life changed completely. From then on, I was not only "Katrin´s son", but the priest-to-be, cherished by Pastor Eyskens. All of a sudden the slaps in the face stopped, either at home or at catechism. They gave way to big eyes and wrinkled faces. Sometimes, on Thursday when there was no school, Pastor Eyskens took me along in his car (Citroen DS, the only one in the whole village) to his original region in the north of the province close to the border with Holland. We went to mark trees in his woods. Eyskens was son of a wealthy family and inherited thousands of acres of pine trees wood land which had to be cleared, meaning that we marked the tree trunks which grew too close one to another with a special knife. The distance was of six yards. Every tree standing closer had to be marked and would be cut.

It did not take me long to understand that all these woods would pass-on to the Holy Church of Rome when Eyskens died, since the vow of celibacy does not allow to have descendents. Later on, I learned that because of priests' celibacy, plus the sales of perpetual holy masses paid for with fertile land, plus the millions of years of indulgencies paid the same way, the holy church had become the biggest landowner in Europe. This mechanism over the centuries meant that the biggest parts of farm lands in the Flemish villages, belonged to the Vatican.

From then on, my buddies called me "the little pastor", some for joking, some out of envy and some out of respect. All the women became very nice to me as if I were Eyskens' son and that my future glory would illuminate the whole village.

My future state of priest did not mean that I kept from meeting the group of buddies in secret and hidden places, once a barn, once a cellar, once a cave where, between potatoes and apples, we looked at each other's pricks and masturbated each one for his own account. Nobody however was able to produce a drop of sperm. This was, so to speak, my sexual initiation.

On a vacation day we went, Eyskens, my mother and me to visit the little seminar of Sint Truiden. A small town lost among wheat and sugar beet fields, prairies full of fruit trees and greasy-green meadows sown with black and white cows, their tits almost hanging to the ground. The seminar was lodged in a castle standing in the middle of the town, just a few yards away from the market place where Eyskens parked his automobile. In the middle of the marketplace stood a – I don't know whose - statue. I do remember that the man had a sword in his hands and that he looked angrily at the castle-seminar. The four sides of the square were full of cafés and restaurants, some with terraces and here and there a clothes or tool shop. I think it is true, what the French say about the Belgians: "every two houses is a café" where, for hours and hours, the elderly and the not so elderly sit drinking one of the forty four kinds of beer that every respectable café has on its card.

A young man, much taller than I, a last year – also called Philosophy- student was assigned to show us around. The castle is a three story, grey stone building which enclosed on two sides a dusty playground and on its two other sides is closed by a six meter high grey stone wall. In one corner stands a cement imitation rock with a cave, three meters high, in which a white stone carved, full size virgin, with a blue scarf around her waist, looked down on two cement benches where the sinners were supposed to kneel and pray.

The ground levels are occupied with classrooms, the chapel and a big dining hall, another big hall is full of pulpits: "the study room". On the second floor are the dormitories divided in small rooms, with wooden walls on three sides and a movable curtain to close them. Each den has a bed and a locker. At the entrance of each dormitory stands a life size statue of the holy virgin. I do remember her, because the virgin of my dorm will be responsible for the loss of my holy vocation. Each dorm had huge windows with heavy curtains which gave onto the central courtyard and playground. These curtains also will play a role in the lost of my vocation. The third floor hosted the teachers' rooms and the saint of the saints, the office of the Superior of the Jesuits. Master on board after God and as God did not talk very much, supreme master of our lives and our vocations.

I was excited, intimidated, humble, anguished and impatient. Yes, this was a world, nothing to do with the village anymore. I felt that there were doors opening and maybe I was going to escape from my future as proletarian metallurgist as was programmed. Each time we passed other groups of visitors, each one composed of a mother holding proudly her offspring by the hand, I tried to find out if maybe this one or that one was going to be a friend. But we hardly dared look at each other. All were dying from anguish and petrified with the prospect of the life that was to become ours.

The Hedonist

What did it mean to become a priest? It's a long time ago, but I remember quite well that I was enchanted with the perspective of passing my life without working. Priests don't sweat; they don't follow the wheat, or sugar beets, or potatoes furrows on their knees. They don't have to clean the weeds or sow potatoes, covering them with bare hands. They don't line up the beets after taking them out of the earth with backbreaking movements of a small shovel. Then, always bent, cut off the leaves making piles of them, loading them on a wagon towed by a horse or a tractor and discharging them on a big pile close to the farm, where they will be left for fermentation under a plastic canvas, until they are served in a stinking sickening smell, as cow food in the winter. A pastor does not do all that; he has clean hands and clean clothes. Praying for our salvation does not make you dirty. Walking through the village, everybody and especially the women come out to salute you, kiss your ring, kneeling. The men folks take their hats off when they pass you. To listen to everybody's sins and absolve them, which means that you know everything about everybody, all that was not to displease me, I did not see any big inconvenience to this career, anyway much less than being a metallurgist or a farmhand. The disadvantage of course was that one does not have access to the enchantment of women, which at that time I only imagined and guessed how it was. But I already knew that this could be arranged. In the pubs, when I acted as an aid for cock singers or pigeon racers, I overheard chats. They said that everybody called the pastor "father" except his children who called him "uncle". I did not completely understand it, but I deduced that there were ways that a priest could make arrangements with this barbarian rule.

No, really, I could not see the inconveniences of priesthood, looking after the spiritual health of your parishioners, which does not get you dirty and smelly.

The two following months previous to entering the seminar as a student of the Jesuits were the best of all I lived in that village and hence for the rest of my life, because I never returned to Heur. It was a splendid summer. It started with the cherry harvest which we went to pick in the top of the trees on high wooden ladders we could not move alone. At the same time, we filled our bellies knowing perfectly well of the coming diarrhea. Then, followed the wheat harvest, once cut and tied in bundles, days before, it was loaded on enormous two or more horse-pulled wagons on top of which we sat to hold it all together and have a look at the second floor bedrooms of the houses when the windows were open; they all were because the summer was hot. Often, when close to a meadow with a drinking pool for the cattle, we bathed just as we came to earth. Once all the wheat in the barns, the potatoes harvest started, more harsh because you had to crawl on your knees through the furrows. I kind of liked to plough the earth with my bare hands looking for the tubers. The whole village participated, one day working for this farmer and the other for that one. The women, almost all big and with huge bellies, brought enormous quantities of lunches, beer, coffee and gin to the fields. Their arrival was the signal to fall on the straw bundles, in the shadow of the wagons. Jokes started to be told, always with a double sense insinuating sex, which made the women laugh undercover. We, the children, did as if we did not hear or understand, but with our ears wide open. Later on will come the sugar beet harvest, but by that time we were again at school.

It looks like I am describing a painting of Brueghel the Elder from the fifteenth century. But that's the way it all went. With the small variation that the wheat was not hand cut, but by a mechanical saw pulled by a horse or a tractor. Tractors were making their first appearance in these years, preceding the cars. In that season, as if sexuality goes better with summer heat, our secret masturbation reunions were more frequent. The pals with a few years more than me, produced sperm: a few white, milky looking drops. This caused them great pride, and made the rest of us, "the dry ones", jealous and invidious.

Little by little, we counted the days that were left to make the great voyage to the other world where spirituality would be the reason of existence. For days my mother and aunts were sewing my name on all my belongings, including socks and towels.

Lightly, almost floating, I descended the village street to the main road and the tramway with my mother's sisters and one uncle who was to accompany me to Sint Truiden. A summer storm, one of the ones that stay in the memory of the peasants, made that we got to the castle in Sint Truiden soaking wet. I was duly registered as a future catholic priest with vocation decided by the pastor Eyskens and my mother. That night, the first one away from home, excitement kept me from sleeping.

The Jesuits who are in charge here are not the Marists of Tongeren. From the first day I understood that what was important here was to obey, to be humble and submitted. Consequently, everything was prohibited.

The measurement of the degree of obedience is prohibition. The more interdictions there are, the more occasions to commit a fault and less possibility of achievement there is. Perfection becomes impossible and culpability appears and grows; this is good and pleases God, or at least, the priests. If you had to walk in silence around the playground, to the chapel or to the refectory, it had to be in perfect silence, the minor disobedience was immediately punished. Everyone had to understand that to obey, to conform to the rules are the ways that God and the religion require from you. There were Jesuits at every corner, just to remember you to behave as the obedient Adam and not like the rebellious Eve. To be submissive at every moment to the desire of God and the Vatican is the supreme quality of priesthood.

I did not understand it all. Nevertheless, I did my utmost best to discipline myself to the extreme. But that was not easy. Submitting myself to the Jesuits that constantly had an eye on me, I submitted myself to God? Somewhere I thought this was a little short, but what the heck?

Days were regulated like clocks. At six, first prayer, followed by sprinkling water in your face, teeth brushing and for some; shaving. Six twenty: mass. Seven: breakfast and first study. Eight: classes of Latin, French, Old Testament, history, followed by lunch, second study and recreation. At two, we kneeled again in the chapel to listen to vespers, followed by more classes of New Testament, mathematics, religion, geography and thirty minutes of recreation in which we played passionate matches of football. Seven: dinner, followed by one and a half hour of study and homework. Then, silent meditation at the chapel, lights out at ten thirty. Saturday afternoon showers: 10 seconds to get undressed and wet, 10 seconds for soaping, 5 seconds for rinsing, all this on the rhythm of a Jesuits whistle. No time to ever look at your body even less touch your penis.

On Sundays waking up was an hour later. In the morning after the great mass there was free study, which meant that either you stayed praying in the chapel or you went to the study room. In the afternoon, after the great vespers, we could leave the seminar. This meant that; in rows of two by two and praying Ave Marias in Latin, we walked through the town and into the fields and meadows, always staying in a row. Going home was three times a year, one week for

Christmas, one for Easter and two months for vacations in the summer. This was the menu through which they wanted to make convinced priests out of us, obedient and saints; so that, at our turn, we would preach obedience and submission. Behavior that most pleases God and his representatives.

Rosa, rosa, rosam, rosae, rosae, rosa. Rosae rosae, rosas, rosarum, rosis, rosis. As far as I remember, Latin and Greek have declinations which they share with Russian and German. The rosa, rosa, rosam song was the easiest one. But how much anguish and sweat were ours with the other ones: days and nights were filled with declinations of Latin verbs. Playing football, I declined. Kneeled in church I substituted paternosters with declinations, in the john, I declined. After a few months we passed on to Latin texts to recite from memory: The conquest of Gaul by Julius Cesar and his legions? I knew it by heart.

Punishment for all kinds of faults, among which not to decline properly, was to have to memorize and recite pages and pages in Latin at the priest office-sleeping room. Standing or kneeling close to him, who sat in an armchair, the punishment always started with him passing his hands through your hair or caressing slightly your face. They almost all did the same: With one hand on your shoulder they pulled you toward them. With their other hand they caressed your knees, going up between your legs. To me that produced such a panic that out of pure nervousness, automatically, I started laughing. This had a dismantling effect. I got out of there with a moralizing sermon on obedience, discipline and submission. I was one of the few who escaped: I was not a subject suitable for pederasty. Let's see if something was left to make a priest out of me? When we knew that such or such had a date with such or such priest to recite Latin, we felt sorry for him, and looked at him with compassion. We knew what was going to happen.

With two hours per day studying the testaments for two years, and liking it, I became a specialist in both books. The Abraham, Saul, Solomon, David, Jacob and so many other stories enchanted me. So much so, that I had a problem making the difference with the Ulysses, Hercules and Paris stories.

*

Sometime later, I went to look for the authors of these writings, because someone must have written them. The Old testament, in the version we actually know, covers a period of a couple thousands of years before our era, when to venerate and praise the gods passed from the stone version to the written one, it then became easier to take your God along in a book that you could put in a bag, than to hustle around with stones, statues and temples. Religion became mobile. Hundreds of authors participated in the editing; leaving something here and adding something there, depending on the political correctness of the moment. Facts and stories were rewritten, put into perspective, or dropped. In the end, a collective work over a couple thousand years. Which made me think that Yaveh did not dictate anything but that the book is a very human compilation, written by the winners, as it always is.

It's the same with the other holy books: the Koran of the Islam-the submitted ones - and the New Testament. The first Koran was written twenty five years after Mohamed's death and the Hadith - the other holy Muslim book — only in the ninth century, i.e. two centuries after the assumption to heaven of the prophet, on a white horse.

The New Testament and Jesus' story has the same history. Not a single evangelist knew Jesus. The actual version of the story originates with very late political decisions, when a certain Eusebius of Caesarea, contracted by the Roman emperor Constantine, constituted a literal body based on 26 versions of the evangelists, out of which they extracted the four official ones in the fourth century. There is no use or case to deny the clear hand of man in the sacred writings of our monotheist civilizations. But I am anticipating, we'll talk more about that. For the moment, I am just an apprentice priest in a Jesuits' seminar, having great problems with some of my teachers' pederasty customs.

*

By natural defense, inherited from my mother, I resisted the hands of my teachers under my shorts, hiding in a high level mysticism. If my surroundings were impure: the body, the flesh, the hands of the Jesuits searching for my penis with on their faces an expression of cruelty, the lies, the hypocrisy, then my world shall be pure: God, the Holy Virgin, The Holy Spirit.

By the end of my first year as an apprentice priest I was living in a complete fiction of mysticism, incredibly tormented, tortured, martyred. I was getting crazy.

Seeing a woman's legs made me turn away. I hardly talked to anyone, hardly ate, passing hours and hours praying all the saints and the holy virgin of Lourdes in particular. When I knew nobody was looking, I crawled on my naked knees on stone paths until they started bleeding, flagellated myself with ropes, hurting my body as much as I could. That hell went on for the whole of the two months vacation and just about when my mother was ready to tell the pastor Eyskens that I had gone crazy, I was saved again by this profound peasant common sense I inherited from that village.

At the occasion of a first communion feast for one of my many cousins, one of the participants was a faraway acquaintance on my aunt's husband side. A girl I had never seen before, from the region of Antwerp. She was a little heavily bodied, a couple of years older than I, beautiful with big blue eyes. Shamelessly, in church, she came to sit beside me and at the feast table she took place right in front of me, away from the adults. First I did not know what happened but then I felt that she was seeking my legs with her naked toes under the tablecloth. I acted as if nothing happened and studied profoundly my soup plate. However, I could not prevent a great sweetness invading my body. I didn't dare to look but our feet were mingling. Her game conquered me. When the party was getting to the drunken part of it, we escaped. I did not look at her, but she took my hand and led me to the barn where she pushed me into the hay stack and came to lay upon me. She put her mouth on my closed lips. That was my first kiss ever. Completely abandoned and incredibly excited I dared to caress her legs while she kept kissing and sucking my tongue into her mouth. Her thighs felt soft and humid. I managed to turn her over and come on top of her rubbing my penis between her legs and my chest on her almost naked breasts. In an instant I experienced an ejaculation and felt the warm liquid running down my legs leaving a big wet spot on my pants.

Campeche, in the fall of 2007

Dear Cousin,
I don't know where you are or where you live; neither do I know   if you are still among us. To you I owe that my life changed and that I will never be a pedophile priest   nor a fornicating hypocritical missionary, nor a Machiavelli minded   bishop: To you I owe that I don't have a problem with the kneeled ones, but that I will never be on the side of those who brought them to this humiliating position. All my life you have accompanied me at one moment or another. It is now

39

The Hedonist

*half a century that, thanks to you, came to an end, and in such a
harmonious way, my devastating mysticism.*
A warm embrace to you
Your cousin, Jean Pierre

*

My second year under Jesuit rule was brutally brought to a stop in the
month of May, when they threw me out without honors. This made me
as happy as someone leaving a prison. My grades fell at a vertiginous
speed, except in the classes of the testaments and history, which I
studied from a more and more critical viewpoint, as if they were
amusing children tales. I had a problem swallowing it all. My
mysticism gave way to disgust but I did not loose faith. That would
happen much later.

The first call for my finishing career happened on a late
afternoon when, as we often did, we played Tarzan (without Jane).
The defiance was to put the curtains of the dorm windows in the
middle of the open window. Climb on top of the two meters high
wooden wall of our bedrooms. Make a dive to the curtain, three
meters away, hang to it and let you being flown out of the window and
back. When my turn came and I was sweeping out of the window
clenched to the curtain, looking down I saw a Jesuit looking up. They
did not like the challenges of youth.

The second happening that put definitively an end to my
vocation took place the day that some of the priests-to-be had
decided to lay the virgin statue of the entrance, in the supervisor's
bed. The dorm supervisor had a small room on the other side of the
dorm with a key locked door. We did not like each other; several times
he had surprised me reading after curfew at the light of a battery lamp
under my blanket. I did not really participate in the event, since there
were many hands carrying the heavy full size virgin all across the
dorm. At ten thirty we were all under our blankets waiting for the
"reaction" of the hierarchy to what we considered was a good joke.
The "reaction" did not take long to show. And what a reaction, in the
form of a swamp of black togged Jesuits, lighting up every single
lamp, whirling all over the dorm and getting us out of bed. Forcing all
of us, kicking bottoms and punching faces, against the wall and on our
knees upon sticks and rulers they had brought along. With in each
hand a pile of books to be upheld high above the shoulders, shouting
and screaming Ave Marias, of course in Latin. Those psalm melodies
entered so far into my brain that even today, fifty years later I still

know them.   We had to stay like that until the leaders and their aids denounced themselves. Man of little faith, not very sure of my vocation to become a pedophile priest, when I felt that the stick under my knees was plowing into my bones and that I was bleeding, I decided to end this bad joke and denounced myself. At midnight, I was again on my knees in the saint of saints in front of the Superior father who was so mad that white foam was to be seen on his lips corners. Because I just did not comply denouncing my supposed aids who helped me to carry the statue, he menaced to kick me out of the seminar. Although I knew the pain this would do to my mother and to pastor Eyskens, I was not caring anymore. The more the three or four Jesuits kicked and beat me up with their sticks, the less I was willing to endorse the role of the traitor.

Two days later, during which I was held in a completely isolated room, I found myself standing in the town square, in front of the I-don't-know-whose statue with his sword menacing the castle. Holding my small suitcase under my arms which still were slightly blue and hurting I was feeling pride and relief for having saved some seminarians who today, forty-nine years later, probably are respectable pastors in their communities. Maybe some are pederasts, who knows?

A few years later, the Holy Catholic Church switched to the use of modern languages, abandoning the use of Latin in the liturgy. The study of Latin is thus the most useless thing the seminarians from Sint Truiden have done in their lives, among many other useless things.

*

The links with the village were broken. In the following years I returned a few times to Heur to say hello to my mother. As said, my father died at fifty five for having too long and too closely looked into the mouth of the magma monster. Death surprised my sugar aunt Geraldine when I was making the revolution in Cuba.

Last year, at the insistence of my sister Mia I went to visit the village. The church was closed and abandoned, there was no pastor. Naturally: I was the predestinated guide of the faithful herd. The big farms from "below", which for centuries had dominated the economic and social life, had been dismantled because the distant heirs had made their country homes of them. I have to add that the families of the big farmers just died off, for lack of descendants. None of them ever married. The great idea they had about themselves prevented them from getting married: no one was good enough for the Picard, Van Dooren, Van Eyck, Stafkens. All of them died very devotedly, but single. Almost nobody still has singing roosters or flying pigeons. The village feast hall – where I learned to dance – remember - is in ruins. The Saint Cecilia marching band has stopped playing long ago. Everybody has a car to go to mass in Tongeren. There is still a pub because thirst still exists and the soccer team stills plays because you have to do something on Sunday afternoons. Heur has become a dormitory for employees and a few craftsmen.

Before closing this basic chapter which determined the way of life I was going to take, here are some conclusions:

If I ever had had any homosexual tendencies, they were brutally and forever interrupted. The innocent games of masturbation in barns, fields and caves with my village buddies passed from fun to repugnance and rejection. I don't know if I have to thank the pederast Jesuits from the seminar for the confirmation of my heterosexual character. Maybe yes, maybe no, but that's the way it is.

*

From the seminar, I jumped in a short time to the military school. I was seventeen. In fact I jumped from one brainwashing to another, from one depersonalization process to another. In two years, I experienced the two possibilities that a poor youngster had to get away from his destiny in Belgium in the fifties: the church or the army. Both will be catastrophic. The pleasant thing was the change in my musical culture, switching from Gregorian credos, Te Deum, Requiem and Kyrie to Bill Haley, The Platters, Louis Armstrong, Jerry Lee Lewis, Lionel Hampton and other Beatles and Presley's.

The school for Flemish officers of the Belgian army is in Zedelgem, close to Bruges. It was pleasant and sane not to have to ignore half of the world's population, the female part, and to adopt another vision of history. Nobody talked about religion but about maneuvering, handling small arms, basic tactics, French and some more courses. The cycle of military training ends with a yearlong assignment to an infantry unit in Germany to protect: liberty, capitalism, democracy, His Majesty the King, western culture and liberalism against the imminent invasion of soviet and communist barbarians.

"If the Russians attack, in the actual state of things, they will be at the English Channel in seventy two hours" a captain told us in a chat on strategies. They always said "the Russians" never "the soviets". It was somewhat demoralizing to know that you were there to stop an invasion, without any chance of success. Besides that, you were supposed to give your life to stop an invasion that couldn't be stopped. But youth fairly well withstands strategic military incoherencies. We were convinced that nobody could get by us and trained hard: maneuvering, shooting, crawling in the mud and all things that go with infantry in times of peace, even if that peace did not look well established.

The German population, mainly made up of half mature widows, fifteen years after Hitler committed suicide in his bunker, ignored us. At this point they did not want to have anything anymore to do with soldiers, especially not with the occupiers. There was no doubt that each one of them at one point or the other had supported their Nazi leaders and that we, boys playing war, were not at the level of their warriors of the superior race.

It's somewhat absurd to play war and, as all armies in times of peace, the Belgian army was boring. Night curfews were at 10. We shared the protection of Soost, Westphalia, with the Canadian and the United States armies. The Canadians had their curfew at 12 and the Americans had no curfew until morning. So it was said that the Belgians danced with the girls, the Canadian flirted with them and the Americans "plucked" them.

The only way to get out of the military career was to commit a big fault, something close to desertion but not quite it. This, at least, will get you back to the mother country. I did it and it worked. My crossing of the Rhine River was delayed by three months, because of an upcoming shooting contest between allied troops. My chest did not carry any decorations for bravery in combat but I proudly displayed a sharp shooters insignia: a copper rifle, more or less where my hart was pumping. I was really good at it: charge the bullet into the cannon chamber; put the safety button to "ready"; move the distance ladder to where I thought it should be; put firmly the rifle into my shoulder, align the distance ladder, the triangle on the point of the gun's cannon and the target (never anything else but paper boards) hold breath, test softly the first resistance of the trigger and then softly press. I knew how to do all this. The instruction sergeant shouted all the time:
- Press the trigger as if it's your girl friend's tits.
At that time I had no experience at all pressing my girl friend's tits. But I knew how to shoot. We won against the best rifles of the Canadian, United States, French, Dutch and English armies, present in Germany at that time. In a great reception, in which for the first and only time in

my life I shook hands with generals, they gave me a medal. I was nineteen.

A few days later I crossed the Rhine and saluted the guards of another infantry regiment in Antwerp. The seventh Line Infantry.(don´t ask me why it is called that way)

Antwerp, the medieval heir of Bruges, when that inland port was eaten by sand and mud in the 14th century, business moved to Antwerp, now a city of excellent taverns, pubs, restaurants, clubs and, for being a harbor town, brothels. The myth of its origins is about the same as the David and Goliath story: a young man by the name of Bravo, killed a bad giant by the name of Antigoon who, from his castle "Het Steen", imposed taxes on the ships navigating on the river Schelde. This river communicates the inland city with the North Sea. In fact, the boy Bravo was a free trade agent. To show his victory over Antigoon, Bravo cut the giant's hand off and threw it into the river. They both have their statue in the town square, Antigoon lying down and Bravo throwing his hand. In the Flemish language, to throw a hand is said: "hand werpen". Some pretend that the origin of the place name "Antwerpen" comes from there. The town square is not really square but more like a triangle, bordered with magnificent baroque style huge stone houses, with very steep roofs on each of which thrones the statue of the patron of the Guild occupying the place before. Today, Mac Donald´s and other funny stores took their place, together with huge cafés and restaurants. The very illustrated and famous sons of Antwerp are: Paul Rubens, Van Eyck, Quentin Metsijs, the father of modern printing Plantin, and more. At a stone draw from the square, going through a narrow street, which they call a throat cutter, stands the imposing gothic cathedral, home to a few huge paintings of Rubens. I remember these well, because they had plenty of very white, somewhat overweighed, naked breasted women.

About Metsijs, there is a beautiful legend. Metsijs, a painter, fell in love with the daughter of the head of the blacksmiths' guild. Who of course did not want to hear about his daughter marrying a vulgar painter. There was nothing else left for poor Metsijs than to become a smith, which he did. To prove his art and his love he executed, only using a hammer and a pincer, a magnificent ornament for a well, with roses and leaves, which still can be seen besides the cathedral. Turning the corner, leaning against the wall of the cathedral stands a sculpture: Three or four masons, cutting stone blocks and a master-mason pointing his finger to the top of the tower. I remember it, because it was one of the few sculptures I saw, where the honor goes to the workers and not to the payers. This, of course, before the realistic proletarian art produced centuries later by the communists.

Of course there is a Jewish quarter, full of diamond cutters, close to the railway station and the Zoo. I cannot leave this description without telling that many streets were full of windows with more or less beautiful half nude women displaying their charms. Antwerp is not an insignificant place. And there I was.

*

Talking about Jewry: by the size and shape of my nose you could etiquette me as a Semite; by the shape of my curly rebellious hair also; by the size of my ears also; even by the name of my mother – Lycops. But the comparison ends when we come to my reproductive tool. To be born in the middle of the Nazi occupation maybe was not the best moment to get circumcised, if such had been my parents' intention. Fortunately it was not. So I have my reproduction tool intact. I am very happy with that. Thinking that the foreskin has a concentration of a thousand nerves terminals, of which two hundred and fifty are major ones, there is reason for satisfaction and gratefulness. Why do the Jews, as in many other things followed by the Muslims, take so seriously this corporal mutilation? This, by the way, is a flagrant case against human rights, being nothing less than cutting a healthy part from a healthy body of a child, who did not ask for this, without a valid medical reason. Isn't that the definition of mutilation? Why?

The disappearance of the foreskin (which some populations dry, eat, keep, pulverize, burry) leaves a circumferential scar which, with the time and the rubbing against cloth materials, hardens and loses its sensitivity. The drying up of this surface and the disappearance of the natural lubrication suppress sexual comfort. The same reasons and some more, are valid for the horrendous custom of excision (extirpation of the clitoris). Nothing justifies these mutilations. The medical or sanitary reasons have no substance. What are left are the religious ones. There is no use to name them: they are even more absurd than the supposedly hygienic ones. The Jews proclaim that it is the symbol of the contract passed between them and God. To make it simple and return their theories: If God wanted us not to have a prepuce or a clitoris, he would have made us without these parts. But some rabbis, mullahs or other holy men pretend to know better and more than the Big Boss himself. Is it a matter of suppressing pleasures to gain heaven? What is heaven worth without a clitoris, the

45

only organ which purpose is pleasure? Is that the reason why all the tenants of monotheism are after it? To erase it, deny it, some physically, some spiritually. This is pure barbarism and a crime against wellbeing, equilibrium, nature and life. The astonishing thing about this crime is that the victims applaud.

*

The military quarters of the seventh Line regiment of his majesty the king of the Belgians are hosted in the Antwerp suburbs, but only a fifteen minute tramway ride from the city center. The seventh infantry is really a caricature of camp life in time of peace. Nobody believes in its utility but everybody plays the game in exchange for receiving a small paycheck by the end of every month. Those who could afford it, rented apartments in town and stuck to a functionary presence among the barracks. The other ones took advantage of free lodging and food. Anyway, the fence had enough holes in it to leave and come as you pleased at night. The inconvenience was that you could not bring girls to the barracks. Of course, I belonged to the second group, waiting for demobilization and return to civilian life. Which I never had known so far, having passed from paternal authority, to the Jesuits in the seminar and from there on to the sergeants of the Belgian army. Up until then my life had been under strict surveillance.

Times were good, after all. De Gaulle was governing France, Adenauer Germany, and Churchill Great Britain. All of them guaranteed peace and stability. I remember that "The Great Charles" said in one of his rare passages on the radio that "The Russian people will digest communism as I digest my breakfast every morning", a prophecy that came true to the letter thirty five years later. Khrushchev sat in the Kremlin steering the cold war and Eisenhower in the White House doing the same thing. Nobody wanted war. (Except Fidel Castro and Che Guevara in Cuba, but that's for later).

*

Years later, in Latin America, I found out that in about that same period, Eisenhower had done his utmost best to screw up the relations of the United States with Latin America for a long time. He did not understand that the demands for more democracy, justice, wellbeing of these peoples did not necessarily make them

46

communists and allies of the Soviets. When somebody told him that the Latin generals taking power everywhere by form of very little democratic military coups, were bastards, he replied "I know that they are bastards, but they are "our" bastards". That's how the United States foreign politics towards Latin America was defined for many decades: Pure waste.

*

My money was scarce but allowed me three or four times a week to make a tour of the half dozen bars I liked; drinking beer, singing Flemish nationalist songs and double meaning ballads, dancing with the few girls that frequented them.

One huge wall painting in one of these hangouts stayed with me all my life. It was at least five meters long by one and a half high. Five skeletons were sitting at a bar, each one with a huge jar of beer. One was covered with a military cap with five stars on it, one with a working class cap, one with a lawyers' hat, one with a bishops' miter, and one with a crown. A concentrate of relativity of things in life and a lesson of philosophy and existentialism, which pointed at the very essence of society; at the futility of honors, money, status and values that the common mortal is supposed to pursue, even at the cost of loosing pleasure in life. Religions pull their existence from the fear of death and the unacceptability of disappearance. Therefore repeating an unbelievable amount of prohibitions, sins, by which we accept to live a little less every day, so that the final act will be less difficult. That's paying the same bill twice.

At the same time, we are making happy legions of preachers, priests, gurus, ministers, shamans, pastors, rabbis, mullahs and ayatollahs. To live less, in order to die better. What do you think about that?

*

Passing from military to civilian life happened almost unnoticed: I stayed in Antwerp, rented a room and got a job in a travel agency by the beautiful name of "Vlaamse Toeristen Bond" (The Union of Flemish Tourists) of clearly Flemish nationalist orientation.

Although it was June the weather was shit, a soft cold rain had been falling for two days, a typical "shitty summer" as the Flemish calls it. On Saturdays, the Vlaamse Toeristen Bond only works till noon; the perspective to walk twelve blocks to my room, light up the coal stove which was my only source of heat, make a sandwich which

served for dinner and wait until the evening to go out, did not enchanted me. So I stayed roaming the streets of Antwerp. When the water was sprouting out from the edges of my shoes, I stood in front of the tavern with the painting and pushed the door. The place was half dark and completely empty, except for Wilhelm who sat at the bar with a pint of Rodenbach, a dark beer made of sour cherries, in front of him. We saluted with a head sign without pronouncing a word. I also asked for a Rodenbach to a waiter who was washing glasses at the other end of the huge bar. I knew Wilhelm for having seen him hanging around this bar and others and knew that he was a "defrocked" priest. Nobody knew why he turned away from the church: he didn't get married, had no known girlfriend and was not gay either. As always, he was well dressed and part of his face was hidden under a goat-style trimmed beard in which some white hair showed. We emptied half of our beers in silence until when, pointing his finger to the painting, Wilhelm opened his mouth to say:
- I like that painting. It is he best I have ever seen.
He had not looked at me, but fixed the painting.
- That's what I think too. Which head you were closest to?
- The Miter!
- I too, although I got close to the Kepi as well.
- I know you were a seminarist. Good that you escaped. Why?
At this he turned a little on his stool and looked at me with smiling eyes.
- Oh, a story about a statue of the virgin, and you?
He turned back on his stool towards the painting
- Couldn't stand and believe anymore the Jesus story.
We lifted our glasses and emptied them. I waved the waiter to fill them up. Long minutes of silence passed.
- Can you imagine how many books were burned and their authors with them, so that the only three books of monotheism could be imposed? The Christian barbarians burned all the libraries of the Greek and Roman philosophers to stay only with one book. Thousands of bonfires were lit all over Europe for those who believed in other books.
I never had heard him talk that much and was surprised by the subject, but then not that much. I suspected Wilhelm to know a lot and of being somewhat frustrated.
- It's the same for the other sacred books, isn't it?
- Unfortunately, it is. Do you know that in the name of their book the Jews committed the first genocide in human history, when they took Jericho?

- No! But now that you mention it, I believe that you are right, the description of it is very bloody.
- Barbarian.

The Rodenbachs got finaly in front of us; the waiter was not in a hurry. He must have been convinced that he was going to pass the afternoon with two nostalgic drunks. Emptying half a glass of the sweet and sour liquid kept us from talking. We cleaned, simultaneously, our white foamed mouths with the back of our coat sleeves. I was feeling good in Wilhelm's company; that made us two not to know where to spend the afternoon. After a while I wanted to start the conversation over again:

- Jesus existed, then?

Wilhelm took a long breath, pushed his glass, turned his bar stool around and looked at me:

- Of course he did. What I don't know is if he existed as Hercules, Cyclope, Zarathustra or as the son of Mary and Joe in flesh and blood. If he did exist in flesh and blood, it is sure that he was not just anybody. Those who believe he existed, created him a genealogy all the way back to Adam, passing through King David: you remember the boy who killed Goliath and once a King had the bad habit of killing all the messengers who brought him bad news?

- Yes, I do remember. In the seminar we learned to recite his genealogy, like a psalm. Psalms are the preferred musical style there. I still remember the tune but forgot the words.

We laughed softly, Wilhelm emptied the remaining liquid in his glass and I took off my shoes to empty them of the water which I threw on the floor under the strongly reprobating eyes of the waiter. It was not much water, but still it could have filled a small glass. He turned back to the bar with his two elbows sustaining his head, fixing the painting. As if in a monologue he pursued:

- No, no, Jesus wasn't just anybody: he had rights to the throne of Israel. Bad luck, the throne was occupied by the collaborationists with the Roman occupier: Herodias, ready to defend his throne at any cost, even helping the Romans to pursue and kill all the members of Jewish resistance movements. As happened here during the war: there were many resistance movements and many led by familiars of Jesus. A guy by the name of Theudos thought that he was Joshua, the prophet of the salvation. He came from Egypt, where he was living, with four thousand followers to liberate Palestine and push the Romans into the sea. He pretended to dry up the rivers so that his followers could advance. The roman soldiers decapitated this Moses before he could show his hydraulic skills. Others: Jacob and his brother Simon, sons of Judas of Galilee, related to Jesus, headed a revolt which finished with their crucifixion. A grandson of the same family of liberators, Menahem, rebelled in the year sixty-six kicking off the Judean war which ended with the destruction of the temple of Jerusalem and the dispersion of the Jewish people all over the earth.

Discretely, I notified the waiter to fill up our glasses. Without paying any attention, the ex-priest Wilhelm continued his monologue:

- History is full of these deeds of Jewish resistance to Roman occupation. This is the political environment in which Jesus appears. Resistance is legitimate: wanting to get rid of the occupying armies who impose their language, their laws, their beliefs and their money by force is justified. But believing that one can oppose and defeat the most experimented, trained and best equipped army of that time with the sole power of faith, is transforming these just causes in defeats. God and the banners of faith waived in the face of the Roman legions don't have the sufficient weight. Now, that Jesus was crucified this is very possible: a lot of people were every week and crucifixion was by law the destiny of rebels resisting domination of the Roman Empire.

I was just forgetting to drink. The more Wilhelm talked, the more I got fascinated. I dared not move, neither move my Rodenbach out of fear that he would stop. But he did not, and fixed his beer and the painting. Fortunately we stayed alone in the hangout.

- Up to here, all this is possible. The rest is a fabulous fairytale of the marvelous life of Jesus invented by his followers among whom, a prominent one: Paul of Tarsus, Saint Paul.

Here he stopped and at once emptied his pint of Rodenbach. I dared:
- Oh, the epistles!
- Yes, the epistles! Unfortunately, Jesus did not write a word, Paul charged himself to fill up the empty space with what he thought Jesus should have said and done, what we should believe and not believe and how we should behave, creating a hero, an exceptional man. Mark, the evangelist who most likely accompanied Paul in his travels around the region is the first author of the marvelous life of Jesus in the year seventy. To make the story understandable they adjusted it to the beliefs and marvelous stories of their time. Mary was a virgin? No problem; Plato, centuries before, was born the same way. The son of Joe is son of God? No problem, Pythagoras, whom his followers took for Apollo himself, was too. Jesus talks in the name of someone more powerful? No problem either: all the prophets did so. Jesus behaved enigmatically: so did Pythagoras who never wrote a word except once with a stick in the sand and erased it immediately. Jesus died for his ideas? So did Socrates. And so on...and so on...What

made me doubt is that Plato, as did Paul, believed in a life after death and in the immortality of the soul: between the two there are almost four centuries.

He lifted his head and all of a sudden must have realized that I was there and that he had another beer in front. I had not noticed either that the waiter had brought two more. The density of Wilhelm's monologue had put me in a second state of mind, forgetting the surroundings. Panic got me when I realized that maybe he was going to stop.

- Why did so many believe the story?
- Look, my half-seminary friend, what follows is all politics: the

language of the evangels is a political language so as to convince its listeners that their announcement is the truth. They created truths repeating fictions. Add to this the militants, the military coup of the emperor Constantine, the long-lasting bloody repression against those who believed something else, and here you have the triumph of Christianity.

- But yet we are liberated from this, aren't we?
- Don't think so. The de-Christianization in Europe started when a sin was not a crime by essence anymore, which permitted the development of science, justice, democracy and liberty. But that was only yesterday. Remember the millions murdered all over the continents in the name of God: The inquisition with its twelve million deads; the crusades; the conquest of the Americas and Africa; the torturing, plundering, rape, exterminations, assassinations, exploitation, genocides and the very Christians: Hitler, Mussolini, Franco, Salazar and more… These millions of murders kept stuck in my throat. Just imagine what our life could have been if the holy church had not gone to merciless war against science and philosophy, since the burning of the first philosophers' libraries and for the one thousand and seven hundred years which followed?

We emptied our glasses, my bladder was next to explode, I excused myself, put back on my shoes, and went to empty it. When I came back a group of people of whom I knew a few, stood around Wilhelm, kissing, hugging and laughing. Someone put music on the jukebox, something by Elvis Presley, a lot of coats were hanging on my bar stool. Yet it was late to go to my room to get dry clothes, which would have been wet anyway just walking back. I stayed in the joint with wet socks and wet shoes, waiting for Martje to appear and

51

watching Wilhelm who apparently got rid of his nostalgia, since I saw him dancing and laughing a lot. When he passed close to me he said:
- The problem is that I know too much. Have fun and don't think.
That, I thought was stupid. I have fun thinking.

*

I had fallen in love with Martje, a fleshy, angel faced, smiling Flemish girl. We met one Saturday evening at the tavern of the painting. We danced and squeezed one against the other and we kissed on the cheek. I tried to apply the lessons heard from my sergeant to squeeze softly her breasts to what she replied with an accelerated respiration and soft moaning, excited to death. After three weekends, moaning, kissing in the dark and squeezing her breasts- as my sergeant had told me to do - I was surprised to find myself one Sunday afternoon at her home. Her father was a big shot at the parish of Antwerp and a "signoor". The very proud authentic natives of Antwerp call themselves "signooren" which means that not only they, but their parents and grandparents were born within the heart of the city. The "signooren" have a great, very great idea of them. (The word comes from the Spanish title "Señor" a souvenir of three centuries of occupation by the Spanish crown). This "Signoor" had made seven children to a little, round, very submitted and obedient woman. Martje twenty years from now?

Hardly seated, the man asked if I knew something about the bible. Yes "Signoor", about the bible I knew a few things. After a brief examination, he showed me oil paintings by a friend of his, a horse painter. I liked them, the strength and beauty of the Gembloux working horses, the ones I had handled, cleaned and driven in carriages and plows in Heur. It looked like I got through the examination with honors. From that moment on I was allowed to court his daughter. Unfortunately Martje, a schoolteacher, was convinced that the pearl of her virginity, sleeping between her legs, was worth marriage. So I stayed with sex-hunger and frustration and she stayed a virgin. I did not want to harm her, I never could harm a woman (which later on will put me in very peculiar situations), so my engagement went on and on.

In these times I read a lot, everything that fell into my hands, novels of any kind, essays of any nature, history of everywhere. Between two dates a week with Martje, two four-hour a day sessions of selling vacations, I swallowed books.

Months after getting into civilian clothes, I sold an airplane ticket to a Mister Van Dam, destination Ouagadougou in Upper Volta (today called Burkina Faso). I found out that the place is south of the Sahara desert in French West Africa. That was a change from selling vacations to Rimini in Italy, Dubrovnik in Yugoslavia, the Swiss Alps or some beach on the Costa Brava in Spain. Van Dam told me that he had a lot of work and that he was looking for a hunter of exotic birds and crocodiles in Upper Volta. Later on, he turned out to be a diamonds smuggler.

Little by little, my head was filling up with African adventures and emptying from marriage with Martje. Fortunately, the engagement ended in a stream of tears when Martje one day saw me somewhat familiar with a female colleague of the agency.

The road to Ouagadougou was open. I decided to walk it.

A few weeks later, I took the train to Brussels to climb into a plane for Paris for the first time in my life and from there another one to Ouagadougou. At that point I was taking myself for Stanley in search of Livingstone.

I did not realize it then, but that plane took me away definitively from Belgium, where I would never return to live. This does not mean that I don't have, especially in present times, a lot of good reasons to be very proud of that little country.

*

There is not one day that the local press, the Mexican television or a politician does not throw a vibrant homage to family values. As if that concept were the only source of affection, love, security, destiny and the supreme moral value of existence. The biological family –of which it is understood that it coincides with the social one – is here in Mexico a source of favoritism, nepotism, corruption and overprotection: all things well learned in the family. In reality, the family is more a factor of segregation and to some point of racism (85 % of Mexican primary school youngsters resent having an Indian, even less a Black as classmates; this is family education). So what are the great qualities of the Latin-way family?

Seeing Brussels disappear through the DC 4 plane window, these family values, fruit of a biological accident, will cease forever to be mine. The families that will be mine for the rest of my life are those of men and women chosen, who gave me their friendship, often their love, because we share values, opinions and ethics in a given place and for a certain time.

The Hedonist

Bye small world, I am going for the big one - without being aware of it at that moment, but that's what happened.

*

This night was of all spectacles. Millions of stars were concurring in brightness, several satellites cruised the firmament as to remember that, in all the natural magnificence, there is also the presence of Homo sapiens.

The fish that is supposed to help us make a living is a typical fall spawner. This means that conditions of equal daylight time and night time must be respected, and that the first northern winds coming from Canada cooled the water temperature by several degrees, producing a thermal choc. Without these conditions Sciaenops Ocellatus will not reproduce. Once natural conditions are as they like them to be, the female will produce an "appeal mucus" which works as a seducer. At that sight, the males start swimming behind and around her. The closer their moment of spawning, the more insistent are the males. These are the same codes as those of a night club. Finally, when the males cannot hold on and courting is judged to be enough, they make a drummer noise, squeezing their frontal head bones one against the other. That's the signal. A few hours later there are fertilized eggs floating all over the tank. Fertilization of eggs is external, which means that the female let go her ovules and the males their spermatozoids and that the spermatozoids have to swim to encounter an ovule and fertilize it. Once I watched this process on a giant electronic microscope. There is nothing more stupid on earth than a spermatozoid. Once he has found an egg he just keeps bouncing and bouncing, head on, at the same place, although there is only one possible entrance. The poor ovule feeling the assault at the wrong place tries to turn on its own axis to put the entrance in front of the stupid assailant before this one dies of pure exhaustion. Could it be that women are more intelligent from the ovule stage on? For the scarce chances there are for an ovule to be fertilized and for the even less chances a larvae has to survive, the female produces enormous quantities of ovules, up to 250,000 per kilo of her weight. Nature has its ways to maintain equilibrium.

Since eight o'clock we have been checking the egg collectors hung on the water outlet of the breed stock tanks. The future of this sea farming company and the welfare of sixteen families depend on the sexual desires of one dozen fish from six to eight kilos each: Their offspring converted - by our dedication - into fish to be sold within one year to the better off United States consumers, make up our business.

Having gotten to my sixty-fourth year of age and being dependent on sex desires of a dozen , is the material result of my life story. The crazy thing is that I like it, with all the stress and anguish included.

There is no sense in collecting fertilized eggs if the larvae food – a plankton named Rotifers- is not at the right level. For weeks we have been hatching and enriching rotifers, destined to become part of something bigger than themselves, a destiny for sure more exciting than to die of old age on their fifth day of existence. But there was no one yet to accomplish the cycle. Although it is not known what a rotifer thinks, "Ave Cesar morituri te salutant" must be their salute. (Hi, Cesar, those who are going to die salute you). To maintain the food production at optimal level, we enrich the sea daily with hundreds of millions of zoo plankton. At least they are not lost for everyone.

One million four hundred eggs, well fertilized, with the spermatozoids firmly hanging in the ovules, was last night harvest. Every two hours we collected, washed, disinfected, counted and sewed them in the larvae tanks in our self made, somewhat rustic, but very productive hatchery of sea fish, (the only one in Mexico). Taking into account its size and how much it had cost us, we must have the most productive hatchery in the entire world.

Don't think that I am the only fool who passes October nights surveying the horniness of fish. Oh no! We are six to share this passion, fever, excitement and stress: Patricia, Willy, Patrick, Roger and Roberto are as crazy as I am.

My French partners all come from a small village in the south of France, Besse sur Isolle, not too far from Marseille: vineyards and craftsmen. More Provencal than Besse, you die. Patricia is our queen, a beautiful woman, always smiling and good humored, I guess of around forty, an unusual common sense and an independent mind specific to the women of that region. She came to Campeche to visit her buddy Willy for three weeks, that was four years ago. She somehow, with her inborn common sense, holds the whole thing together and going.

Patrick is companion to Patricia. Man of little words. Voracious reader, something he says he had never done before, he swallows books. Up to the point that keeping up with providing books is a problem, since his Spanish is still not good and books in French are not available here.

The Hedonist

There remain Roger and Roberto, the Mexican human elements of the hatchery team. They are in charge of everything, since interchangeability in this trade is essential. They know everything about rotifers, artemias, larvae and bacteria. They are brothers in law, living in a small town, thirty miles away, with the beautiful (!) name of Champoton. (There is little else to say about the place, except that it does have some kind of stone house on the waterfront, built by the Spaniards after they lost a battle against the local mayan cacique right here, therefore they called the Champoton Bay: "the bay of the bad fight" while the mayans call it "the bay of the good fight). It is likely that the spermatozoids in this town also work in a closed circuit. I don't know much about them. All of the Mexican team, after the fifth pay get girlfriends, at the tenth pay they get married, and around the twenty first pay they get children. Victims of their ignorance about condoms or pills but above all of the great science of young girls to wrap them up in their enchanting charms so as to get a husband as soon as possible, if necessary by way of pregnancy. That's the way life goes in small Mexican towns.

Even if this first night of watching fish erotic life (there will be many more) started with a new bad moon – bad because it appeared with its legs up into the air - dawn was a marvelous spectacle. With the skyline turning from dark blue to light blue and the stars keeping shining as if the Milky Way struggled to put up a last resistance stand. Finally, after days and days of nerve breaking waiting, with the larvae tanks empty, more than a million eggs were swirled around and waiting in a few hours to become part of life. The pumps were snoring regularly and peacefully, the trickle of the larvae tanks well adjusted, the UV lamps all lit up, the biological filter, where we cultivate bacteria which are supposed to consume the ammonia, all well circulating, the lights turned off (because larvae spawn in the dark and stay that way until they get hungry), everything is in its place.

Here we are, the fish makers of Mexico, drinking the last coffee (at my age it's decaf), talking about fish, larvae, eggs, juveniles, fish cages, about previous spawning and how magnificent all this is, experiencing, deep inside, the great feeling of satisfaction that grows with a job well done. If many warriors have their nights of vigil before battle, politicians their election nights, we have our spawning nights.

CHAPTER II
ILESHA – ABIDJAN- WASHINGTON-SAN FRANCISCO

Ouagadougou: two miles of a four-lane asphalted avenue with, on both sides, government buildings, a hotel taking itself for a five star, ending with the Presidential Palace almost lost in the savanna. Four paved streets on each side of the central market place at the opposite side of the presidential palace. All the rest is red dust streets with on each side mud walls. The houses in Ouagadougou are behind walls and divided into several also mud rooms all giving into a central - cooking-washing-chatting-sitting patio. Nobody has a direct access to the street and nobody from the street can look inside. Everything was marvelous to me, even the cockroaches and the iguanas I found beautiful.

On Van Dam's recommendation, I looked up a French embassy employee who brought me to a mansion, on the main avenue, I was supposed to live in. I don't know what marvelous things about my finances Van Dam had told this civil servant, but when I was told the rent money, I only stayed one week and moved out to the small hotel on the market corner. Even if the cockroaches were enormous and walked all over the room, if the shower water had a very suspicious yellow color, the ceiling ventilator seemed to take a whole minute to do just one turn, I felt happy. The place had a bar-restaurant, hangout of the "petits Blancs" (small whites). Those whites who stayed in the ex-colonies, who could not leave for one reason or the other: craftsmen, entrepreneurs, ex-military, shop owners, butchers, bakers. All of them: big talkers, big drinkers, and with a big heart.

Van Dam was supposed to show up soon and bring me money to finance my bird-expeditions but, just to show my bravery and dedication, I decided to rent a pick-up and without asking more went on a hunting-buying expedition to Dori, way up in the Sahel zone which runs from the Atlantic to the Indian Ocean, just south of the Sahara. Yes, I knew something about trucks, about surviving with a tin of corned beef, another one of instant coffee, a bag of biscuits, a kilo of sugar and some sardine tins. On the contrary, I didn't know anything about birds, African roads, the suffocating heat and even less about its people. I had no idea what it was like to adventure alone with an old pick up truck trying to find out where the road is. In the Sahel everyone traces his own road wherever he likes, guided by intuition and guessing. I learned, and fast.

Dori is about three hundred kilometers north of Ouaga. Little by little, I passed from Mossi territory into Peul (also called Fulani) country and from a red dusty road to a grey and yellow sandy one. On this road which further north will lose itself in the Sahara and Algeria, the last Mossi peasant's village, named Kaya, is where I wanted to spend the night.

It was impossible to enter the village with the pick-up, so I parked a hundred yards away under a huge cotton tree. My first visitors were a cloud of half-naked, big bellied, skinny, children. They stayed at respectable distance just staring, while I displayed my straw woven carpet. That village is a fortress, surrounded with a grey mud wall of six meters high with, for what I could see, a sole porch looking like a cave entrance. After looking at each other for about half an hour asking which one was the fool, the group of children made way to let about a dozen of adults approach, led by what I took for the village chief: a high, erect man with curly hair and a grey beard, from shoulders to sandals enveloped in a sky-blue large tunic, locally called "boubou", richly embroidered around the neck and chest. I stood with my back against the cabin door and when they stopped in half a circle around me I saluted:
- Good day.
The blue boubou came forward and in excellent French, much better than mine, responded:
- Good day, who are you?
Shaking his hand, which was very rough but firm, I said:
- I am a bird hunter and I am going to Dori.
A silence followed for a couple of seconds while we looked at each other's eyes. There was amusement in his and a smile came on his face, which made me see a row of awful looking brown-yellow teeth.
- So, you want to buy birds?
-Yes, but they have to be beautiful and very much alive.
In reality, I still had not asked myself how I would acquit myself of my new job as a bird hunter: I only knew that these birds had to be exotic enough to please the Belgian fans of exotic birds.

Now the blue boubou man was really laughing, imitated in this by the rest of the peasants, some of whom had their axes over their shoulders, all wearing a knife in a leather holster attached to the rope that also served to hold their pants up. The blue boubou turned his back to me and talked in moreh - which is the language of the Mossi - to the peasants who approved shaking their heads up and down. In the meantime, I surveyed my little belongings in the truck, by now overwhelmed by the children. Everything was still there. When the blue one turned back to me, he screamed something and the cloud of children flew from the truck as a bunch of chicken seeing a fox. The blue one put himself in front of me and showed me an impeccable military salute, with his sandaled feet, his heels touching each other. The palm of his right hand turned outside, as do the French. Instinctively I too stood at attention and brought my right hand to my forehead in the best military salute I had ever performed.

Thinking of it today, there were standing face to face an old soldier of all battles, who fought for liberty, and a young twenty-one year old bird hunter, saluting each other, impeccably, in front of an African mud village, lost somewhere in the Sahel. All this impressed very much the audience who looked on in complete silence. My reaction, of pure reflex, must have pleased him, and without lowering his hand from his forehead he shouted:

- Corporal Auguste Sawadogo, chief of this village.

To which I replied:

- Sergeant Jean-Pierre Goffings of the seventh line regiment of his Majesty the King of Belgium.

We lowered our arms and shook hands again. After a small pause, Auguste asked me

- You don't have Pastis?

It took me a moment to grab the question, after which I murmured

- Yes, I think I have some left.

While I searched in the couple of carton boxes of my belongings for one of the half bottles of Pastis I had brought along by recommendations of my buddies the "little whites" from the hotel bar, a row of women had brought huge straw carpets they displayed on the side of my pick-up. We sat. I, my back against the fore wheel of the truck and my audience in half a circle around, with August right in front and the Pastis bottle between us.

Pastis, for those who don't know it, is a beverage based on anis, with a quite nice degree of alcohol. It's only drunk diluted in water and ice. It's the typical beverage of all the southern regions of France. I waited for someone to bring the water. Auguste offered me half a cola nut: chewing cola is what gives that awful coffee color to their teeth. I really did not know what to do with it, but for hospitality sake I bit a piece of it. It's very, very bitter. I felt my mouth contracting as a chicken ass just after laying an egg.

There was no time to realize it, but when I turned my head, Auguste had the Pastis bottle to his mouth. I never had, and never will see again someone drinking Pastis like that, right from the bottle. I expected him to spit or something, but nothing happened. With calm and careful not to spill a drop, he just put the bottle, with a quarter of

liquid missing, where it had been just seconds before, and cleaned his mouth with the large sleeve of his beautiful tunic.
- What's your name?
I had said that before, but I presumed that it was just a way to start talking again.
- Jean-Pierre.
- Do you know Paris?
No, I didn't know Paris.
August started to give me a detailed description of Paris: its avenues, the metro stations, the Latin Quarter, the Seine River, the monuments, Pigalle, Barbès and more. No Parisian policeman could have done better. When he finished he took another long drink, happy to see that I had abstained.
- I fought for General de Gaulle, with Leclerc.
I understood that it was in the French army that he had learned to drink Pastis that way.
- Where? I dared ask
- Everywhere, Tobruk in Libya, Monte Casino in Italy, Provence... but also in Indochina and Algeria.
He followed on with an extensive description of the battles and campaigns of the French army in the ten post-war years. This was my first encounter with an authentic war hero of the Second World War. It will not be the last one in Africa.

*

To give reality to his resistance movement against the Nazis and the submission of France, de Gaulle from London, with the help, very difficultly obtained, from Churchill and Roosevelt, ordered his best General to organize a French colonial army and attack the Nazis and the Italians in the north of Africa, crossing the Sahara desert to become the spear point of the liberation of France. Leclerc recruited in all the French sub-Saharan colonies of West and Central Africa. All of them achieved heroism, especially in the slaughter of the battle for Monte Casino in Italy, where half of them died. I am a poor historian but I believe that that's the way it happened.

*

I did not know very much about World War II, but this corporal sitting there on a straw carpet, drinking Pastis as if it were Coca Cola, was a real hero, deserving all the war medals a nation can give. Night had fallen, stars like they are only to be seen in this part of the earth, did not let the night install itself completely. The Pastis bottle was dead since a while, fallen on the field of honor. Auguste was slightly drunk but did not lose posture when with dignity he gave me a last salute, inviting me to spend the night in his house. Which I, very politely, with a lot of thanks and lies, refused, preferring to spend my first night in the Sahel among the stars and close to my few belongings.

I was woken up with what I thought was a rooster philharmonic orchestra. After two glasses of instant coffee and a couple of biscuits, I started the motor. To my surprise the gas tank needle showed the same amount of gasoline. The last image of Kaya, which still hangs in my memory, is a large row of women and children, in the low light of dawn, walking into the bush towards some mysterious well or a water point, all carrying basins or buckets on their heads.

Peul herdsmen and their sheep, animals I had never seen before: high standing, short-haired, white from head to half of their belly and the other half to the tail black, crossed my road The distinguishing thing about Peul pastors is that they walk in front of their herds which follow them glued to their heels, no one passes ahead, belly to belly all at the same pace. Here, in a territory of little pasture and even scarcer water, the animals are completely dependent on their pastor and on where he leads them: their lives depend on him and they know it. The Peuls are tall, skinny, bronze skin colored, which makes them different from the other populations of Burkina Faso (which stands for "land of the faithful", or something like that)

Not one of these herdsmen I crossed all along the road to Dori, thought that I was worth a glance. Walking straight up, gazing at some point beyond the horizon, their long sticks over their shoulders with their arms and hands loosely resting over them, they walk their way. Around their necks and hanging on their chest are a lot of necklaces and amulets. They didn't go a meter out of their way when approaching me, not even looked at me. Where were they going? Where did they come from? That's their business. Where was I going? That was my business. We had nothing to say to each other.

*

Later on, I learned that the Peuls are divided into several tribes all along the south of the Sahara desert and that they are of Berber origin, an ethnic group dominating the north of Africa before the Arab invasions. That explains their brown skin color and the absence of anthropological negroïd characteristics: they don't have curly hair, neither flat noses, nor big lips. You could easily mistake them for a well tanned Italian or Spaniard.

Besides these physical particularities, they have a lot of cultural ones which distinguish them and very few practice excision. Yes, they are Muslims, but soft. They do believe that the prophet was God's messenger but they believe in a lot more things too.. Known to be rebellious to any authority that does not come from the family, the clan or the tribe, they are proud and superior minded. In pre-colonial times they raided the Negroid populations of the south and enslaved them. A habit they shared with all the other Saharan and Sahelian tribes. Their wives are very independent, even when married they possess their own cattle and sheep herds. Years later in Chad, I crossed the case of a poor Peul herdsman who had lost all of his animals because of the render pest epidemic, except for a few cows, who was complaining because his wife did not want to lend him one of her steers to rebuild his herd.

According to a typical Peul's marriage contract, the woman comes to live in her husband's family with her own herd of livestock, her servants, some younger sister and her belongings. The product of her herd: milk, calves, belongs completely to her. The more children she has before marriage, the more she is searched for as a spouse, because she proved her fertility; something very sought after in her husband's family. The husband owes her so many blouses and clothes, necklaces, bracelets and sandals per year and of course he has to fertilize her. And if all this is not to her liking, one day she takes her cows, sheep and goats, puts her children on a donkey and rides off, back to her family. Then, the families go into a round of talks for weeks for the reconciliation of the couple, or to agree on how to split up the dowry. I'll tell you more about the role of the dowry later on.

Among the Peul tribes, the most famous ones are the Bororos, the only tribe to resist Islamism and still practicing a pure nomadic life. They are known all over the world because of pictures and films which show them in their annual gathering where they compete in beauty contests for men and appear somewhat feminine. Fifteen years later I will frequent closely Bororo tribesmen in Chad, three thousand kilometers east of Dori. There, I realized that they are not only exotic models for ethnological reviews; they are above all free men. Free from outside religious influences. Free to go and come wherever they please following the rains which, depending on the season, go north or come south, towards or back from the Sahara desert. Free from any control, whatsoever, from any government. To be a Bororo is a myth and a reason for envy.

*

Dori. A dozen sand and dust streets imprisoned by walls of mud houses. To the south, on top of a slight elevation, the "administrative city": half a dozen, one-floor cement buildings in which live the administrators: the sub-prefect, the vet, the chief of police and his four keepers of peace, the schoolmaster, the doctor and his clinic, the postmaster and oh! miracle, a church. It's an on-the-side village. Separated from the real one by a football field, and having little to do with the real village. All the representatives of the Nation are people from the South, negroïd. The Peuls from Dori, as all the other Peuls, must just consider them as potential subjects to be raided and sold or used as slaves. There is nothing to be administrated in Dori. During three quarters of the year, the main body of the population is walking around the Sahel with their livestock, leaving behind the elderly who cannot keep up the pace, the too small children, still no good to help out herding cattle and some former Negro slaves, to take care of them.

All this was told to me by the two missionaries, one French and one Italian, both around thirty five years old, both tall, with large beards hanging over brown cassocks held together with a rope around the waist of which hung a big cross in the Franciscan mode. They were here to make Christians out of the Peuls and offered me hospitality in a spare room.

They looked very happy and amused by the diversion I represented. What had they done to the bishop to be relegated to this corner, in the middle of Muslim tribes?

The Franciscan and Dominican religious orders for a long time competed to see who would burn more unbelievers, witches and scientists during the holy inquisition in Europe and who more blessed the conquering Spanish armies in the Americas. Here, they were to bring salvation to cattle tribesmen who were not there. For hundreds of miles around they were the only white people.

We got along fine, the Italian talked a lot. He wanted to know everything about me: the seminar, the army and my new vocation as a bird hunter. My doubts about the holy faith and the holy church from Rome were not as strong as they are today, so we almost met up in a fraternal communion. They were assisted by a Mossi servant who was an excellent cook, but the spaghettis were cooked by the Italian, while he was telling us how his mother, a saint, prepared spaghettis drowning them all at once in the boiling water and according to how they fell interpreted the response to a secret question she had formulated. Depending upon the result of the falling spaghettis, that holy woman was good or ill-tempered. We passed dinner talking and talking. This father was the first Italian I met in my life. Later on I'll meet many more: all talked a lot and at one moment or the other they all talked about their "mamma".

The Frenchman did not say very much. He must have heard the Italian stories a thousand times. With the end of dinner and the graces said all together in Latin, night fell and we passed on to the roofless terrace where the Mossi servant had laid a carpet, cushions and two petrol lamps. Little by little, the sky lightened up with a billion stars. From the village, a smell of cooking and burning wood came up to envelop the terrace; at large, a powerful radio was playing languid Arab songs. Some dogs barked but stopped as suddenly as they had started. The French served mint tea, strong, very sweet, very hot, Arab style. Comfortably lying on our backs, we pointed our noses to the sky and finally, in silence. Even the Italian lost his speech with the spectacle of the universe which seemed to fall upon us.

Some time passed before we heard somebody approach, clapping hands, the way people around here announce themselves: it's like knocking on a door when there are no doors available. Followed by a soft voice "father, father" The Frenchman rolled to his side and leaning on his elbow:
- Come on in, mister sub-prefect.

This was funny, because we were lying down on a terrace with no walls or doors to trespass. Out of the dark there appeared a tall man, large, athletic, and lost in the darkness of which his clothes and skin had the color. He took off his shoes and crawling on his knees, got around to shake hands. His hands were twice mine and mine are not small. Finishing the greeting ceremonial, he went to lie down beside the Frenchman and out of his pocket dug up a bottle of Johnny Walker, half full. The bottle made the circle, filling up our small tea glasses. The music coming from the village increased in volume, some women or girls' voices, accompanied by drums, sang what must have been a love song.

There was nothing else in the world I would have liked more than to lay on my back on a carpet in the desert with a glass of whisky and accompanied by women voices. The sub-prefect and the French were engaged in a low voice conversation. For once, the Italian did not speak but we emptied quite a few tea glasses of Walking Johnny. Passing some glasses, the Mossi servant came to whisper something to the Italian's ear. My companion got up with a smile on his face, which to me looked a little nervous, and disappeared into the dining room. Rolling a little to my left, so as to have the kitchen door in sight, in the dim light of the petrol lamp I saw clearly a female figure going out of the kitchen door followed by the Italian.

Though my sexual experience at that time was close to zero, I nevertheless had heard of the "missionary position": the lovemaking position (woman below, man on top) as the Africans called it when they saw the missionaries fornicating.

Early in the morning, the night still in power, I was woken by a voice screaming loud and clear, from the distance:
- Allaaaaaaaah Akbar, Muhammad razou Allaaaaaaah.
The petrol lamp had given up and I was alone on the terrace. Vaguely, I remembered that in the center of the village stood a building a little taller than the houses, like a tower. I figured that it was the mosque where the voice came from. Sleep caught me again and I woke up when the sky was already blue and the servant, I never knew his name, gave me a cup of smoking instant coffee and a large smile. The two missionaries were already having breakfast and talking. My head was heavy and I needed to go to the bathroom.

An hour later, the servant started to walk through the "administrative quarters" ringing a hand bell, bringing it up to his shoulder and lowering it to his knees, just as I had done so many times in Heur.

I can say that I have seen many surrealistic situations in my life, especially here in Mexico, where surrealism is a way of life. Nevertheless, that mass there in Dori, with a dozen and a half Negroid Mossi men and women in Peul Muslim territory listening to a mass in Latin and singing Gregorian music is one of the outstanding occasions.

I stayed five days in Dori, one of which I passed crawling in a mud pool trying to approach a bunch of crowned grouses that, apart from keeping distance from me, sent regularly a sentinel to fly over to see where I was in my progress towards them. They are magnificent birds: from foot to head they stand over one meter, very gracious, with black wing feathers, white-yellow chest, a long black peak, blue eyes and a crown of small yellow feathers (hence the name), and red thin legs which also could belong to Flamingoes. When I thought I was close enough to try an assault, I realized that I did not know what to do with them. I had not even brought a rope.

One of those evenings, spread out over the big carpet with all the length of my body, after the ritual and the discrete leaving of the Italian through the back door, with the French father we listened to a live concert of Georges Brassens, broadcast by RFI radio. My primitive French did not allow me to understand everything, just one word over here and another one over there, but enough to grasp that this troubadour was very disrespectful of the priests, the church, the pope, the fatherland, the politicians and many more things which smell of conformism. (Later on, with my French being better and better, George Brassens will become my favorite poet). The French missionary next to me laughed out loudly and I followed him without understanding what was being said, but just for the fun of this tough voice, the public applauding loudly and the guitar sound coming out of the black short wave radio. When the half hour of pure and completely surrealistic pleasure, because of the Dori environment, came to an end, my companion turned off the radio, pushed his pillow closer to mine and with his face at two feet from my nose, he looked straight into my eyes and asked:

- Do you happen to know who Saint Helena was?

His eyes had an inquisitive but soft expression with a kidding sprinkle. If there was something I did not want to talk about, at that moment, it was "the life of the saints". I just figured that Helena sounded like a converted prostitute who became holy for whatever reason.

- No, my dear father, my seminary experience did not last long enough to know who Saint Helena was.

He smiled.

- She was the mother of Emperor Constantine, the one who made Catholicism become a state religion and ordered to write the evangels we know today.

- Are you saying that he ordered to write the evangels? Were they not written by the four evangelists?

- The four evangelists are a selection of the twenty-six existing before Constantine and the Nicaea council in 325. Constantine and his Christian counselor by the name of Eusebius from Caesarea, put in that place by Helena, felt the necessity to make some sense and coherence in the existing confusing Christian literature.

From half asleep, I became completely awake.

- Why did Constantine want to do this?

- His empire was falling to pieces which worried him a lot. He came to power by way of a military coup, defeating Maxense and understood the advantages of getting associated with a religious monotheist sect that preached total obedience to the temporal power holder and the acceptance of poverty and misery without rebellion, as recommended by the writings of Saint Paul. To disobey the emperor is disobeying God: which politician would not like a law like this one? After his triumph, he wrote into the Roman laws everything that was recommended to him by this religious sect of Jewish origin.

- Wait a minute, father, this is politics. What became of the divinity of Jesus Christ and his teaching?

- A joke, which passed through a vote at the same council with a narrow margin.

- Are you telling me that Jesus was appointed "son of God" by a vote?

- Yes, that's the way it went, does it surprise you?

The hell it did.

- Well, yes, I have never heard that before.

I turned my back to him to adjust my pillow, but also not to show my face. I was dead scared. We took a sip of tea, which was cold and bitter.

- But we left Saint Helena, let's go on with her.

He cleared his throat and continued:

- She was a little worried because her son, the Emperor, had killed his own son, instigated by his second wife who convinced him that his son was seducing her

- Constantine killed *his* son?

This was getting better and better, it sounded to me like a horror story.

- Yes, yes and a lot of other people too from his own family and allies. To buy the absolution of her son's sins, Helena went on pilgrimage to the Holly Land where she discovered the Titulus and the three hundred years old holy cross of Jesus; the Golgotha, which just happened to stand under a temple dedicated to Aphrodite, which she ordered to be destroyed. She created the churches of the Nativity and the Holy Grave and named the Olive Garden. For all this and some more things, Helena was declared a saint, her son forgiven and declared the thirteenth apostle. She became the first holy Empress.

This last sentence was said with sorrow and followed with long minutes of silence. I did not know what to say or think.

- What happened afterwards?

My companion moved to reach his tea cup while talking:

- After that, the Catholic Church had an armed arm and started to use it without restriction to create a totalitarian state. The philosophers were assassinated, their libraries burned and everybody who was not convinced of the truth of the new religion was persecuted and put to

death. Only the Inquisition accounts for twelve million deaths all over Europe, which, by the way, saved the holy Church of Rome. Not believing whatever the Vatican said you had to believe cost you your head. In these conditions, who will not believe in Santa Claus?
All this sounded incredibly coherent and realistic, but so what?
- So what about us, father?
- We don't count; we are individuals without any value or importance, just   grains of sand in the Sahara to be stepped on whenever they please.
I guessed who "they" were. By now, my companion's voice sounded very depressed.
- I am just telling you this so you know how and why you were sent to the seminar and I became a missionary in Dori, one thousand seven hundred years after the story of Helena. I wish you a good night.
He got up and with his pillow under his arm and in a whisper of his cassock, he went to his room. I stayed there for a long while, getting lost among the stars feeling that, whatever I believed before and after this chat, I was not the same anymore. One thing became sure: I started feeling very well about having been kicked out of the seminar.

It was clear that the faith and the will to civilize and save souls of these two missionaries were at their lowest level. They didn't know what to do with their days. They mounted horses and organized races with the vet. There, I learned to ride camels, which would be very useful some years later.
The vet had studied his trade for seven years in the Tropical Veterinarian School of Maisons Alfort in the Paris suburbs, one of the most famous Vet schools in the world. He too, had his doubts about his utility in Dori, taking care of cattle that was only present a few months in the year, and which the herdsmen hid from him for fear that he would count them and that they would have to pay taxes. Very sociable, with always a large smile painted on his face with deep scarves on the cheeks, he told me that he expected that his service in Dori would be short. He talked about Paris and the working class struggle. As almost all the vets from Maisons Alfort I will meet later in my life, he was a convinced Marxist-Leninist, but at that time this was Chinese to me. To go to the Vet's post from the church, one had to cross the whole village. It was my first physical contact with a Muslim community of which I would gain a large experience later on. (Large enough to conclude, that of all the monotheist cultures, Islam is by far the most retrograde, archaic and obscurantist religion of them all).

The road back to Ouagadougou was as upon a cloud. I felt delighted with my first contact with Africa, happy to eat the dust of the road out of pure romanticism. I made a long curve in the bush to avoid the village of Auguste: there was no Pastis left. The vet, the missionaries and the sub-prefect of Dori had taken care of my reserve.

I reached Ouaga well into the night, passing in front of the mansion Van Dam had recommended to me. Van Dam, who to my surprise, wearing big dark sunglasses, was seated on the dining room table with in front of him several Voltaïcs in majestic large tunics. Before I entered, I heard Van Dam shouting. On the table lay a blue cloth with a lot of small yellowish stones. My apparition, in shorts, very dirty, my hair standing straight with the huge quantity of dust, made an impression. Everybody fell silent. The Mossis looked astonished and frightened. I went to salute Van Dam to see closer what was on the table: small stones disposed in several heaps of different sizes. Van Dam held a magnifying glass in his left hand. Rising on his legs, spitting through his teeth, he said to me in Flemish:
- Get out, imbecile!
I acted as if I didn't understand and kept looking at the diamonds.
- Disappear! He looked very angry and menacing.
The Mossis too had risen and wrapped up the stones in the blue cloth. Van Dam barked at them to sit down, which they did very reluctantly. The sun glassed partner pushed me to the door. I did not resist, made a few steps and went through the door, not without shouting "Good night everybody".

So I learned that my associate in the bird business was a diamonds smuggler. Besides that, fhe did himself get by as a textile investor who had an investment project for a factory. That was his business card with the government. I heard this from one of the Mossis who waited for me at the hotel door next morning. I asked him to find a craftsman who could make me a backpack in exchange for my suitcase.

Thirty-six hours later, I stood on the road from Ouagadougou to Togo with a goatskin, very smelly backpack hanging from my shoulder and with my thumb in the air. I would have liked to stay a while in Upper Volta, but without Van Dam.

From ride to ride, eating dry toasts, accommodated with bananas and green oranges, it did go smoothly. Until I don't know how I found myself imprisoned for two nights and three days in Bawku, Ghana. I didn't want to go there, but the road to Togo was

69

interrupted because of a fallen bridge or something like that, so the truck I was on, had to cut a corner into Ghana. Ghana at that time was ruled by a sort of socialist dictator by the name of Nkrumah with a very bad reputation. I'll never know why I was imprisoned. They pulled me out of the cabin and walked me to the prison with two guns pointed at my back. The following day they – half a dozen policemen and custom agents - let me out sitting on a bench, my back against my new home. I sat there for hours, the only thing they asked me was: "Do you want Ghana woman". No, I did not want a whore, neither had I the money to pay for her. Two days later, lightened of all the few things I carried, I was "liberated" by the representatives of her "Majesty the Queen" as they called themselves every morning when they rose the flag on a very crooked wooden pole, with all the pompous screaming and shouting they were capable of. Then I got the scare – I'd say panic, of my life. In the afternoon they took me out of the cell which had been my home for a few days, and had me walk away from the road, down a hill, towards a dense wood in the valley, with two rifles pointed at my back.

All of a sudden I realized my situation. Forty years later, I still remember in detail the anguish, fear, panic and resignation that seized me. It became clear that they were going to shoot me in the back and just let me rot away there or rather serve as dinner to some wild beast. Nobody in the whole world knew where I was. I thought of my parents, my aunt Geraldine, Heur, my sisters and started to weep. I wanted to throw up but did not have anything left in my stomach, nothing came. As if hypnotized, my feet took me to that bush which I was sure was the last thing I was ever going to see from this world, my bones and belly would be eaten by hyenas. When was that damned click-clack from the charging rifles going to come?

The click-clack never came. Getting to the bush, down in the valley, I dared to look over my shoulder and saw my assassins walking back up the hill, holding their rifles with the canon over their shoulders. The fear of my life had been for nothing. I fell under a tree and passed the night there, an awful night, crying, feeling as miserable as possible, desperate, sleeping for short whiles interrupted by horrendous nightmares. Never had I been and never again will I be as miserable as that night in that wood, waiting for death. When dawn came, I walked as a drunk up the hill, sweating, shivering with cold, found a road, and lost conscience.

I woke up three days later, in a monk cell of the Apadongo catholic mission in Togo. Someone had found me on the roadside and carried me to the mission where for three days and nights I was delirious with malaria. That's what the fathers told me. They had feared for my life. I still have malaria, fortunately not often anymore. It took me a week to get back on my feet and continue south: a whole week in which I served mass everyday but talked very little.

In Lome, Togo, I got a visa for Nigeria. Why Nigeria? I don't know but that's where I went.

I'm not painting Lagos, I don't have a clue how the place looks like today, but forty years ago it was the biggest mess you can imagine. Dirty, bad smelling, dusty, traffic jams that lasted for hours, they called them "Go slow", it was more like not going anywhere. Every time there was a state visit, they had to cut off water for a whole section of the city, just to make sure that the hotel where the foreigners were staying had enough water. Lodging was in a Salvation Army Boy Scout compound in the center of town.

Through the Belgian embassy I found a job in a forest exploitation camp in Ilesha, about two hundred kilometers north of Lagos. The man in charge wore the name of Goossens, Flemish from Antwerp. About sixty, grey hair and equally grey well-trimmed beard, blue eyes, a bit bellied, and too much far everywhere. There was another Flemish working with him, Johan, an always laughing young man, a very, very cool guy. So cool that one day he called me from his room, asking me to get his cigarettes, which I found in his jacket pockets hanging on a chair. He was lying on his side, with his penis connected to a young girl with frightened eyes. He just wanted to make a pause in whatever he was doing, smoking a cigarette. I didn't have time to react or be surprised at the picture I was contemplating and even lit up his cigarette before fleeing from the room. From him I heard that Goossens was on the run for having been a Nazi and participated in the Flemish Legion that fought for Hitler in Stalingrad. He had fled from Belgium in 1945 and stayed hidden in Franco's Spain for years. It was rare to me that a racist Flemish was exploiting a forest permit in Nigeria. There are funny things in this world. Later, in Chad, I met a French expert from the United Nations who strongly recommended me to take vacations in South Africa "before the negroes screw up the place". It's a pity that the FAO does not require any moral values from its experts. But what are we going to say if for years the Secretary-General of the United Nations, a certain Kurt Waldheim, was an ex Nazi.

In Ilesha, a relatively big Yoruba town, I learned the beautiful trade of forestry: To trace and build forest roads for tractors, and lumber trucks; to select and cut hundred years old majestic trees, standing as cathedrals; to calculate cubic meters of lumber, mark them, load them on to trucks and finally float them in the Lagos lagoon to ships waiting in the harbor, with European, American and Japanese destinations, where they will be converted into furniture, walls or floors.

The destruction of the forest, just to take out one single trunk was tremendous. The roads for the bulldozers to go and get them out, the three or four giants that fell along and were left there to rot, because of less commercial value, the enormous zones for maneuvering and loading, the temporary camps for the lumbermen, the truck roads; all this made of the virgin forest a "civilized" zone. Fortunately, in those days, trees were still cut with hatchets, which slowed down the general destruction. From three to six wood cutters would climb on a three meter high, very fragile platform made up of poles around the tree trunk. For the tree is only exploitable from where the trunk becomes straight, above the root curbs. The structure balances back and forth at each hatch swing. Only very precise synchronization of the butcher movements – let me call them this way because that's where it comes down to, butchering the forest - kept it from tumbling down. The only way to get this synchronization, since they could not see each other, is singing and swinging the hatchets at the rhythm of the songs. A counter movement and the whole structure with the butchers on it would disintegrate - that happened several times, with the consequent disaster of wounds and cuts. It was all very nice, almost Hollywood movies like: the songs, the noise of the hatches cutting into the fresh timber, the athletic naked Yorubas swinging their hatches, standing on slim poles three meters above the ground. Yes, John Ford would have been happy with that scene. What's less beautiful is when the giant, wounded to the heart, starts hesitating on which side it is going to fall and everybody starts shouting "timber, timbeeer" and runs in the opposite way they think it is going to fall. Sometimes it does not work out, when the tree decides to fall the other way. Accidents of legs and bodies badly crushed were not rare. I don't remember how we communicated with the Yorubas: I chewed three English words and they, five. It must be that their cheerful character, their way of making a joke of everything did the rest.

Ilesha is a town, so there is a catholic mission and schools. Johan took me to the weekly Saturday cultural happening of the white people in Ilesha: English school teachers –men and women- a couple of forest people like us, and the totality of missionaries, monks, nuns and even two adepts of the American Peace Corps, with whom I sympathized somewhat: they showed us pictures and served tea and coca cola. That's where I saw Sir Hillary climbing the Everest. All this was pleasant and very civilized.

Our English neighbor was unforgettable. Every Tuesday, Thursday and Saturday, which were the days when the mail got to Ilesha, he had his breakfast served on the terrace giving to the street by his servant and also white jacketed and white gloved cook. When breakfast was on the table the "boy" (that's what the English and the French call their servants in Africa) would go to the post office and get the mail. Coming back, the boy would walk down the street waving the newspaper, shouting: "The Times, The Times". Our neighbor would throw him a coin and receive his newspaper. After which the boy would go in by the back door, put on his white jacket and gloves and proceed serving tea to the gentleman who, lighting up a pipe, enjoyed his at least one week old Times. It was an immovable ceremony.

We, hidden behind the garden fence, laughed our heads off with the eccentric spectacle. Of these old colonials, who could just not hang up their past lives and go back to whatever home was, I'll meet many. All of them had something loose in their heads but all were real gentlemen, jovial, serviceable and with high civic and moral values.

Goossens, the Nazi, was putting high pressure on us and expressed himself only with grunting, shouting, screaming, humiliating us whenever he had an occasion. He instructed me to convoy the lumber trucks to Lagos and survey the loading to an East German ship. I stayed four days in the harbor of Lagos, living on the ship. Day and night I convoyed lumber through the Lagos lagoon, docking them on starboard and craning them onto the ship's belly and deck. The last day, Goossens came to inspect and with his usual shouting ordered me to go and pick up furniture at the German embassy and take it that same night to Ilesha. Which I did, but at three o'clock in the morning I found myself with the truck in a ditch besides the road. I had fallen asleep on the steering wheel. Later on, that same day, in his office, Goossens got into a disproportionate temper for the damage I had done to his truck. He put his red face with white foam in the corners of his mouth close to mine and lifted his hand to slap me. Before I knew what I was doing, I used on him, instinctively, one of the self-defense grips I had practiced in the Belgian army, immobilizing his arm, kicking his feet from under him, kicking towards his genitals which I felt right on the top of my boots, letting myself fall on him with a couple of punches to his nose which started to bleed heavily. It was done in a second; he didn't have time to scream. I sat on the Nazi who was moaning, crawled in a fetus position and holding his balls between his legs with both hands.

I stood up and slowly walked to his desk and grabbed a bronze horse statue about thirty centimeters high. Seeing me coming Goossens asked for mercy. His nose kept bleeding, with the blood filling up his mouth. He crawled away to a corner weeping.

I opened all his desk drawers, looking for a gun and money. There were both of them. I put the gun under my belt and from a pile of dollars took what he owed me – two months.

This was the first time in my life I punched someone to harm him. It did not come out bad. I locked Goossens in his office, took the key to Johan to whom I told the story. He laughed, as if liberated, threw the key out of the window, put the gun in his suitcase and offered to take me to Lagos right away. Ten minutes later we were on the road, making up the story he was going to tell Goossens. We did not enter Lagos and said goodbye on the road leading to Dahomey (today Benin). That same night, I crossed the border but not without another problem. In the no man's land I had to hide on the side of the road in a ditch filled with water, high grass and rotten wood to let pass a border patrol. Probably they were scared, because they talked very loud and announced themselves dozens of meters away. Infantry commando training served to something.

A few days later I was in Abidjan, capital of Ivory Coast, lodging in a small hotel in Treichville, the biggest of the many "red zones" of the city. Soon I got a job as a forester for a company named "The woods of the Monza" with an exploitation permit in Abengourou, close to the Ghana border. The same evening of my contracting I was sitting in a First World War truck with a drunken chauffeur of the same age, who stopped at every village to buy a liter of red wine. Every time we passed another vehicle, he closed his eyes, hung on to the steering wheel and never took his foot off the accelerator pedal pushed to the floor. I passed a couple of scary moments but we got to the lumber camp all right.

Work was the same as in Ilesha, with the exception that things were better organized. The woodcutters were Mossi and Bambara immigrants from Upper Volta and Mali. Those who did not do much, or rather nothing, were the Ivory Coast nationals. The chiefs were French, from the camp's mechanic to the supervisors of whom I was one. We,"the whites" occupied a beautiful compound, with nice houses and flowery gardens, well kept by a team of gardeners. The houses were displayed in a half moon all around the saint of saints, the mechanic's workshop where everything was repaired, from trucks to bicycles and watches. The Master of this workshop was a former ship mechanic, a magician of mechanics. We became friends. There were four singles and two couples, one of which the woman was particularly beautiful and showed it, displaying in mini shorts her really well formed and generous buttocks finishing in extremely long legs, a honey bee waist and a Sofia Loren breast, her mouth always heavily red painted and black long hair falling to her hips. How many rivers of spermatozoids I had running with the image of that woman, wife to the chief of the lumber camp.

Three times a week, we organized a night out to Abengourou with dinner in the "Campement", a small five room hotel and restaurant owned by a couple of wine growers from the region of Bordeaux who one day got tired of listening to their vines growing and established themselves in Abengourou. Food was as good as in any French restaurant in Los Angeles. With our stomachs filled, we went then to the open sky movie hall to see an Italian made peplum about mythological and ancient historical stories: The treason of Dalila, Hercules, Cesar's murder etc...The show was in the public, with some three hundred people shouting, applauding the heroes and wooing, spitting and throwing anything at the bad guys. I liked it all, the job, the forest, the people. The pay was good and spending was little.

Every month, – we worked seven days a week – the company gave us four days of leave in Abidjan. There was no need any more to lodge in the Treichville "little whites" hotels. I took a room in the "Hotel Ivoire" something like a local Hilton, two blocks away from the Presidential palace. There is no need telling you more. Except that the very first Friday, I met in the hotel nightclub, a woman quite a bit older than me but with a beautifully well proportioned body, very romantic, wearing a sensual suggestive dress. We danced, it's much to say, we did not move more than a few centimeters. It was all about gluing our bodies' one to the other and just move enough to excite each other with furtive movements of legs between legs, soft kisses on cheeks and shoulders and slow caresses on the backs. Each one of these preliminaries encountering response, I got a painful, tremendous erection witch hurt and almost immediately experienced an ejaculation which filled me with shame for it must have been noticeable because of the large humid spot on my pants. Fortunately these pants were dark, as was the nightclub. It surprised me a little but not much when she whispered into my ear "I want to make love to you". We went to her apartment. I did not come out of it until Monday morning. Finally, and for the first time, all the sexual vigor of my twenty two years found an expression, including a master. This was really my first sexual experience. She was employed by a bank; Marseille was her home, divorced. Her husband had left her to go to live with two black girls in Treichville. That's all she told me in sixty hours. We did not talk very much. This was to go on all the time I stayed as a forester in Ivory Coast.

Hitting the road back to Abengourou I felt extremely weak, very tired, very hungry but light as a feather and happy.

*

Today, 27th of October of the year 2007, is day 23 of the lifetime of the first Sciaenops Ocellatus larvae of the season I talked about earlier. They already are juveniles with all their organs operational and their stomachs full of rotifers and artemias. We feed them in such a way that they never lack food because at the slightest lack of it they start eating their brothers and sisters right away. On their 23rd day of being part of the world's biomass, we start a process of weaning. You can't feed them all their life live food, so they are introduced to a powder like food of which the composition is only known at the University of Gent in Belgium, where the best sea fish food is made. (The Flemish do export some more things than missionaries, ex Nazis and diamond smugglers.)

The weather is awful, rain is pouring from a tropical depression hanging over the Yucatan peninsula, it seems like we are in Normandy where it rains three hundred days a year and which has the most productive dairy cows in the world. This thought is not gracious; we are not keeping dairy cows but tropical sea fish. Rain is no harm to the fish, they are already wet, neither is it for us, we are still waterproof, but at any moment electricity could be cut off as it always happen when Tlaloc, Maya God of rain, opens the water tub over Campeche. Then, everything stops: filters, pumps, air compressors and the air conditioners. Rain means moments of anguish and worry. As a problem never comes alone, I am sure that the electrical small plant we have to keep going the essentials is not going to start either.

Since the larvae finish the vital reserve they are born with - 24 hours after birth - they rely on us to give them food every two hours, day and night. After two weeks, none of the people in charge of keeping them alive has his eyes in front of the eyeholes. We are not enough people to get a proper break in the infernal rhythm that is imposed by the larvae.

*

I was about getting used to my forester life in Abengourou, when I was called to see the big chief of the company of the "Woods of the Monza" in his offices in Abidjan. This company was getting daily about one hundred seventy cubic meters of precious lumber out of the Ivory Coast tropical rain forest. If the reason was to fire me, I would not have to go to Abidjan. A simple note carried by the still and always drunk truck driver would have done the job.

I was feeling very uncomfortable, after one full hour with nothing to do but look at a few forest reviews displayed on a table and admire the secretary. Once in a while she would pick up the phone, get up and disappear behind the big teak door which guarded the entrance to the office of the Big Boss. She was beautiful, with a mini dress which showed long legs that hardly touched the floor, when she moved she seemed to float. But that was not enough to keep me from having the feeling that someone was wasting my time. I hate having to wait. A couple of times I walked to the large window. We were on the tenth floor of a modern building with view over the Lagoon and the bridge that connected "Le Plateau"- residential and business quarters – to Treichville, where life was happening. At large of the lagoon I could see the cranes of Abidjan harbor.

When things came to the point that I just was thinking of sending all of it to hell, a bell rang and the secretary, moving her head towards the wooden door, let me understand that this was my hour. He was a handsome man, tall, slim, with silver hair, as perfect as his office, completely walled with precious wood, ceiling and floor included, and some abstract paintings hanging on the wall, all of very good taste. He was wearing a white shirt with fine blue stripes, short sleeved and with a red tie. He was not alone: in two large black leather couches were sitting, almost lying, two individuals, smoking Havana cigars and drinking whisky. I never had seen them before.

I am not very acquainted with interviews. The only ones I had experienced were defined by very rigid rituals in the seminar and in the army. My preparation for this ceremonial of looks (sustained without defiance) and hand shaking (firm but not too much) showing respect and humility without falling into submission, was scarce. Even without experience, I quickly understood from the joviality and smiles that here, I was not going to be eaten. With an arm movement he invited me to the two armchairs around the tea table in front of the two guys who saluted without getting out of their comfortable position.

The Big Boss sat on the edge of the chair, as I was doing.

- Mister Goffings – he had a mezzo soprano voice, very high, which surprised me.

He took a pause

- Do you know how to read a map?

If there was something I had learned in the army, it was reading maps. I said I had learned that in the Belgian army. That provoked a smile of all the buddies there present.

The Belgians are the French underdogs and laughingstock. There are thousands of jokes, some very good, about the Belgian army and the Belgians, running all over France. Some are deserved. All peoples have their underdogs: the whites have the blacks and vice versa, The Walloons have the Flemish, the Italians the Mezzogiorno. In Switzerland they have the Bern canton. The Mexicans have the Gallegos - and everybody his mother in law.

By miracle, from under the tea table, appeared a map which the Boss displayed over the table, the whisky glasses taking the place where the map came from. There was not much to be said, some tracks, some small villages, few level lines, a couple of swamps and one all-weather road.

When I finished, the mezzo soprano put a white sheet on the table.

- Draw me a road that crosses a river, climbs a low hill and tell us how you go about to measure the distance of a climbing road.

That too, I knew how to do it. The two chair holders - let's call them like that- came to sit at the edge of the sofa to look closer. All approved, shaking their heads up and down while I was drawing and talking. At that moment, I already had a good idea of what they wanted from me. The Boss got up to ring a small bell and the secretary appeared instantly. To my surprise, she gratified me with a smile from under her black hair which was hiding part of her face.

- Coffee, whisky or something else?

I would have liked a whisky but asked for coffee. The maps disappeared from the table and the whisky glasses reappeared. Then, we all fell in the back of the couches. All this was very agreeable. My three colleagues from the wood industry started talking very fast in a language which I did not understand. I detected some French words: it was not French but "Provençal" a tongue of their southern region of France, a mix of Spanish, Italian and French.

The secretary reappeared with three whiskies and my stupid coffee. Looking at me, the Boss with the soprano voice, which I had problems not to laugh at, resumed:
- We bought two permits, one around Abengourou and another one in San Pedro. We thought that you could be our "tracer".

"Tracers" are the commando troops of the wood industry. The companies buy exploitation permits of a region from the government on a map, without really having any idea of what's on it; what kind of timber, number, size, physical limits etc. It's clear that these permits are obtained through a sophisticated system of corruption and under the table monies, by civil servants, ministers and the President himself, who all make fortunes selling permits. Fortunes that are spent buying apartments in the most selects quarters of Paris, villas on the Mediterranean Coast, farms in Normandy and let's not forget the luxury prostitutes of the Madeleine.

In the corporation, "tracers" are the crazy ones who will walk the forest for weeks and months with a dozen and more "carriers", walking straight ahead guided by a compass, tracing physically the permit through rivers, fields, villages, hills or mountains, making a small scar in the virgin forest. For one wanting to be Stanley looking for Livingstone, it was an irresistible offer.

*

For those who don't know about Stanley and Livingstone, here goes the story. Livingstone, a Scottish pastor, scientist, doctor, antislavery militant, buried himself in the Congolese forest in 1849. Nobody heard anything about him for years. The king of the Belgians, Leopold II, who coveted the Congo River basin, contracted Stanley, a journalist-explorer, to go and search for Livingstone, search for the Nile source and plant his flag on the territory. This permitted him to claim the Congo as his private property at the great African repartition conference of the European powers in Berlin in the year 1900. Stanley did find Livingstone after weeks of traveling through the rain forest with several very picturesque adventures. When he finally met Livingstone he pronounced the famous phrase "Doctor Livingstone, I presume". Together they went to search for the Nile source, which they did not find but discovered Lake Victoria. Their story finishes here but not the Congo story. Because of Stanley, the European powers indeed gave the Congo to Leopold II – a territory 80 times the size of Belgium. Not knowing what to do with it, the King decided to give it to the Belgians. Who refused the package through their Parliament. Finally, Leopold II put the Belgian State as heir of the Congo in his will. So the Belgians became a colonial power against their will.

*

I asked for more information about the San Pedro permit, which was close to the Liberian border on the other side of the country. They assured me that there would be local assistance and previous organization. The salary was good, the budget generous and the liberty absolute. The permit trace had to start in one week in a point on the road close to Abengourou. From there on, there were 105 kilometers to be walked, N-NE, 50 West and some 70 S-SW to end on the road from Bouaké. In total a 225 kilometers walk in the forest.

I stayed two more days in Abidjan to say goodbye to my bed friend whom I started to appreciate a lot. It is sure that one cannot enjoy lovemaking for a long time without getting somehow sentimentally involved. When I called her, I felt that she was disturbed and uncomfortable, she had other lovers. That's what made my leave from Abidjan easier. Could it be that I had become a libertine and that in less then two years I had passed from a dedicated seminarist to an apprentice libertine?

*

A libertine is a person who cherishes liberty above all things: All liberties, not only sexual liberty. The figure of the libertine is generally associated with that of the wealthy, the famous – politicians, high civil servants, people with power, stars of all kinds - because they have the money to finance flats for their mistresses and sow their little fruits all over town. This vision, consequently, pretends to grant the poorer, humble and working class, moral values, dignity and honesty which in reality they don't have. Values are a matter of individuals, not of social class. The humble ones, who see the local rich passing in their shining cars with blackened windows, also aspire to a permissive life of insolence and libertine behavior. So much so that, for a long time, for example here in Mexico, to tame the heaviest trade unionists, the most anarchist or socialist Stalinists, it was customary to take them for a weekend to the red zone in Acapulco. The class struggle ends with the sight of table dancers' buttocks.

Far from aspiring to the virtues of eternal vaginal purity, females too have the secret desire to share luxury hotel rooms with the wealthy and famous, envying the employees and secretaries with whom the bosses now and then play "the beast", and who soon can aspire to a promotion as a supervisor, or anything else.

How virtuous can the people be, when they don't have an occasion to be libertine! (Onfray)

Libertinage is a universal aspiration. Few get to it and the average lower class rarely gets occasions to practice it. The goal is the game, copulation which defies the rules, social codes, moral behavior, religion, customs and the ambient hypocritical moralization. It's not necessary to be among the rich and famous to play it. As the French philosopher Michel Onfray says: "When it's not a butcher shop, the world is an enormous brothel".

Libertine experience is not related to social class, politics or religion. Everybody who makes of sexuality a game, a play and nothing else, man, woman, right or left, poor or rich is a potential libertine. The libertine only listens to his fantasies, only searches for pleasure. As said Don Juan: "I do have a natural tendency to give in to the things I like". A libertine always is subversive by essence, because he is against sad sex, sex that makes you feel guilty, routine-sex, in one word: miserable sex. If you doubt, just have a look around you.

*

Although it was not easy because they had to be from the same ethnic group, in a few days we got the expedition together. The Mossis and Bambaras from the forest camp were out. I also needed a fairly good French-speaking interpreter, who spoke the languages of the region. All this gave way to long discussions. The help of the fellow forest men was very valuable; one even lent me a gun and 50 cartridges.

Made up the caravan: Two machete swinging cutters; just behind them, the compass reader and someone to take notes (these two posts were held by the interpreter and myself); two measurers who dragged a 50 meters long, light chain; a painter to mark every ten meters a tree, a rock or a picket and one hunter from the fraternity of hunters – years later I will be initiated to that fraternity in Mali. Our hunter was wearing a very funny hat; somewhat looking like the one Don Quixote de la Mancha usually is pictured with. From his neck hung at least a dozen amulets to protect him against anything, from snake bites to bad spirits. When I saw his gun I felt obliged to give him mine which he accepted very gratefully, caressing and talking to it for some while evoking all the spirits he knew for good luck. He was the free element of the caravan, his job was to better our daily diet getting fresh meat. Although, just in case, one of the porters carried a cage with live chicken.

Behind came the cook carrying my camp bed, followed by a dozen porters carrying everything else we were going to eat or need: rice bags, sugar, cooking oil, two cardboard boxes of tin cans, potatoes, and bottled water for me (I don't have the stomach with immunity defenses my companions have) blankets, a petrol tank for the lamps and a metal trunk with my belongings – among which spare boots, I hate snakes.- and two folding chairs.

All this was carried by young, athletic, strong men like the Africans from West Africa are. Their descendents who, let's say "immigrated" to other parts of the world, gain all the championships in athletics, football, baseball and basket ball - but under other banners.

After a small ceremony in which the hunter killed a chicken to get the good will of the forest spirits, the first machete blow was given behind the small settlement of point A. Everything got organized fast, the cutters who kept an eye on me all the time because I had the compass, advanced rapidly in the fields of the settlement. The measurers had to run to keep up with me because walking through the fields was easy. Later on, in the forest, the roles will be reversed. They'll have to wait for the advance of the cutters. The porters came far behind, since we only needed them every two hours when we made pauses. As for the hunter, he had disappeared.

At noon we left behind the banana, yucca and cacao plantations and entered the forest. All of my companions started to talk loudly or sing, this was to scare the wild animals, especially snakes which don't like noise. Although snakes don't taste bad- they taste like chicken- I don't like them.

In twelve days we got to the first turning point, according to the map very close to the Ghana border (of bad memory). Each afternoon the hunter reappeared. I never knew how he got around, neither where he was coming from. Some days we heard a shot faraway, some days not, but everyday he brought something: an anteater, a small bush deer, snakes, monkeys, some birds. Generally, I preferred one of our chickens or a can of corned beef. The forest was almost flat. The crossing of the river Comoé took us one day. Fortunately this was dry season, which does not mean dry, only it rained a little less. We did not lose anything.

We made a two day break in that half a dozen huts settlement, close to the river. There was nothing we could buy except for a couple of chicken. The chief of the family offered me his hut and told his daughter to take care of me. I did not use her as he thought I would, except for the hot water tub I found close to my bed in the morning. A popular saying in these regions goes : "If a stranger comes to your place, the first day you give him your wife, the second day you give him food and the third day you give him a machete so he goes to work with you". The expression "he did not wash with cold water" means that he did not sleep alone. I slept alone but I did not wash with cold water.

The huts of the settlement were the typical African, round, palm leaves roofed constructions. Set up in a circle around three smaller constructions standing on poles which are the grain reserves. Cooking is done outside with three stones. Leaving, I gave the family head two machetes and a file, for which I got an amulet in return, a small leather box grossly sewn to a leather string. In it was supposed to be a lion's hair to protect me against all animals. I hung it around my neck and did not quit it until it fell apart: it had a goat smell and I did not find the hair. To the girl of about twelve years and already well formed breasts one hundred CFA francs. Everybody was pleased.

The interpreter Josef learned fast the art of reading the compass, write down the kind of trees we crossed and draw the line. More and more, I relied on him. He was about eighteen, smiled all the time and had a great sense of humor which I deduced from the laughter he produced among the crew. The first days he had been praying a lot: waking up, before each meal and at night before he disappeared under his mosquito net, which he hung on tree branches close to mine. After a few days he stopped praying, seeing that I was not a big prayer. I suspected that he had been praying to get my good dispositions towards him. The missionaries of Abengourou had taught him French, which he wrote with very beautiful characters although with a mistake in every word. But that was negligible.

The two nights we passed in the settlement had made everybody good humored. I have no idea how they got around, but I strongly believe that nobody washed with cold water.

The second part of the forest walk was more complicated. There were hills to climb and even escarpments; also several small rivers to cross. The advance was slow. According to the map we were supposed to cross a village, big enough to figure on a map. Indeed, we entered plantations and fields one day before smelling in the evening the odors of cooking and burning wood.

83

The Hedonist

I believe it must have been Holy Week but I am not sure. The day before, I had sent Josef to announce that we were coming, because one does not approach or enter a village just like that. An African village is not a Spanish church. So, when the first huts were in sight we were expected at the entrance of the village like Cesar entering Rome or Henry the Fourth of France coming home from battle. Besides being a diversion, we also brought the expectation of the settling of a forest camp with work for everyone, easy roads and leaving the forest ready for fields after the foresters finish destroying it. All this would increase the volume of financial circulation to benefit the largest number. (to say it as an economist.)

In this triumphal entrance many women came to kneel in front of me and tried to kiss my hand, which I thought was awful. Why did they humiliate themselves that way? Josef chased them laughing but firmly, telling me that they thought that I was a "father" because of my beard. There was only one road in the village which ended right there according to the map, in front of the village chief's hut. This hut was flanked by three square constructions: one was the town hall because a board with "Mairie" on it, hung over the door, one was a shop, because a Coca Cola board with a bottle on it was fixed to the door. The last one was the church, because of the wooden cross planted besides the door and a metal "ring" hanging from a tree branch in front of it which was used as a bell beating it with a piece of metal. This, I had seen all over Africa in schools and churches.

The chief of the village - I don't remember his name – was wearing a French army cap: at first sight another veteran from Leclerc's army. He confirmed this giving me a military salute as had done Gustave in Kaya. After the greetings and explanations which I let Josef take care of, our belongings were put in the town hall and the carriers disappeared searching for lodging. We all were exhausted.

An hour before sunrise; the woman of the African villages move wood, move pots and pans, pounding and softening the corn pasta to make galletas, heating water. In short, they prepare breakfast. This coming and going, with the barking of dogs and the chant of roosters as if they were in competition, without forgetting the smell of burning wood, woke me up before daylight, got me from under the protection of the mosquito net to light the petrol lamp, take a pee, get some water on my face and there I was ready. Just in time to welcome the cook who brought me the first cup of smoking coffee. Since this was Sunday for us, whatever the calendar said, I sent him to buy some eggs for a Sunday breakfast.

Josef entered after announcing himself as usual, clapping his hands, and we agreed to stay for two days in order to update our notes and observations. We decided to start right away, putting the table and the two chairs in front of our lodging in the shade of the flamboyan tree.

It must have been around ten, when all of a sudden, on the other side of the plaza, a "two horses" escorted by a bunch of shouting and screaming children appeared. The "two horses" is a very small car made by Citroën, the smallest, most robust, cheapest to buy and to run car ever made. It looks very funny too: the roof is mobile and made of a plasticized canvas. For those who remember: the English called it a frog.

The motor is hidden under a millimeter thin metal sheet; it sounds like a boat motor and the car has such suspensions that you have the impression it bounces more than it runs. Altogether it looks like a duck's head. As the rear is higher than the front, on the African bumpy roads it gives an unmistakable impression of dancing. To resume: it's the French competitor of the famous German beetle.

The four wheels rolled slowly up to the entrance of the church a few meters away. Out of it came a white Dominican missionary. White is much said, the poor man was covered from head to sandals by red dust. It was a tall man, with a big black beard and black eyes. A heavy rosary held up his toga around his waist. A rarely seen colonial helmet surmounted his head. By now there were so many people surrounding him – among whom some of my carriers- that I thought it was better to stay at my small table and wait until things calm down. Seeing the figure of the father, Josef's face illuminated and getting up, he shouted:

- Father André, father André

In the general noise I was the only one to hear him.

- Do you know him?

- Yes, yes, he was my teacher in Abengourou.

Somebody was beating the ring. Josef tried to make his way to the missionary pushing women and children aside with his elbows and arms.

Half an hour went by saluting, taking children in his arms, making a hundred blessings and putting his hands on a hundred heads. Some women started to clap their hands and began a song, making a cloud of dust stamping their feet to the ground. A few moments later drums appeared, overcoming the noise and drumming to outdo each other. The village chief appeared in a yellow tunic with a picture of President Houphouët Boigny all over it. In his hands he

85

held a heavy sculptured stick, symbol of his authority. In no time this quiet, pleasant morning was converted into a loud fiesta.

When things started to calm down, because father André had extracted from the "two horses" a football ball and all humans under fourteen from that village, having two legs and a penis, were running after it all over the plaza. Then I stood up to salute Father André. Josef had not left his side for a second, so the father knew already everything about me.

André was a jovial and smiling man. Must have been in his forties and still covered with red dust in which sweat dripped, making lines and falling on his chest. We made a brief greeting, promising to see each other after he cleans up, at mass in the afternoon.

Josef said that the father was going to stay for two days, that he had not come to this village for four months. The next day he was going to celebrate a big mass with baptism for those who needed it, communion for those who deserved it and marriage for the couples living in sin. He added that this evening after mass they were going to show the masks. That program suited me: we all needed some entertainment after having been buried in the forest.

When the sun started to make long shadows, André appeared, this time dressed in a really white toga, no more trace of dust, even his sandals were shining. He accepted my invitation for dinner. Our cook had done marvels shopping fresh vegetables, tomatoes, salads, cucumbers: a feast.

He had a soft, low key voice; we talked about everything, only to talk. When we came to the subject of my seminar experience we recited an "Ave Maria" in Latin. After which we laughed about the situation the same way I had laughed with the Latin mass in Dori. I assisted at the mass, more because of good manners than of liking. It was simple, in the local language which André spoke fluently with two dozen women and girls animating the ceremony with hand clapping, singing and dancing. Then followed the fiesta, the dancing and jumping of the masks representing ghosts and beasts of the forest, which scared the hell out of the children who looked for refuge under their mothers' dresses. Certainly for respect to the catholic father, the women had covered their breasts with short blouses, breasts they had at the open air all the time when the inquisitive eye of the church was not upon them, showing a great variety of shapes, volumes and levels. I enjoyed the dances of the women, well synchronized and rhythmic although I felt great pity for the babies they carried on their backs held with a cloth and who were shaken as in a mixer.

Men danced individually. One after the other they entered the circle, executed a few complicated steps, some acrobatic movements, collecting applause and screaming. We watched the spectacle seated in three armchairs: Father André in the middle, flanked by the chief and myself. Even the drums sounded "civilized", nothing to do with the wild hammering of the goat skins of other fiestas I'll get used to later.

It was the following day that the incident occurred, with the distribution of the holy sacrament of marriage, after the mass, baptism and communion. Many people from the settlements around had made the trip at night to be there. The whole family of the settlement we had crossed, greeted us with a lot of affection. There were so many people that the whole ritual was set up in the plaza. All that time - three hours had passed - I kept myself next to Josef, seated against the church wall behind André. For the wedding ceremonies André stood on a bench and the idea was that the couples would line up in front of him. Asking the questions that are asked all over the world and for which the answer always is "Yes, I will". Bless them, congratulate them and give them an image of the holy virgin of Lourdes in all her whiteness, with a prayer on the back in French, which of course nobody could understand or read. With all the family accompanying the engaged couples (many with a baby on their back, another under their shirt and a third one in their belly) it was impossible to find out who was marrying who. André had to ask for every group of people gathering in front of him, who was the groom and who, the bride.

All was going fine, until André came to a couple in which, when he asked who was the bride, a girl of about sixteen put up her finger and when he asked who was the groom, another girl of about the same age put up hers.

Three times André asked the question and three times both girls, surrounded with their family, lifted their fingers. Feeling that something rare was happening, my interest awoke and I asked Josef for a precise translation. André did not proceed with the ceremony and kept silent, not knowing how to handle the case. Then, a very aged man with a few gray hairs on his chin, helping himself with a large walking stick came forward.
- Yes father, that's the way it is, you may marry them.
André got very red in the places that were not covered with his beard
- I cannot.
- Yes, you can, said the old man with a tranquil voice.
- I cannot – insisted André- they are two women.
- Yes you can, everything has been arranged.

87

- I will not. Next.

Nobody moved.

Many people started giving their opinion, even those who stood behind waiting their turn. Rapidly this became chaotic. Some voices started shouting. It looked like everybody agreed that the marriage could go on and that the representative of the holy Roman Catholic Church could marry these two girls as husband and wife. But the father, who already had jumped from his bench, stayed firm in his "No" which was producing a small rebellion.

At that moment I had not the slightest idea about homosexual couples. It looked to me as something awkward and disgusting, so I took André's side. But we were very few who thought like that. The tumult had generalized - however without them taking to their machetes - and André, Josef and I took refuge in the church, closing the door behind us. We went out through the sacristy door and into my hut. I armed the gun which fortunately I had asked the hunter to leave me.

André was furious.

- I cannot marry them! Imagine, two girls, he shouted although there was only Josef and me. I didn't know what to say but dared:

- Why do they think you can?

- I don't know and I don't want to know, he kept shouting.

A heavy silence installed itself, the outside noise was diminishing

Josef said, with a surprisingly calm voice.

- For them you can. You just have to do as if one of the girls is a man.

- But Josef, I can't do that, she is a woman, God made her that way.

We kept silent for a long moment. Indeed how to handle this?

- Heaven, do they tire me. Do they tire me out!

His voice was close to nervous breakdown. At that moment someone knocked at the door. Josef opened and the chief came in. With very authoritarian voice - after all he had been a sergeant in the French army - he said

- It's all right, they will not marry, but you have to give each one a blessed image and marry the remaining couples.

André handed him two images of the virgin and let escape a "For God's sake": he was completely downhearted. He waited a few minutes before going into the daylight, still bright at this hour. I disarmed the gun and followed him. There were still some people in the plaza, but many had left and more were going to do so. In a record time André finished blessing the ones who wanted to fornicate with the Lord's blessing. Then, he said rapidly goodbye, got his things, started the "two horses" and disappeared in a cloud of dust. I stayed waving at him till the jumping and dancing "two horses" completely disappeared on the other side of the plaza. Turning around, I noticed that Venus was shining. Going back to my hut, I crossed the chief who looked desolated and said:

-Yes, he could have married them. He shook my hand and entered his compound.

That evening, eating my chicken with rice and for dessert, chocolate and coffee I had a strange feeling. Something had happened and I did not know what. When Josef came in, I told him that the following day we would go to the settlement of the two girls to pay a visit to their family.

Four kilometers of easy walking in the early morning freshness, on a clean but narrow path, got us to the small settlement. There were the hunter, Josef of course and the two machete swingers who carried the presents; a machete and a metal bucket. I got the feeling that we were expected.

The old man with the walking stick from the day before told me the following story: The most horrendous thing that could happen to a man in his lifetime had happened to him. Regardless of having had many spouses, he stayed without male descendents. Therefore, he could not die because the consequences were that nobody would venerate, call, consult and even feed his spirit. He would be denied entering the sacred forest where his father, brothers and friends were waiting for him. He had failed to secure his lineage. All his offspring were female.

To heal this disgrace, the tradition permitted that two of his daughters marry one to the other; one as a wife and one with the husband role. To fecundate and make pregnant the girl-spouse in that couple, the clan will contract one or more strangers from another village or clan, convene upon a precisely defined compensation of so many goats, chicken, machetes, etc. for each male child that the girl-spouse will bring to this world. Once his contract is fulfilled, the stranger will disappear and never show up again.

Upon the first male child birth, the girl-husband will be invested of all the responsibilities of a father for her sister's children. These responsibilities are well defined and precise. For example: there exists a great complicity and solidarity between a child and his grandfather. They have a permissive behavior. This counter balances the rigor, injustice, harshness of the relations between father and son. Since the father is son of the grandfather; the couple grandfather-grandchild is dominant. If the grandfather disappears, the role is played by one of his brothers. That's the way things get equilibrium. The problem of course surges when there are no sons.

For not losing the potential productivity of the girl-husband, she will of course simultaneously be part of another household in which she is going to be the spouse. And that's it.

There was nothing in this scheme that had the slightest thing to do with sex, as I and André had been thinking. The only motivation and matter was to give a man male descendents and secure that he would be allowed to enter the sacred forest to pass his afterlife with his buddies.

That was a lot for my brain. Questions and questioning did not stop to shock in my head for the entire return walk.

*

We all have personal life experiences: situations, books we read, movies seen, persons who walked a while with us, or simply crossed our road of life and whom forever changed our ways of seeing things. They marked our perceptions, opinions, values which make up one's personality. Everything that we know, are, think, value; our principles, our most secret thinking, somebody has taught us or shown us. Everything comes from an apprenticeship. Says a popular Mexican song: "A stone on the road changed my destiny".

That's what happened to me. My brain of Flemish peasant, modeled by the catholic seminar, came to suffer a serious blow. Nothing in the marriage of these two girls matched my morals and values and heavily questioned my taboos. Still I valued them as just, logic and in harmony with nature.

*

This brings me to another peculiar social behavior pattern I just experienced two weeks ago, when Lluvia- I'll talk later about her- invited me to a social gathering for a christening in Oaxaca, Mexico. The cooking and serving was done by a "Mochi", obviously a travesty, and his mother. What is a "Mochi"?

In some of the villages, each family will designate one of the sons, most of the time the youngest, since childhood, to become the "Mochi" and undergo little by little a feminization process, to become a homosexual and a travesty. In fact, the "he-she" in the end will become the keeper of the mother while the other children go normally about their lives, most of them immigrating to other parts. In many villages and towns, once a year the "Mochis" have their feast. Parading in the most beautiful and sexy garments, with the local band in front, they go to the restaurant or feast ground where they'll have their night.

Intelligent societies find ways towards harmony, rigid doctrinarian societies do not.

*

There is nothing more relevant in my first forest walk as a tracer. We passed through other villages, one close to a lake, where the villagers worshipped some huge crocodiles, feeding them every day with chicken. I don't know why they sanctified these animals; neither to what this version of God corresponds. Maybe because crocodiles are one of the few species left that can trace their background straight to the Jurassic period (by the way where was God in these times?). But does one question faith? Of course not. Faith exists and does not need any rational ground, it sustains itself.

For my second assignment as tracer, I traveled to San Pedro, in the extreme West of Ivory Coast, close to the Liberian border. In these times the only way to reach San Pedro was flying, or by boat. The DC3 that took us there landed in the midst of an abundant, dark forest, although it was barely noon. The company's agent was waiting for me and in less than ten minutes showed me the place: the only three kilometer long road that goes from the airport to the town; a small hotel made of wood, as all the constructions were. The San Pedro River that joins the ocean just a few kilometers away and which was bordered with a fifty meter wharf where wood was floating. The church, standing a little on the side and which had a real bell hanging in its tower, was made of wood boards.

The only thing my contact wanted was to get out of the place as fast as possible and certainly not miss the flight that brought me in. It did not look like this was going to be fun. I went to pay a visit to the father who explained that San Pedro was founded by the Portuguese as a slave port for trade with the Americas. Later on, it was taken over by the slave traders of the famous port of Saint Malo, in France. With his precious help, I managed to reunite a team of tracers, not without difficulty though.

At first sight, the permit was not easy, very irregular with high hills and escarpments. My interpreter was exactly the opposite of Josef: stupid, stubborn, not easygoing and no education. His only preoccupation was coffee and roasting monkeys, of which there were many around. Their smell made me feel like vomiting. He scared me to the point that I was sleeping with the loaded gun, although that was somewhat excessive.

Here another shaking up event occurred. After a week of difficult advance we entered a village that was not on the map and where a kind of English was spoken. This meant that probably I was in Liberia and not in Ivory Coast. There were two possibilities: or the map was wrong, or I was mistaken. I concluded it was the map

For those who don't know it, Liberia is a particular case among the African countries. It was created by goodwill and well-intentioned United States philanthropic organizations, after the civil war and the liberation of slaves. The whole idea was to send back to Africa the former slaves and slaves descendents who liked the idea of going back. (That's where the name- Liberia- comes from and also the flag with stripes and one star). Of course the newcomers established their rules and governed pretty much leaving aside the original and traditional tribes. These facts are a good explanation to understand the continuous unrest and civil wars the country recently experienced.

The other particularity of this village was that the women and girls were very, very provocative and daring. They did not satisfy themselves with looks, but also used their hands. I experienced that with an almost elderly woman who showed me a two-room wooden construction we could occupy. To say it clearly, she put her hand between my legs, and laughed.

In spite of my twenty one years, I already had experienced a lot of weird situations, but this was   humiliating. In this village there was no religious authority to rely on, to make me feel on familiar ground, secure, with a minimum of known rules. Here, there was nothing of that. In a general way, whenever I made an incursion into the unknown there always had been some basic rules I could identify and go by. But here, I did not find any. This made me feel uncomfortable and somewhat lost. Of course my life was not in danger. They knew the price for killing a white man for a couple of cans of coffee and a loaf of sugar. It was not worth it. The unease was moral, a heavy feeling of loneliness which made me decide to go back to San Pedro the following day. I didn't know who got the idea to buy a wood permit in this place, it seemed they bought a cat in a bag. This region was practically unexploitable and it was going to cost a lot of money to get timber out of it.

A big swallow of whisky did not draw away my nostalgia, but it helped. Then, there was a knock at the door. The interpreter I had sent to find out if there was a chief in this village stuck his face through the door. Yes, there was one, and he was even inviting all of us to a village feast called "Name Calling" that very same evening.

This is what happened: Seated in a chair besides the chief, to whom I had brought the traditional presents, I experienced the first round of palm wine being served all along a big circle of people seated on straw carpets . The pumpkin the wine came in was dirty. It was presented by a young girl who, all the time I did as if I was drinking, kneeled in front of me and studied my shoes. I felt watched, so I took a big swallow of palm wine to the great satisfaction of the chief and the audience. Even my interpreter smiled for the first time since we were working together. Then the drums started and a dozen of young girls, naked to the hips, executed very acrobatic dances, stamping the ground frenetically with their feet making dust as if a herd of elephants was walking by. In the meantime, the rounds of palm wine kept circulating and the serving girl kept studying my feet.

Palm wine is collected fresh, there is no processing, merely a gross filtration through a cloth, and left until fermentation in a pumpkin bark. Fermentation is very fast, in a few hours the alcohol degrees double. It smells like rotten wood and tastes....well, as palm wine; there is nothing it can be compared to. After a couple of days a palm wine harvest is not usable anymore for a normal throat. This was going to be fatal to my stomach, so I sent the interpreter to go for the case of beer we had brought from San Pedro.

The feet stamping of the local beauties came to an end. They put more wood on the fire that was burning in the middle of the circle. Huge flames started to lick the sky and lightened up the square. The drums had not stopped for one minute, neither the rounds of palm wine pumpkins. Looking at the shouting and laughing crowd, it became clear that all this was going to end in a tremendous drunken Jamboree.

Luckily for me, the beers came to slow my rhythm of getting drunk. The chief was very pleased with the beer; he got up and made a speech which all applauded. All of a sudden, a woman stood in the circle close to the wood fire. She did not look young, neither old although her tits reached almost to her waist. She shouted something that I thought was a poem but which turned out to be names, as the interpreter told me. When she finished, everybody burst in laughter and screams overwhelmed by the drums. Some men, vacillating, got up and directed themselves to one point of the circle where the husband of the woman-poet was sitting. These men carried all types of things, machetes, tubs, pumpkins with palm wine, limes.

The rules of the game were as follows: Each woman shouted to the face of the world, the names of the men she had been fornicating with, in the past year (or since the last "Name Calling"). Those men had to give a present to her husband. Her husband of course was "called" by other women and in turn had to give part of his presents to the husbands of his loved ones. So, the same presents, or at least part of them, changing owners, got around and around among laughter, cheering, crazy drumming and pumpkins with palm wine going from mouth to mouth. When I asked the almost completely drunk interpreter, whom the children belonged to, he looked at me as if I was completely stupid and with a laugh responded:
- To her husband, naturally!
Indeed my question was a stupid one. I was just not used to societies where biological and social paternity is completely disassociated. Supposedly and pretentiously, these two factors are synonyms in the civilization I happen to be born in.

Later on, experience taught me that a watered down version of "Name calling" behavior exists in many places. The Latin American saying: "The little goat that was born in my stable is mine" is a certain form of "Name Calling".

Disgusted or fascinated by this way of putting the accounts in zero in such a spectacular way? The only thing I knew was that I got caught completely off guard. All the calling women were far from being beauties: some of the uglier ones were the most popular, at the delight of their proud husbands who accumulated gifts.

Palm wine and beer don't go together, so I got drunk and sick, my head was exploding. The interpreter and the cook carried me to my room. The next day, there was another name calling – they could not finish the accounts in one night – but I decided to go back to San Pedro as fast as possible. This place was too much for me. I knew how to live in the African forest on the condition to have some basic rules to rely on. Besides that, as to the matter of forestry, this permit was a disaster.

In Abidjan, my girlfriend – calling her that- did not open. We exchanged a few words through the door. I cried, out of desolation, frustration and misery. Years later – don't ask me why so late – I came to the conclusion that I had been a lousy lover.

*

I still did not know (where could I have learned?) that   male sexuality without   apprenticeship and learning, without the establishing of mutual complicity between two human beings is nothing more than an instinctive and animal-like assault. Penetration-ejaculation: any male animal is capable of doing this, and that's what they do. Female sexuality on the contrary is a matter of culture, more difficult, more secret, hidden, profound and almost mysterious, at the image of the female sexual organ itself. A female orgasm is the combination of feeling, giving, searching and caring. Could it be that for this reason the founding myths of our moral values, rules and behavior are based on the hatred of the female? And that their sexual life is reprehended?

Let's take an example: The original sin, culpability, treason, curiosity, the desire to know, unconformity, disobedience, are all attached to the female: Eve. The male part of the story is: submission, obedience and conformism. For not understanding and being afraid of it, the founding fathers of our values repressed the female part, and everything that goes with it: desire, pleasure, curiosity, in one word: life. It was thus decided that the original sin was transmitted through the belly – according to a certain Saint Augustine. Blood, flesh, libido etc... - naturally associated with woman- are decreed as impure, illegal, illicit. The founding values only admit as respectable the spouse and the mother: The only accepted destinies for woman, there is no place for womanhood. The spouse and the mother sink the woman upon whom rabbis, priests, mullahs, impose domination. There is no space for female sexuality; her body is doomed in all the sacred writings, culminating with Saint Paul; the most outspoken and implacable misogynist of our history. The family works as unique and only skyline, the basic cell of society. Therefore, homosexuals also were sentenced to death – not anymore in our political environment but in many places they still are sentenced to death, very little time ago their destination was to be burned alive – only for practicing a free sexuality unrelated to reproduction and the pattern of father – mother, spouse – husband. The single, says the Talmud, is only half a man. In the Mâcon council, in 585, Valeus book was submitted to the church fathers. The title: "A paradox dissertation to demonstrate that women are not human creatures". What else is needed? Women represent too much desire, too much pleasure, excess, passion, sex and rave, putting in danger male virility and, of course the worshipping of God.

The Hedonist

*

Back to Abengourou where I stayed in the hotel of the Bordeaux wine grower, away from the lumber camp, I met Billy, a North American from Ohio, a member of the Kennedy Peace Corps, together with two more American girls about my age. Their job was to teach English and basket ball in a correct way to the Abengourou youth. Billy was a jovial young man without complexes and owner of a fabulous library of "classics". (A sort of comic strips, with all the classics of world literature). That's how I learned English, plus two hours a day of teaching by Billy.

As a member of a minority ethnic group who wants to enlarge his horizon, culture or business, the only way is to learn other languages. Someone said that: "you are as many times human as you speak languages", I imagine that he referred to the cultural enrichment a language brings. I liked to learn English, the language of cowboys and Indians I had played at, being a boy in Heur. When I learned that thousands of young Americans came to die on the Normandy beaches to help us do away with the Nazis, I liked the language even more. Simply, America and the Americans fascinated me and they still do.

So, when a wood buyer from the United States came to Abengourou, I was already able to sustain a minimum of dialogue to the great satisfaction and delight of the Big Boss of the company. This was very useful because, as most Americans, Joe Harlon did not think that it would be necessary to ever speak another tongue but English to buy wood in Ivory Coast. Later on, I would learn that Americans are not only zeroes in geography, but also in languages and history. It's not surprising thus that, for the great majority: Cancun is the capital of Mexico; Jefferson is a rock band and Europe a London suburb. This ignorance is consequence of their superb self confidence. They are sure to be the center of the world, what actually was true, and maybe still is, but not in education.

The man was short, with eyes profoundly incrusted in their sockets, somewhat overweighed and bald,dressed up in a Saharan jacket with countless pockets, Bermuda shorts down to under his knees, alpine boots and white socks reaching almost to his shorts. The only thing missing to complete a fashion review picture was the Australian bush hat, instead of which he carried a New York Yankees cap. The big boss, of whom I only remember that he was wearing his

96

trousers in rubber boots and thus exposing his feet to mushroom growing, was very pleased to find out that I was able to chew some English. This means that, you don't have to be cultured to be rich. To get rich you have to be smart which is a completely different aspect of intelligence; let's say more pragmatic.

The gentleman in the Saharan outfit owned a sawmill in Virginia. Later on in the afternoon, without any formality, he proposed me to go and work for some time in his sawmill in Bowling Green, VA. He also told me about a forest school in Tennessee where he wanted to send me. Afterwards, I would come back here or anywhere else and buy wood for him. Costs were for me except when working in his sawmill.

In hardly over a dozen of months, I had passed from bird hunter – partner of a Flemish diamond smuggler – to a forest agent and tracer and on to a foreign student in the United States of America. My ascension in the forest industry had been like lightning, as was my learning of life.

*

The eyes of Mister Joe Harlon fell wide open when, a month later, I stepped into his office in Bowling Green, Virginia. Without passing through Heur, I had disembarked in New York where I stayed for five days, lodging in a YMCA and spending the days walking and walking on Fifth Avenue, visiting the lady with the torch, the harbor, learning fast English driven by survival. I don't remember how I got to Washington, neither how I got about to be lodged for two days in the Hotel Lafayette just across the White House. I do remember that from Washington to bowling green I hitchhiked. Everything was enchanting: the people tremendously simpatico, easygoing, friendly, well educated and serviceable. All the women were beautiful and I wanted to marry all of them. From the very first moment; when the immigration officer in the airport said "Welcome to the United States" I fell in love with this country. Love at first sight.

Among all the classic United States small towns, stands Bowling Green, Virginia: one large avenue which comes from the Federal highway to get lost precisely in front of Joe's sawmill. To have an idea of what it looks like, just see any Hollywood movie or a TV series. The whole town exudes wellbeing, equilibrium and security. Sure, somewhere there must be a poor neighborhood, as there is in all towns, where Afro-Americans, or colored people, or whatever you want to call them in a respectable way (for not saying negroes) live, love and suffer. (Not naming things by their name in order to hide them is a trend of modern society. But in the end, negro is negro, white is white, handicapped is handicapped, blind is blind and not: "not seeing well". Poor is poor and not "of lesser income", I don't understand these hypocritical sensibilities)

One day, in Abengourou, I had myself been a victim of these words which don't say what they say. A policeman had stopped my car and sticking his head through the window asked me of which color he was. If I responded that he was black; I was afraid that he could get offended. If I said that he was white, it could be interpreted as if I was pulling his leg. So I murmured:

- You are African.

He put one arm up, as policemen do when they stop the traffic

- No sir! When I am like this, I am red.

Then he brought his arm at shoulder height:

- And like this, I am green. You made an infraction, license please!

This is the only traffic ticket I paid with pleasure in my whole life.

Joe took me to the house of an old girlfriend of his, a mature, fat woman who showed me a room. We agreed upon a price and she went back to the living room to see her wrestling match on a very loud TV.

I learned to classify wooden tables according to kind, color, design of nerves and density, also about inches, feet and yards. Saturdays and Sundays, a huge trunk of lumberjacks of the factory took me along to huge dance halls where live country music was played and a lot of drinking was going on. I learned to dance square dance and blushed with the outright provocative looks of young women, with whom I was careful. Rare were the nights when there was not a fight about women. For not having their stomachs and training, many Saturday nights were spent vomiting in Missus Daisy's lawn.

A couple of Sundays after integrating the Bowling Green community, a factory colleague's fat sister took me to her church where psalms were sung and hamburgers and pies were served after service. It was an all-white church, rather formal and stiff. Nothing to do with the black churches I later on liked to frequent for my outspoken taste for spectacles and gospel music.

There was no such thing as working hours at the mill. With the sun barely showing, one of the colleagues picked me up with his car and with the same sun sinking below the corn fields he would bring me back. Mister Joe, who passed once in a while in the mill, did not talk anymore about the Tennessee forest school, and I began feeling that my future started to look as if I would be a sawmill worker for the rest of my life. My being a foreigner did not impress at all. Most of the workers had a father or grandfather who came from some place in Europe, most of them from Eastern Europe.

Soon, I switched my nationality from Belgian to French because I was tired of explaining all the time where Belgium is. Being French, nobody asked more questions except for things like: "Do you have cars? Do your people enjoy electricity? Do the French have television?". To keep a little bit in touch with something else but wooden boards, every week I went to buy Time magazine or Newsweek at the local drug store. They sold two copies every week. I wondered who bought the other one. Sawmill workers in Virginia don't ask themselves too many questions about history, politics or geography. They knew something about Germany and England and were just introduced to a place called Vietnam, where the war was getting uglier every day.

Malaria changed my destiny for the second time: it fell over me in the sawmill. The chief took me home to missus Daisy where I got trembling, sweating and unable to stand on my feet. Through the mist, I saw a doctor and half an hour later they loaded me into an ambulance which ran all lights blinking to Richmond. Fortunately, Missus Daisy threw my belongings into the ambulance, because I never returned to bowling green and nobody came to visit me in the hospital, making it easy to stay where I was. In the hospital I was very popular: nobody had seen a malaria case in close-up, besides becoming a medical curiosity and also an object of much maternal care on the part of the female nursing corporation, this got even better, when telling them a little bit of my African story. One of them, a young, quite good looking girl, with black eyes in a soft face and long hair, advised me to stay in Richmond and go to school. She had broken up with her lover a little time before; this made her even more attractive and even desired.

Getting out of the hospital she took me right away to the Richmond Professional Institute, where her father, a very serviceable middle aged man, accepted to sponsor me and wrote me up for some courses. I choose: American Diplomatic history, History of rights and laws, English, Communism and Literature. This left me enough time to choose in the long list of "student jobs" something to keep me alive and eating. In the year I stayed in Richmond I was: a waiter- of course-, night guard in a mental hospital – where I learned the use of the straightjacket-, driver in the local Hertz agency, teacher of French-which was cheating because it was not my language, but nobody noticed-, night watch and receptionist in an upper middle class apartment building – where I had to wear a tie -, lorry charger in a Cigarette warehouse, fast food cook, dishwasher and many more trades.

I learned everything about the "Boston tea party", Jefferson, Washington and the signers of the Independence with special mentions of Franklin and Henry (the one of "Give me liberty or give me death", not the French football player), The Monroe doctrine, Hamilton and the long list of American presidents; Lincoln and the civil war, the melting pot and also the notions of "working class", Lenin and ugly Stalin, the elements of the cold war and the functioning of the "détente"; had no more secrets to me . Also the way justice and the so many cases that make it work, became familiar and I have to add: Chaucer, Shakespeare, James Joyce, Steinbeck, Baldwin - and my all time favorite: Mark Twain, of whom I still think he was the first American writer, while those preceding him wrote Anglo-American literature. Twain is only American. I swallowed it all as a hungry wolf.

Kennedy had been assassinated almost two years before and Johnson was president. Before one year there, I felt so American that I presented myself at the marine recruitment office (don't ask me why). They turned me down because of malaria. In less than a year malaria saved me from two big stupidities. A few months later, I will walk in front of the White House shouting "Hey, hey, L B J, how many kids you killed today". But that's for later.

I shared an apartment with two students from the area, one of whom had serious problems with sex coming from his profound belief and observance of Christian rule and morals. The Richmond Professional Institute had something to do with a church but I don't remember which one.

Richmond is a beautiful city, with wide avenues and huge trees boarding them. In the middle of the main avenue there are many statues of all the confederate generals, most of them on horses with their front legs up in the air, meaning that their cavalier died in battle.

I felt so good as an American that I also presented myself for candidate to the presidency of the catholic students association from the State of Virginia, nothing less. I masticated grossly some English, I was not American, I just came to Virginia etc... All that was all right to become president of the association. I passed the first election round with good possibilities of being elected. Apparently I showed conviction and had charisma. That's the greatness of the United States of America; there is no other country on earth alike in this respect. Could it be that they are where they are for being efficient above all and not wrapped up in relatively poor and secondary considerations, such as "where were you born"?

Nobody in the whole State of Virginia will put forward such a poor argument for preventing a few months old immigrant to become President of a State student organization.

In this catholic student organization I met very odd and old young girls and boys. In conversations, I learned that the majority of the girls were convinced that they could get pregnant kissing (especially the famous "French kiss"). The chaplain of the organization enforced that belief. This young father supervised the ideological orientation and the virginity of the group. At that time in Virginia, sexual education was as poor as it had been for me in the seminar. I think that things have gotten better since then. Without ever speaking about it in a normal way; sex was the obsession. The subject was present all the time, everywhere: in looks, undercover conversation, insinuations, and silly laughter.

If you want to look at how repression and abstinence leads to sexual frustration, take a trip inside America. The counterpart of these virgins and heavily acne suffering faces was a small group of students from the art and theatre faculties. They seemed normal and well liberated of the overall repression in the matter, the contrary of my roommates. I admired them.

*

Yesterday, the 12th of February 2008, the Governor of New York was dismissed of his functions because "they" (the sex obsessed and frustrated hypocrites) discovered that he was frequenting a prostitute. It is hard to understand why a fornicating governor is, per definition, a bad governor. In the name, of what? Does anybody have the right to get into the bed where two adults have decided that they are going to do what people do in a bed? For having loved life completely, entirely, for having tried to heal his pain of living in a hypocritical society, sexually repressive and psychologically sick of sex, Mister Governor had to excuse himself publicly – with his pitied wife besides him – and resign.

At this rhythm and in this time: neither Jefferson, Adams, Washington, much less Franklin or Roosevelt and many more, not even the puritan Eisenhower, ever could have been Presidents of the United States. All of them loved life, which included mistresses and lovers, and also prostitutes. This did not prevent them from creating the marvelous country the United States are. The hypocrites who rule today lost something important along the road.

I like prostitutes although I never had any business with them. I like the idea of this sort of women who take on the healing of life, the pain of living in a denaturalized world in which desire is cruelly sanctioned. I like these woman offering the sweetness and gentleness of their bodies with easy pleasures to those who are in need of becoming more human. It is inhuman to make the human species live in a state of sexual frustration.

Of course, all prostitutes are not at the level of the lady who copulated with the NY governor. On one side we have: The Mayflower hotel in Washington, caviar, champagne and the high society ejaculators: Presidents, Cardinals, Governors, Diplomats and Princes. On the other side: the benches, the cheap boarding rooms, the bohemians, the romantics and the poets, the wife or the husband poorly loved or vice versa, the poor and the miserable. The cause however is the same: the bad unsatisfactory feeling of living in a society that ceased to be human and natural, sexually speaking.

*

I was not elected President of the association of Catholic students of Virginia. In the final debating round I had to admit that I did not have any money. To have money is a "sine qua non" for being President since the President has to pay out of his own pocket the visits he is going to pay to the other schools all over the state. I left the race with all the honors and a standing ovation. By that time I did not care too much, my sympathies went to the small students group from the school of arts.

Finally I lived "juventus ad libidum". Vacations bored me. So as not to waste time, I wrote up for summer school at William and Mary in Williamsburg. One of the first colonial settlements and which escaped modernism, an open air museum. Everything is as it was in the 17th century: the inhabitants dressed up as in colonial times to the delight of the tourist. The University campus is one of the most beautiful I've ever seen, hidden amongst century old trees. I registered for courses in political science and literature. This time I learned all about the donkey and the elephant taught by a passionate elderly anti Nixon gentlemen. He swore that Nixon would never come back – he called the ex candidate:"tricky Dick" – of course he was dead wrong. We talked about Africa, colonialism and the African policy of de Gaulle which he did not like and of which I didn't have a clue. He advised me to take advantage of my experience and keep studying politics and African sociology.

The eternal waiter's job – this time in "the Carriage House" at the entrance of town – took care of keeping me alive. I also got a turn as a trolleybus driver with tourists, for which I dressed up as a servant of his highness the Governor of Virginia and of Their Majesties the Kings of England.

The University of Virginia – or was it Virginia State? – gave courses about Africa, so I went to see them. Just to find out everything about segregated universities. This one was full of negroes and it was only then that I realized that at RPI there were none of them. A gentle middle-aged man received me and with a lot of diplomacy made me understand that I would be the only white student of all his institution and that such a thing maybe would be a problem to some of his teachers and students. He did not want any problem. He oriented me to the American University in Washington DC.

Indeed there is a University with this pompous name, at the top of Massachusetts Avenue. The first thing that one has to do when coming to Washington is to go to the university cafeteria and consult "student's jobs". After only two days in the YMCA, I got a comfortable basement room in a huge suburban house in Bethesda. The mission was to take care of the paralytic William Lawson Junior of fifteen years of age, son of the lawyer William Lawson and his wife Margrit. My work consisted of lifting Bill out of his wheelchair and put him on the john, clean his ass, put him back in his chair, keep him company, put him in the bathtub, wash him, entertain him – I learned to play chess. Walk him around the block pushing his chair, take him to the movies, to the restaurant, which meant that I had to hustle him in and out the Lincoln and put him to sleep at night. The guy weighed around seventy kilos and I did feel it.

I was not rich but lived as one. Why do you need to be rich if you can live like one? OK, I had to carry the biomass of Bill, but that was paying little for living that way. For not paying public transport which in Bethesda does not exist, I used the Lincoln for my escapes to Washington and keep an eye on the University. I got food – cooked by a Scottish maid which is not synonymous for bad food -, was lodged comfortably and made a salary, which of course was not enough to pay only one hour of class at the American University

School of International Affairs. Let's see how I got about to convert myself in a student of this very select institution.

Came the day of registering: the rule of the game was that each candidate had to select his courses, which title was on a board hanging behind the person teaching the course, sitting next to a small table with a spare chair; one had to have an interview with the professor who – if accepted - signed and gave you a perforated computer card. I did not know very well what I wanted to study but there were several inspiring course titles with "Africa" in it. I thought that this would be my best chance and I was not wrong. When my future professors learned that I had lived in Africa they got very enthusiastic and wanted me in their courses. Once the four computer cards gathered and properly signed, the student-to-be had to go to the last three tables, close to the exit. On the first one they took your cards and put them in a huge closet which was the computer of those days, and which vomited a sheet confirming the registration. At the second, they gave you the bill to be paid. The last table was to pay or present the credentials of the tutoring institution that was going to do so for you. My problem was this last table. I never got that far. Hiding behind other students I just turned back and slowly, as naturally as possible, walked out through the entrance door.

I had no idea how expensive an education could be. I thought it was a right and those thousands and thousands of dollars written on that sheet, besides that I could not pay them, were shocking. Each trimester I will have to play the same circus.

The fellow students of the School for International Affairs were sympathetic men and women   with scholarships from the Pentagon, the State Department and a couple of church organizations with missionary tendencies. One was an "Afro American", as they said in those days. Later on they will be called "colored people" which supposes that white is not a color, which makes whites transparent. The professors were three: two transparent-Americans, one of them a pastor of the Presbyterian Church- the third one was South African, ex-representative of the ANC party at the UNO; of course, this latter one was not transparent at all.

. No one of this teaching group ever had set foot in Africa, except Doctor Villakasy, the South African, who taught "African politics".

I was a fraud, a free wheel; sure they thought that I belonged to the KGB. Common sense told me that at least three quarter parts of them belonged to the CIA. But we got along greatly. Everything that should and could be known about African political parties, the tribal social relationships, the value and social security role of the dowry (which is not buying a wife as westerners often think), tribe alliances etc....The afro American fellow student was obsessed with the slave trade, which could be understood being himself a descendent of one. We passed hours and hours with this theme: the process, the beneficiaries, the tribal origins, the trade, even the ship plans of slave traders. In brief: everything about it, but nothing about the essence of it.

Years later, in a conference, in Cuba an Afro-Caribbean writer – sorry, forgot his name - to whom a journalist asked what he thought of the slave trade, calmly responded : "Considering what Africa is like, he was very happy that his great-great-grandfather got a seat on the slave boat". Looking at it from that angle...?

*

What about it? The right to have slaves is clearly written in all letters in the Bible, in which it is recommended to the Jews not to take slaves from their own people. In the actual Nation-State context, this means that Mexicans can take slaves in the Unites States but not from Chiapas. Let's pay tribute to the founders; since they were the first, we owe them many rules and inventions still valid in our society. Many pages legitimize and regulate slavery in the old fundamental writings of the current faiths. There is not much respect for the fellow neighbor who does not belong to the same family. The non-Jew does not enjoy the same rights as a member of the chosen by God himself people. In such a way that those who stay outside – the whole world - can be treated as objects, things, merchandise over whom the owner has rights of life and death. The book of Genesis defends slavery and what previously was a right of war, fruit of conquest, later was converted into common trade.

Saint Paul in his writings legitimizes total submission to the ruling authority and goes far beyond the war and conquest justifications of slavery. Christianity does not prohibit slavery and to clean a little bit the bad conscience slavery could produce, they just wrote into the dogma that all those living beyond Cabo Verde – North African coast- did not have a soul and therefore could be reduced into slaved of the Christians. In the 6th century, Pope Gregorio I, prohibited access to priesthood to slaves. In the middle Ages, thousands of slaves worked for the popes' agricultural domains. The great monasteries used them without restrictions: the cloister of Saint

Germain des Prés, in Paris had more than eight thousand slaves working on it.

Of course, Christians are not the only ones, Muslims did not do badly in this matter and some of them still do. As with the Jews (of whom Islam is a poor copy), Islamic law prohibits to sell Muslims as slaves but in no way peoples who have other faiths. Nine centuries before the transatlantic slave trade, the trans-Sahara slave trade started this commerce of humans. An estimated ten million people were deported into slavery by the followers of Allah, the very compassionate one. It's somewhat awkward to see the followers of Malcolm X combat western civilization with the Islamic tools. It's like fighting fire with a flaming torch.

To resume: all the holy books – Torah, Koran, Bible - justify slavery, considered to be a destiny for sub-humans who pray other Gods than theirs.

Of course, these considerations did not enter the minds of my colleagues learning African history at the American University in Washington DC.

*

Even if Bill Lawson permitted me to go in a Lincoln to the University, I could not hold on to the rhythm of combining; taking care of him and do respectable work at the School of International Affairs. I got out of the bourgeois existence of a rich student to pick up again the bohemian way of life in a room close to Washington Circle and got a waiter's job at the Jockey Club of Washington. The cafeteria of senators, high civil servants, diplomats and high ranking CIA agents; where the whole Kennedy clan, presided by God-Mother Rose, a disaster of prepotency, with her nose way up in the air and having forgotten since long that her fortune originated with booze smuggling, came for lunch every Wednesday.

Every spare minute, and that was not much after: courses, waiting in the jockey club, library, was spent on Washington Circle, temple of soft marginalization, the starting hippy movement, the flower people of peace and love . The heavy marginalization of misery or poverty was in the Negro neighborhoods, somewhere on the outskirts of the city, in Baltimore or Virginia. There were always bongo players, guitar scratchers, chess players or just hanging around people on the Circle. Lying on the lawn, there was always a possibility of conversation about anything with anyone, a lot of flirting and reading at the light of the public lamp posts, costless. Liberated from

106

Billy, his seventy kilos and his obsessive parents, Saturdays and Sundays in small groups – most of them with some secretaries from one or the other administration- or alone, I walked my legs off visiting the monuments, the Smithsonian and other museums.

Little by little, I became a convinced adversary of the Vietnam war and whenever possible, together with the afro American from my course, we went picketing in front of the White House. The Jockey Club hours became unbearable, so I sold myself as a French language lab supervisor for four hours a day (I still was far from perfect with my future national language). Proof of my many facets were the nights passed away, singing and drinking in an English pub in a chic tavern on Wisconsin Avenue, where Irish, English and German melodies made us laugh loud or cry in our beers.

*

In the School of International Affairs a whole trimester was dedicated to African colonization: The facts, the aberrations, but also the different philosophies of colonialism. The French based the concept on: "integration"", pretending in the long run to make of every colonized a descendent of the Gaule tribes, good daughters and sons of Marianne, patriots of beautiful France. The English thought that this was outrageous, they did not want to imagine that one day the House of Commons would host originals from the colonies like the French who filled their National congress with colonized members. The English philosophical concept of colonialism was "separation": Each one in his place and God guarding the sheep, with the segregationist laws in the middle. The extreme logic of the concept led to the South African apartheid system. Another variety of colonial philosophy was the Portuguese concept of "assimilation". The Portuguese did not bring their women along in the colonization adventure, which gave birth to a complicated institution of "mulatoes","asimilados", "half asimilados", and   "indigenous", each one with different rights and obligations. Here you passed from one status to another by examinations. The Spanish colonization of Latin America was designed along about the same patterns as the Portuguese: very legalized segregation.

In German and Dutch, there are two words which perfectly define the philosophical foundations of the different types of colonization, they are: *"Gezelschaft and Gemeinschaft"*. If you want to know more about the exact definitions of these, there are excellent encyclopedias.

107

The Hedonist

The French colonial philosophy implied that all colonized one day would become citizens with equal rights. Consequently, one day the French Congress, the Senate and the executive would be dominated by: polygamous, black or brown Muslims, third world lawmakers, just by the principles of majority rule and one man one vote. It was up to de Gaulle to save France for a second time from inevitable Islamization by quickly distributing independence to everyone. This is what the Algerian French colonials never were able to understand and which resulted in the bloody Algerian war.

I beg for indulgency if you do encounter some shortcomings. This is all I remember. After all, today I am a sea farmer in Mexico.

*

Finally, what are the basic philosophies of colonialism? In my opinion the French philosopher Michel Onfray (whom I recommend to all) puts forward the most trustworthy analysis. "Colonialism is the exportation of the colonizers' religion to the four cardinal points of the earth, by means of imposture, physical constraint, mental pressure and armed force." For its part, the Jewish religion choose not to be part of this expansion and the Jews elected to establish themselves in only one territory without searching expansion beyond. Zionism is neither expansionism nor internationalization. This, because of the simple fact that to be a Jew you have to be born one – through the mother's linage. Therefore the monotheist Jews stay out of the chapter of overseas colonialism. They aspire to a closed society and in no way to establish an empire over the whole surface of the planet as the two other religions of the Book want to do.

The catholic religion is master in the destruction of civilizations. Before Christianity, the Roman legions assimilated and incorporated the civilizations they conquered. They simply integrated the Gods of the conquered peoples into their own pantheon. Some even went as far as making offerings to the enemy's Gods before battle, just promising these new Gods that they will stay Gods and become part of the Roman Pantheon. After the coup of Constantine they no longer assimilated, they destroyed. The discovery of the New World in 1492 is not only a discovery but also a destruction of other worlds. Christian Europe wiped out an impressive number of indigenous societies in the Americas. Once the cleaning up done by soldiers and mercenaries, the priests came along with: saints, processions and crosses, predicating love of mankind, the evangelical vetoes and some more biblical joys as: original sin, guilt, hatred of woman, body and sexuality, the "natural" tendency of Catholicism towards mass extermination is old and still in use. The latest one is the Tutsi genocide by the hands of the very catholic Hutus in Rwanda in 1994 – just fourteen years ago- covered up, defended and supported by the catholic institutions and the Pope himself. This latter one, much more dynamic to help the criminal priests, monks, and sisters to escape from the prosecution than to offer excuses to the Tutsi people. One million deaths in three months (they did much better than the German Nazis). Silent and accomplice of the Hutus, in, the massive murdering, silent and accomplice, after the discovery of the disaster, did Pope John Paul II write a letter to the President of Rwanda saying to be sorry for the facts? To regret? To disassociate himself from the murderers? No, he wrote instead to ask that the murderers would not be executed. He never had a word for the victims.

This is the essence of colonial philosophy. Of course this is not taught in any school and less at the American University, where the atmosphere started to heat up for me.

*

There came the moment that I could not hold the rhythm. A big term paper every trimester, a weekly presentation to the whole class of a chosen subject, plus daily documenting and assimilating the contents of courses, all this became too much. Time going by, things became worse. In the end, when time invested to stay alive interfered with time I had to spend trying to do a good job, I started translating - in a certain way, cheating. In the French bookstore of Georgetown I translated entire chapters of Claude Levy Strauss, Meister, René Dumont and many more. All these sociologists and economists are of world fame and were completely ignored by my teachers, just because they were not translated into English at that time. That's how American teaching was: ignorant of a good part of world knowledge. I suspected something wrong when one day the very distinguished PHD Randall rejected one of my translations saying that it was not good enough. It happened to be a literal translation of a chapter of the French sociologist Levi Strauss; poor, poor Randall.

All this does not mean that I could not fall in love with a French student from Strasbourg. I don't know what she was studying. It was not really important; she was there to have fun. She rented an apartment in Georgetown, which shows that she was not poor. I moved in immediately, saving money. We had fun, she was always good humored and not very pretty which was compensated by a huge libido.

At the University, things became squeezed. Someone was getting aware that I did not comply with something. I figured that it took them time to figure out what. One day I received a letter from the Dean telling me that they had no trace of my existence. I showed it to Villakasy and together we went to the administration office where Villakasy; showing my term papers, notes, and credits, told them that I did exist. There were only two months left to graduation in Master of Arts in Political science and social affairs with an African specialization.

The magic of learning however had gone since I had realized the ignorance of the PHD Randall. These faults of the teaching staff can be traced all the way to American foreign politics. The lack of profoundness and social sensitivity: Vietnam, Cambodia, Cuba, Latin America and of course the Middle East and Iraq, are just demonstrations of fatal political errors which can be traced back to the lack of knowledge and sociological sensibility. Someone just forgot to tell them that not all is rational, logical and simple in other cultures which are not: white, Christian and rich. The intentions of American foreign policies are always good, generous, noble, but are executed with the Randall mentality and the "American common sense" simplifications.

It was time to break up camp. My Strasbourg girl friend rented a car and one early morning we left - without asking for the invoice - off to California, where we arrived three weeks later.

*

I just had stolen an education. One of the best available normally reserved to the civil servants with diplomatic careers, policy makers, and CIA agents. Funny, but I did not experience any feeling of guilt. I don't know that there is a juridical code to specify the crime of stealing an education, or what maximum penalty it is punished with. I consider it less criminal than steeling a candy bar. Isn't education a basic right? However, I hope that one day my finances permit me to ask for the check at the American University in Washington DC. I learned from this experience in what time I am living; why things are the way they are; to distinguish between intelligence and imbecility. No, I have no guilt feeling for this theft. I did not get the diploma, neither a graduate ceremony, but that's the least. I went through this for the sake of learning and not to make money out of it. The idea about making a career and turn knowledge into money never occurred to me. I don't know why.

To learn is to become aware that you don't know anything, as said Socrates. With my fellow students from the Pentagon, the State Department, the CIA and the protestant churches we were enriched by precise and theoretical knowledge. We read it all, we saw it all, we knew it all, with the exception of the raw reality of African society in blood and bones. It was supposed to be a training of free men and women with knowledge of the causes. But it came out to be a manufacture of domestics for the administration, obedient to the rules and customs. Without realizing that one more technician of sociology, philosophy etc., is completely useless. The search for harmony with the world and its people as they are- and not as they are supposed to be or as the school owners would like them to be – is not the purpose of education: neither in Sint Truiden, nor in Washington and still less in Campeche.

We were not taught the irony of Socrates who questions, destroys the truths of the moment or "a la mode", who despised egoism as unique ethical imperative, the consent of barbarism, the disdain of ideas, the will to have powers, and fascination for fictitious successes, admiration for third rate politicians: All this was not on the program.

The world today is the result of what the educators did yesterday.

*

This is not a tourist guide; therefore there is no use in telling you the trip across the United States. But everything was fine. When Hollywood appeared through the car window; Denise already had organized it all. She seriously wanted us to become engaged. She had already talked it over with her brother, a powerful man in the steel industry business in Strasbourg – of which she owned half - and with whom I was supposed to take a job. She did not talk about marriage but it was as if it was done. The script of the movie: I'll become the second in charge to an industrialist, we will be living happily in a big house in the suburbs, and another one in the mountains to ski in the winter weekends, and a third one on the Riviera to do nudism in the Summer. That we'll have many children and that's it: Happy end of the movie.

Regardless the pleasure of her company, the thousand and one affinities of all kind; something inside told me not to take the highway that Denise had traced. With the pretext that I wanted to take courses at Berkeley, I would stay for a while in the USA while she had to go back for a family matter. We said so long in the San Francisco airport with a thousand passionate kisses – for sure amidst a lot of scandalized people- and many promises. A TWA hostess came to separate us saying, with a large smile, that the airplane was closing its doors.

Many weeks later, when eventually I had an address, I received a long letter in which there were many things, except the degree of love that I expected. Months later we met in the Café de Flore in Saint Germain des Prés in Paris. She was on the point of getting married, I too, but not one to another.

I tried to take some courses in Berkeley where world-famous professors in sociology and anthropology were teaching. But it was impossible. On the campus yet nobody was talking about courses and teaching but about psychedelic revolution, peace in Vietnam, social and sexual liberation, women's rights and more. We were hippies and darn happy. Early in the morning, which means around eleven, groups of young people would gather around the cafeteria and on the lawns. Blessed cafeteria where bread, water, coffee, ketchup and mustard were free.

Passionate discussions happened everywhere about anything, interrupted by smelling flowers and giving them out to everyone, including the policeman who stood at the Campus entrance to protect I don't know who from I don't know what. We kissed, caressed and flirted without restrictions. Of course the "joints" circulated at surprising speed. That's where I discovered that I am not an exhibitionist. Our heroes were some GI's coming back from Vietnam who told their war stories, burnt their military cards and spat on their medals. They were very popular and venerated among the girls. Sometimes we went to spend the day in Sausalito, free territory which belonged to the homosexuals, lesbians and all types of rebel communities.

I did not understand very well against what we were rebelling. In the last weeks I spent in the American University in DC, a student movement had started to make some noise. The big claim was to have access to the girls' dorms after 10 PM. A couple of times I went to scream along in front of the Dean's office. It was more like a feast, a joke with much irony. This was rebellion?

Berkeley was anti-war with a mystical background. The psychedelics were giving way to the Jesus freaks. A rebellion without a route, except for some vague claims of sexual liberty, against the system, but without questioning it; Against the war, money as a supreme value; against savage capitalism but no question of ever talking about changing it. Most of my hippy friends and sweethearts were so apolitical that it did not occur to them to challenge the system. We were just happy to predicate love, adore flowers, and smoke pot. How nice this superficiality: everything goes. Living a complete form of nihilism, relativism, to disconnect completely from reality, for which there is no need to face it, is an agreeable way to live. Society, reality, bourgeois values, the war, barbarism were not liked. So, let's climb one more staircase and simply deny the existence of all these awkward things.

This is about all I can get out – philosophically speaking – of the hippy movement which we sometimes take for a revolution, if not social, at least cultural. It is not surprising that nothing, or so little, stayed from this movement.

*

Taking them for what they are not, imagining themselves in configurations away from reality, mankind sometimes avoids tragedies but passes besides many good things in life. By way of preferring fictions and tranquilizers as children who need a nice story to sleep. Preferring faith that calms, to reason that disturbs. The mental cost of this lying to oneself is monstrous and sometimes overflows in movements which are escape or safety valves to the pressure of life confined to perpetual fiction and lies. The will to avoid taking on reality up front is unimaginable. The desire for a nicer looking spectacle than reality – even if this implies living with a complete fiction – is shared by all. Most of mankind prefers to live in a fairy tale, with stories and myths than in the reality which obliges to see the cruel evidence of the world and of life. To exorcise death, we dismiss it. To avoid having to resolve the problem, we abolish it.

Having to die is a mortals' business. The ingenuous believer knows that he is immortal and that he will survive the general hecatomb. To help him build that fiction of immortality there are individuals who dedicate themselves to traffic with that fiction. The business of "life after life" is one of the most prosperous of all times and secures to the traffickers a reason for their existence at the same time that they heal their own fears and frustrations.

The trick, the swindle, of course, goes far beyond insuring the needs of the exploiter of anguish.

The submission of society to all traffickers, spiritual guides, mullahs, rabbis, priests, gurus, who promote fictions in order to hide the existential anguish, comes sometimes to such a boiling point of absurdity that it has to adjust. In their fight against science, culture and reason, the religious fictions have to adapt and maneuver. These adjustments, since history exists, never were by consent but by means of wars, rebellion and bloodshed. The "Christianization" of the Gallic tribes by the newly baptized King Clovis was done by simply cutting the heads off, of those who refused to convert to the new beliefs of how to exorcise death.

*

It must have been my preservation instinct - my mother's legacy- which told me to step down from the "Peace and Love" cloud I was so comfortably sitting on. The risk was to get lost for good in this unreal and artificial world. With my few things in a backpack, I left California and the hippy period to go back to DC which was the only place I was familiar with and where I knew how to move.

Just off the record: I passed four days in an enchanting jail cell of a small town close to Milwaukee. Just for hitchhiking on a highway, which in this place was prohibited and sentenced by jail. Since the judge did not pass before four days, I stayed for that time host of the judicial system of the United States of America. Food was furnished by the only restaurant in town and the sheriff left me a meter high pile of Mickey Mouse comic strips. Four days of free food, hot water showers, a good mattress, a well heated room, a serviceable sheriff and a laughing judge thinking that, four days of jail were enough for my crime - besides of being quite expensive to the community – left me with a very good opinion of American jails.

I fell back on Washington Circle and the Jockey Club but without term papers and the African Specialist who never had heard about Levi Strauss.

CHAPTER III
PARIS- HABANA

Her name was Marie Chantal de Riac, about thirty, daughter to a French General, French teacher and part of a linguistic exchange program. She was about ready to go home to her native Neuilly, somewhere in the Paris posh suburbs. We met on the Circle, talked a lot and kissed a little. I fell in love. Problem: She was a virgin and wanted to keep the hymen intact. Together we drove in a hired van to New York where she was supposed to board the cruiser France to Le Havre, France. I got on the ship, with a visitor one dollar ticket in support of the Seamen Widows Association. I stayed on as a stowaway. She fed me sandwiches, bread and fruit she hid in her purse, coming from the excellent ship's restaurant. We passed the day reading in comfortable deck chairs, walking back and forth, playing very stupid social games or in the pool.

What had to happen, happened: an officer found me at three in the morning, sitting on the carpet of a passage between cabins. Nobody was supposed to come through there at this hour, but the guy just came out of a cabin zipping up his pants. The rest of the voyage I spent in the cruiser's jail, which was not disagreeable at all. After three days of sleeping anywhere I was glad to get a comfortable bed. In Le Havre, her mum, a little woman looking dried up and her father-general waited for us. We installed ourselves in her place and barely two months later were we married in the most bourgeois fashionable way in the church of Neuilly-sur-Seine. She, in a traditional white wedding dress and I in tuxedo and top hat followed by a reception at the Military Circle. Yes Sir. That night in a big hotel the sheets showed big, ugly bloodstains. The way things are supposed to be in the world of bourgeois Christians.

We moved to the small Normandy town of Elbeuf, where she had an assignment as an English teacher. I contributed a little to the family economy, selling life insurances and encyclopedias to the peasants around. We made love day and night, something that to my surprise she got bored with, trying with difficulty to give us a more civilized sexual "rhythm". I too, I got bored, not of making love, but of the small town and the life I was leading. Besides, I started looking, with animal desire, at one of her school colleagues who apparently did not object.

I began to go to Paris more and more often, with the pretext of registering at the University to get a French equivalence of my incursions in the American academic world. Very happy with the fact, Marie became pregnant. Little by little I became aware that this was her goal for our sacred union. Becoming a mother was the prime objective of her life at that time. I was content to have made her happy and given her what she really was after. In a certain way I was paying a debt.

The Hedonist

On the 22nd of March of the year 1968, in my 25th year of earth dweller, I presented myself at the University of Nanterre in the Paris suburbs. A few blocks of cement gray buildings, a huge parking, also gray amongst a carton-wooden "slum of North African immigrants and to complete the sinister picture of that campus the sky was also gray with a fine, penetrating to the bone, misty rain falling for hours. Finally I got a appointment with a sociologist, specialist in Africa, to talk about my academic equivalences.

This date will become very important because that day the student movement "22 of March" was created, spearhead of the historical May 68 student movement which two months later will bring the French Nation to its knees. By accident I was there and lived it all, it was going to change my life again.

I got there early and the professor, of whom I remember he was Belgian, had barely started a magisterial course on Rwanda social and political structures in a half empty amphitheatre. This is a lot of people for that subject. With foresight this professor was predicting, with short films and slides, the roots of the civil war between Hutus and Tutsis that was going to devastate Rwanda thirty years later. Yes, sociology well understood has a political utility. The ethnic group which was not heard of in that civil war was the Pygmies, third component of the Rwanda social map.

At the end of this lecture demonstration, I applauded very loud standing besides the last row of seats, just beside the door. All of a sudden the door swung open with a smack, I took it fully in my face and fell between the seats. By the time I got up, with the firm intention of asking for an explanation and if necessary to butt the authors' bottoms, a group of people shouting and pushing stood on the speaker's platform. Somebody tried to take the microphone from the professor who resisted and therefore was brutally pushed and received a blow on his bald head with the microphone. My first reaction was to go up front and rescue him, but when I got to the platform I had to renounce. First, because I did not see the teacher anymore and secondly, the shouting and screaming group had become about a hundred. I kept pushing to get to the point I had seen the bald head disappear. All of a sudden I was face to face with a young man, smaller than me, but fatter, with very clear eyes under an abundant bush of red hair, the kind of red hair I had never seen before. He had the microphone and smiled at me while he was trying to get upon the conference table for which I gave him a push in his big ass. He was the guy named Daniel Cohn-Bendit who in a few weeks will become the headache of the French government, including the

General de Gaulle. Once upon the table, he raised his arms up in the air and the whole bunch of boys and girls screamed: "Revolution!".

The redhead screamed in the microphone: "Comrades" and tried to calm the crowd without much success. "Comrades" is the password all the leftist combatants identify themselves with, from the worst of the Stalinists to the softest social-democrats, comrades is the war cry. Looking into the theatre, I saw the bald headed professor sitting in the last row. Extracting myself from the platform, now completely loaded with screaming people electing themselves to the board of directors of the revolution, I had not the slightest idea what all this was about. I got to him and presented myself. To which he reacted by only lifting his head with eyes full of desolation and sorrow. Then, he looked back at his shoes, showing me his very bald skull, while murmuring "How can they do this to me? "

I did not have the answer and for a while we kept silent, looking at the redhead enumerating an endless list of demands and complaints.

- How can they do this to me? The bald head repeated.
- What is going on professor? What do they want?

Again he looked at me with his clear eyes full of deception and sorrow. I did understand that it was not the moment to raise the subject of my academic credentials.

- Demands and more demands. They say that the university functions badly, that the programs are bad, and that they want access to the girl's dorms after ten. I agree with all that, I am on their side.

At that moment the redhead indeed was screaming that this was the symbol of a bourgeois university. That sounded familiar to me.

- That's true, said the professor asI admired a very nice bulge growing on top of his head, there where the microphone had landed.

In silence we looked at the bourgeois youth rebelling. The amphitheater was getting fuller and fuller, more and more groups of students were joining the shouting.

- Comrades, at this moment we declare a general strike until the complete satisfaction of our just demands, shouted the redhead.

This was greeted with an enormous tumult. In one corner some started to sing "L´Internationale" which I heard for the first time. I liked it.

The bald head got up.

- Can you help me to recuperate my films in from projection booth?

Of course I could. Pushing people in front of me, we made our way to the projection booth, for by now the theater was full. The booth, on top of a small staircase was completely abandoned. The bald head knew how to handle the projection machine. While he reeled his films I looked through the projection hole and enjoyed the spectacle with a panoramic view; all were standing, some on the chairs. The platform was filled with supposed representatives of different faculties. The redhead was still holding on to the microphone and each time he announced the arrival of another faculty there was more shouting: "Strike, strike,"

The bald head arranged his films in a black leather handbag and we wrestled against the current to the door. We shook hands:

- Better we see each other tomorrow, if this brothel, because that's what it is, is over.

On which he walked away, his back bent as if the whole weight of what was coming was crunching him. I would never see that man again.

Back in the amphitheater, I had to stop halfway down the aisle. The place was packed and more were coming. Daniel Cohn-Bendit was proposing the creation of a student movement and a strike committee with representatives of every faculty. The movement's name was "Twenty-second of March", because that was the date. It was legalized by a vote of raised hands.

Happy to participate in something and for not staying behind, I raised my hand too. I was not a student yet, I had no clear idea what it was all about, but it seemed the right thing to do.

So, I became a member of the student movement 22nd of March, lighting the wick of the student rebellion which will bring the country to its knees.

I really liked him, the red haired leader, he knew how to maneuver a crowd, had an incredible speaking talent, follow up in his ideas, a tremendous willpower, a good sense of organization and humor. Yes I liked him. He used concepts and words that were new to me: Democratization of the University, a student quota for peasants and proletarian descendants, abolition of exams to end with the arbitrary protectionism of the bourgeoisie, student participation in all the university councils, access to girls dorms - this I did understand - and more, and more. We voted and voted, shouted and screamed, applauded and when the redhead had completely lost his voice, I added my voice to all those who voted the indefinite strike. The last vote was to take the offices of the Dean.

Night had fallen and chased a day that never really came to wake. The parking light poles were wrapped up in small grey clouds which did not even let the light reach the tarmac. The outside grey contrasted with the lights and splendor of the amphitheater and the lights showing in each one's eyes.

Packed as sardines in a tin, we kept shouting in front of the administration building, also grey and wrapped up in grey as anything else on that campus. I don't know how it happened, I only saw that the Dean had come out of the building to talk with us and was received by a whistling concert in which of course I enthusiastically participated. From far, looking above the forest of heads and shoulders, we saw a turned over garbage can moving from one side to the other among laughter and screams. Under that garbage can was the respectable Dean trying to get back into his building. As if scared by their own daring, the demonstration dissolved, laughing and shouting youths running away in all directions.

As said, my date with the professor did not take place the next day, nor ever. Long before reaching the campus I walked along a long, long line of parked police buses belonging to the famous CRS antiriot squads. They had taken over the campus during the night. The first big mistake made by the government and the minister of the Interior a certain Fouché.

Then started a few weeks of confrontations with the police,, a matter of throwing stones and running. The University was closed and the CRS were eating their lunches in the amphitheatres.

For some days I got away from the university, trying to earn some money selling insurances to the Elbeuf peasants, and taking care of Marie.

Back in Paris the word circulated: "A la Sorbonne" and a few days later a student demonstration was called at the Denfert-Rochereau square, close to the Observatory. We walked down the Boulevard Saint- Michel, past the Sorbonne and walked right in. Not a policeman in sight.

That's how it all started. The next day the statue of Victor Hugo on the Sorbonne square was wrapped in a red cloth. Someone had written on the staircases: "The stairs weep", There were inscriptions everywhere:"It's forbidden to forbid". In each amphitheatre there were debates going on about everything and anything, from the Vietnam War, the dialectics of socialism or the cleaning services in the toilets. Even one forum I listened to, promoted to create a highway from Saint Michel Boulevard to the Normandy coast. Everybody talked and said what they thought had to be said. Everyone, from revolutionary poets or phony politicians, marginalized social or unsocial people; every tendency who lived in Paris and its suburbs was there. Information got in that more and more universities in other cities had also gone on strike.

After the students, or whatever they were, occupied the Odeon Theatre, two blocks away from the Sorbonne, I moved to there. A permanent debate-shouting was installed in which I did not participate, but I listened a lot.

Then came the day that the government decided to clean up the place, by means of squadrons of helmeted, shielded and stick waving CRS. The confrontations started immediately: We, trying to take the Sorbonne, with shielded, masked, helmeted CRS keeping us from doing so. I screamed my ass off "Fouché to the wall, liberate the Sorbonne". Every afternoon and night we tried to reenter the university. Soon the barricades appeared, made of cobblestones – very handy to be thrown at the police squads – cut trees, furniture, cars, some of them burnt; anything; we played at cat and mouse with the CRS in the streets of the Latin Quarter. When they took a barricade, we built another one a little farther or behind them. We ran, shouted, sang revolutionary songs, some from the Spanish war or the Mexican revolution, we kissed and hugged a lot too, sharing the few sandwiches that we could get hold of, handed out by the inhabitants who gave them, or threw them, through their windows. We vomited a lot, our lungs loaded with tear gas generously distributed by the police.

One day we marched to the Renault factories in Boulogne Billancourt, in the suburbs to incite the proletarians to join the revolution; which we obtained because many unions were joining the strike. That means that the workers lay off and the union heads, so as not to lose the control of this spontaneous movement, declared the strike.

Little by little the country was paralyzed. (I just can imagine the back and forth phone calls between Paris and Moscow since Moscow controlled the French communist party and the French communist party controlled the most important working class unions.)

Then, all of a sudden, one night, the police disappeared from the Sorbonne and the whole Latin Quarter. We shouted Victory. In the following days the Sorbonne was converted into a touristic place. The middle classes and bourgeois from Paris came to visit us, along with their wives and children dressed up as for Sunday church or going to the circus. Many brought us food and beverages.

The neighborhood was a battlefield. Not a single cobblestone was in its place on all the Saint Michel and Saint-Germain boulevards. Many trees were cut. Burnt out cars were lying everywhere.

In these times when I was a perfect political illiterate. Slowly but surely a political consciousness process was invading my mind. The just cause, for which it was worth fighting, was the proletarian cause, socialist, and justice for the underdogs of society, just distributor of the wealth, generous, shoulder to shoulder, fraternal and free in all matters. This was the new paradise. Finally, and for the time my life is going to last, the socialist cause will stick to my skin. This looked very much like the teachings of a certain Jesus who had been kicked into my head with fists and sticks.

The square of the Sorbonne, with Victor Hugo still wearing his red scarf, was converted into a small market place, something like a school festival. With the difference that instead of ball drawing stands and duck fishing pools, the hot dog or sandwich sellers, the stands were three dozen tables occupied by the comrades of the one thousand and one revolutionary organizations and political movements that existed or just popped up. There were the stands of the first environmental movements, at least five variations of women's liberation front's, at least three variations of Maoists, and as many Trotskyites, the free unionists, the Stalinists who pretended that Khrushchev was a traitor, the anti-Leninist Marxists and their contrary, the defendants of Pol Pot and one small desk of the Guevarists. This one captivated my interest more than any other, although I had only vaguely heard the name at the American University or reading the newspapers. I got into a passionate discussion and hours later, I signed myself up to participate in an international student camp in Cuba. The name of this summer school camp was "Campamento Cinco de Mayo" for Marx's birthday.

In the meantime, the official unions and the political parties of the left took the lead of the social movement that evolved in the whole country. Bypassing the original student movement, some, because they saw a splendid occasion to get from the government the fulfillment of their ever "just demands", the other ones because this was a dreamed of occasion to overthrow the government of de Gaulle and sit in his seat.

The tenth of May there was a giant Unitarian manifestation which mobilized the full artillery of the official unions to make sure things were going the way they wanted them to go. We descended the Boulevard Saint Michel, marching towards the bridge of the same name. This was an ocean of red banners and singing and shouting people. I marched with the original group of the 22nd of March where the faces were familiar. When we got to Saint Michel plaza there was a huge bottleneck, because the bridge, narrower than the avenue, could not carry that many people. Who cared? We shouted, sang, sat down, danced, convinced as we were that this was the revolution. I started to have some doubts when seeing, from the middle of the second bridge, that the ocean of people was not turning to the left – towards the Elysée Palace - but to the right toward the Sebastopol avenue. There was not a policeman in sight, but the security squads of the communist union CGT guarded access to the streets which led to the Elysée. When I moved near to Cohn-Bendit I saw him really worried. We kept walking until getting lost, hours later, behind the East railway station in a working class neighborhood.. This was not the picture we had in mind. Angry, we went back to the Latin Quarter for a last great standoff with the CRS. Our eyes out of their orbits, because of the clouds of teargas that enveloped the whole neighborhood, our legs which did not want to move anymore, shirts and pants with several holes, we ended up feasting in the café "The Smoking Dog" in the Halles: the Paris stomach, where between eleven at night and six in the morning everything that will be eaten in Paris changes owners. Many times I gained good money renting my arms and legs for a few hours charging and discharging cages of tomatoes, potatoes, quarters of sheep, pork heads, cow legs, anything; these were hours of rush and running. At six o'clock there passed the municipal cleaning up services and anything that was still on the street was converted into garbage.

General de Gaulle gave his press conference, of which I remember the famous phrase "Reforms: Yes. Shit in the bed: No". Three days later, the Gaullist party and supporters mounted a counter demonstration on the Champs-Elysée. An ocean of French flags descended the avenue. De Gaulle dissolved Parliament and called for general elections. And won them in a landslide way.

*

What had happened in these three months, besides that personally I came out of it as a completely different person? A student movement which started with some almost childish claims and demands, like the access to girls dorms after ten, had paralyzed the country, brought the government to resign and call new elections to legitimize itself, obliging the President to go to Germany to verify the loyalty of his army.

Hundreds of books and thousands of articles tried to explain and did explain. Up to today, the actors and spectators lose themselves in conjecture and hypothesis: a social explosion, a poetic breach, a nihilists overtaking, a social crisis, a rejection of the consumer society, a union movement, and what more? Freud would have called it: "the killing of the father", rejection of authority, of hierarchy, of the models, of bourgeois values. The movement left an inheritance in which everyone is going to find whatever he likes to find; The spirit of liberty and libertinage, of independence, of ethical existence, the power of criticizing and of resistance. The leftists, to whom I belonged, dreamed of a social paradise for tomorrow in which all the power will rest with the working class. From the feminists and the entire women's liberation movements – of which many became anti-men movements – the gay and lesbian movements, and the illumination of Mao's little red book: Everybody was there. And when everybody is there, nobody is.

I believe that the nihilist side of the movement was understood by de Gaulle. Like all the men of action, it is in action that they realize themselves and find solutions. He understood the unrest and was going to take care of it, talking directly to the people above the heads of the political parties. That's where he found the roots of a new legitimacy of the social contract that he had passed with the people of France. Doing so, he raised against him his own allies, all the political dwarves, the opportunists, the careerists, and of course the left, which in their own programs never had dared to propose such progressive measures. All of them sharpened their knives for his political murder. All those who followed de Gaulle on the throne, had in their pockets the knives for his murder. Confirming Marx's saying that: "History repeats itself twice: once as a drama and once as a joke"

*

Let's go back to my new reason of being: "the revolution", generous, optimistic, just, and utopist. I felt very strange in my marriage to Marie Chantal who enjoyed above all her growing belly. My new inclinations: marxist-socialist-guevarist did not help at all in the harmonization of relations with the general's daughter. So I had no bad feeling at all when I flew off, with my French fellow revolutionaries, to the "Fifth of May camp "in Cuba.

*

For those interested in landscape and nature descriptions, I recommend having a look at how the western Cuban province of Pinar Del Rio looks like in any tourist guide. The air ticket was cheap, including hostel – to give it a name- and food. We had the privilege to be invited by the Cuban government as well as the thousand and some other "youth from all over the world". Mass tourism had to wait another twenty eight years to have the privilege to see Cuban shores and landscapes.

From the airport, where we were received by a swinging orchestra and dancing girls moving to pleasant rhythms, we were immediately taken to the camp. I choose an upper bed in a kind of warehouse full of bunk beds, with bathrooms at the entrance. Identification hung around my neck: Name, country and a small photo on which I looked like a young premier with great ears and a big forehead covered with curly black hair. I haven't changed very much, except for the hair color which by now is very grey and white, some say silvered. But that is because they like me.

On the first day, I got lost and asked my way to one of the many girl guides. She talked so well about my shirt that I ended up giving it to her. There was nothing else in exchange. The first days nothing happened, except the arrival of more and more revolutionary pupils from all over the world. There was always some orchestra playing, sometimes only made up of a few guitars and a bongo. I met many people, among whom a group of Belgian Walloons. I got in a verbal fight with them from the very first moment. I fraternized with the Cubans, to be honest with the Cuban mulatto females. Girls with a loose tongue, who talked and talked, and also with "cool" behavior, easy to talk to, very smiling and with sensual looks that always seemed to invite to a horizontal position. They were also very revolutionary, although I did not understand very well the obsession with material things which had cost me my shirt. "Revolution" was, to me, to disconnect from the material goods, of bourgeois values like a nice shirt and elevate you to spiritual heights to fortify yourself for the just cause of the people in struggle. Even if I did not get the final goal of such a noble cause either.

At dawn on the second day, the event was inaugurated. Several commanders of the Cuban revolution spoke with English interpreters. I don't remember all that was said; they talked about the Cuban process, Moncada, the example of Che Guevara and invited us to be good revolutionaries because "the duty of a revolutionary is to make revolution".

It ended with a dancing party in which I met an Australian and a couple of English people drinking beer at the bar, very skeptical conversation about it all. I figured they got to the wrong fiesta, wrong country and at the wrong time.

The next morning, we climbed into some trucks with picks and shovels. The idea was to plant the nearby hills with coffee trees on terraces. As the natural earth apparently was no good for coffee trees, we had to make holes of one, by one, by one meters, to fill them with good earth and plant a small tree. A French FAO coffee expert explained that that was no use. Once the roots reach the walls of the hole and touch poor stony earth, they would die. We rather thought that he was a disgraceful counter revolutionary and we laughed at him. Because to us it was sure that our revolutionary fervor would make coffee grow, even in the Sahara.

In the afternoons there was a very varied program of conferences, debates and visits. Each delegation of each country exposed how the socialist revolution would take place in their countries. Time gone by, I just am amazed by the volume of information the Cuban secret service collected for free. We had paid to come here to inform them and on top of that we made their coffee plantation holes.

At night, there was a show with outstanding Cuban artists. The one I preferred was, and still is, the one that I keep considering the biggest Cuban artist: Bola de Nieve. Black as the blackest charcoal, small, much overweighed, with the same lips as my son Hervé, authentic West African lips. Bola de Nieve wept when he sang boleros. From a kilometer away you could see that he was very gay, which was very badly looked upon in the socialist society, Castro style, misogynic and macho. Forty years later, and despite the construction of a new society and a "new man" it still is the same.

When Bola de Nieve sang " Drume Negrito", even stones would become sweeties; with "Flor de la Canela" trees would smile; with "Monsieur Julian" the hills would laugh and with "Ya no me quieres" we all wept like little boys. One night came the Aragon orchestra, impossible not to dance. Culturally speaking this was really a treat. They also brought to these muddy hills the national ballet with Alicia Alonso and the National folkloric ballet. Even the poet Nicolas Guillén came to encourage our revolutionary fever.

I knew- in all senses of the world- Isabel Monal, a professor of the University of Havana in Marxism-Leninism who also studied German, just to be able to read the old Karl in his original text. This to tell you that she was a serious person, halfway beautiful and very generous; we talked about African sociology and African politics. Her knowledge ended with the writings of Che Guevara when he tried to start up a revolution in Congo – which ended up with a disaster- and something about the Lumumba episode. Of course, her reading of the

Lumumba drama was exclusively Marxist-Leninist which is a high flying intellectual acrobatic exercise. Somehow she got it all together. As for me, the difficulties I encountered to match Marxist orthodoxy with what I knew of African reality would bring me some problems later on.

Isabel introduced me to the University Dean, who came also to visit the camp: We convened for a date at the university.

The visit to the University of Havana is worth the trip. Indeed it is he first university of the whole continent, even so that the original did not stand where the present is, but was created in downtown old Havana close to the harbor. A white stairway, with in its middle a bronze statue of a woman seated with her arms spread out and the classic inscription "Alma Mater", brings you to a well shadowed campus. These stairs have been the scene of dozens of demonstrations and meetings in which Fidel Castro played a major role as student leader. Of course, this was pre-revolution. Since the victory of socialism, students are not anymore supposed to have reasons to manifest their discontent, since the revolution took care of all their needs. (Except freedom). Since 1959, the stairs only serve to commemorate and support meetings. Sometimes Fidel Castro himself takes the main role, for hours and hours the maximum leader monologues about the march of the world, the imminent end of capitalism, of imperialism and North American domination. (Still in the waiting up to today).

The University is situated upon a hill, like a castle, from which descends a large avenue all the way to the Malecon and the sea. The faculty buildings are huge, with Greek columns, distributed around a small square with centennial trees.

Very informal, the Dean received me his feet upon his desk in an office covered with precious wooden walls and ceiling, and with a marble floor. After brief introductions he proposed to me, in an impeccable English, to dispense courses on African affairs at master level, and this as soon as possible. Isabel was present at the whole interview without losing one second the beautiful and very natural smile on her face.

The Dean led me to the patio. We shook hands firmly and so I got nothing less but a job as a postgraduate professor at the University of Havana.

I took the day to visit the colonial old Havana which was dirty, falling in ruins, almost abandoned, with empty shops and others closed. All this would undergo some restoration decades later with

UNESCO funds, but in 1968 it was really a mess. I tried to get something to eat at the "Bodeguita del Medio", made famous by Hemingway sipping there his mojitos. There was nothing to buy, a few bags of powdered milk and a dozen small boxes of tomato concentrate. Besides, to buy you had to be the owner of a libreta: the famous food rationing system of the socialist paradise (still in use forty years later). In the Bodeguita they did not even remember what a mojito looked like. But at that time all that was not important to me.

I passed the night on a couch in Isabel's apartment, which she shared with her mother and a sister with three children. The next day I had a taxi bring me back to the camp, which finished my financial reserves.

*

Don't think that at my advanced age, at which most Europeans are sent home to keep care of their grandchildren, their dogs and cats or their garden, I have nothing else to do than to tell you my story. Not so. I am still in combat and have to move a lot to keep my sea farm enterprise alive and going. The way things are going, there is a good chance that my only retirement will be the crematorium or in the: "drunks' hole" at the Florida Indian style. (If the occasion arises I'll tell you that too). One way to keep the farm going of course is to sell our production of *Sciaenops Ocellatus* at the best possible price to my only client in Miami. That's what we did today. What is specific about these exports is that they are the only farmed sea fish produced and exported in the Republic of Mexico and that they are not legal. Yes, I am a fraudulent exporter, not an illegal one, because the product passes through regular custom services once at the airport, but still they are a fraud. Probably we are the only legal fraudulent exporters in the world.

I think it is worth it that I tell you the story so you understand better how things work at the bottom in lower middle class Mexico, mostly unseen, or only by small entrepreneurs who, in spite of the persistence of all the civil servants to kill them, want to live.

After a dozen years of practicing the very honorable and exciting trade of creator and operator of "off shore sea farming" in the French Mediterranean – another story you'll come through later on – I came to Mexico with a sea farm project and great desire to make my farm a prosperous one at the same time that we introduced Mexico to the technology of sea farming. Something that simply did not exist and still does not exist really in this country, except for our farm and lab.

First, I was surprised to find out that we were the only integrated sea farm in Mexico since the trade is on the road for at least forty years. Secondly, I got disgusted finding out that nobody was interested.

In a very ingenuous way I wanted to do things the way they are supposed to be done, respecting rules and laws. One thing is that the rules and laws to grow fish do exist but the trade does not. So I introduced our request for a sea concession and the right to put fish cages floating on it, the way this all is written up in the fisheries laws. One article in these laws says that if the administration does not reply to the request in 45 days, the concession is granted. After a good 45 days, I politely asked the director of aquaculture affairs of the Ministry of agriculture, livestock and fishery to grant us the concession by application of that article of the law. This is called a "positive ficta". What a monumental error that was, and a demonstration of ignorance of "the Mexican way". By that time I was supposed to know more about idiosyncrasy. The law here is not "dura lex, sed lex", but an object of negotiations as any other; buying a car, socks in the market, a house, all is negotiable. My friends laughed their head off and recommended strongly to go to Mazatlan, see that guy with at least an attaché case full of banknotes. Instead I kept asking the civil servant in charge to grant us the concession according to the law - and he kept ignoring my demands. In the meantime I installed the farm, hatched fingerlings, grew them to commercial size and exported them to the US.

Two years went by. Finally, I decided to try to implement the law by means of a lawsuit against the government. I was gently advised not to do this because they would simply close the farm. So, from 2002 to 2007 I became a fraudulent sea farmer and exporter of fish as we did again this morning. Corruption is the main reason for the absence of Mexican development. This perverse system in which the civil servant can use his power as he pleases and "pump" money, consist of the following: without a duly established concession document, you can't get a register and without a register you cannot get the "Guia de Pesca" and without this paper you cannot move any fish in Mexico. Since there is no register available, if you don't subscribe to the generalized corruption, you are pressed to line up. It's that simple. In conclusion: for years we hatched, grew, packed, transported and exported fish fraudulently, just avoiding the road controls. Once we get to the airport, the product becomes legal and part of the Mexican economy, and enriches the country with our contribution to increasing the circulating financial mass (just to say it like an economist). That we created employment and contributed in a general way to the economy does not matter in the slightest to the people in charge and paid huge salaries to make this country grow. There are many, much too many of these in power to give Mexico a chance. This high level corruption practices are the surest way to keep the country where it is and apparently nobody is doing a darn thing about it.

The surrealist French writer André Breton was very happy in Mexico. I am starting to understand why. Except that my business is not poetry. I had better stop here because I am getting mad and we better go back to Cuba in 1968. So, apart from trying to connect me to you, dear friend, a couple of hours a day, I am also running a real life as a small entrepreneur, a fraudulent exporter, making my living as a producer of real wellbeing for some Mexican families.

*

I went back to Cuba the same year that I wed; made student fiesta at the Sorbonne and witnessed the birth of my son Jan in a "top level" clinic in Neuilly-sur-Seine. Marie was happy, her mother and her general of a father were happy and seeing them happy, I was too. For them, a wish became fulfilled; Jan is the only male descendant of that branch of the Riac family.

In my head I was giving African sociology classes in the University of Havana. The fact of having an offspring and heir did not particularly touch me. I was happy just to see Marie very happy achieving her dream of motherhood. I don't know if she ever had other dreams in her adult life. We said goodbye with many promises, it was understood that she and Jan would come to Havana as soon as my things looked a little stabilized.

*

For a moment, the Dean of the University of Havana looked at me with surprise and amusement. It became clear that he did not expect me in the slightest and that yet he didn't know very well what to do with me. However, we agreed that my career as professor would start in a month - which became two – in the meantime he assigned me to the Hotel Deauville on the Malecon for accommodation, in expectation of a university apartment. I looked for Isabel without success.

Havana in the pre-soviet period was a social experiment, a psychological event, a political workshop, materially speaking decadent, a cheerful brothel. Economically a disaster that apparently nobody cared about and politically a tropical tyranny, I mean an open sky prison. For those who did not agree with the regime of course it was hell.

I shared the hotel Deauville and its some 150 rooms, huge restaurant, night club- where every night played a full live band to a completely empty floor- with a Spaniard who happened to be a priest. A sinister and surrealistic experience to be, so to say, the only client in a hotel that once belonged to the Cuban-American mafia and where hundreds of people crowded among the casino tables, now closed.

Passing the days walking in Old Havana, in Vedado and Miramar, I was surprised that people came out of their homes to ask me questions like: We're you from? Where did you buy your pants and shoes? What are you doing here? Unfortunately my very primitive Spanish did not enable me to make a conversation, for which they tried to compensate with some English words, pronounced in such a way that, even then, I did not understand. I never had seen people that eager to learn, to know. Ten years of isolation from the outside world had made them curious. I will learn fast also that misery creates miserable people.

In the movies I discovered the Masajista Itchi films, the Japanese version of western pictures. Itchi is their John Wayne, even better: a blind Samurai who in spite of this small inconvenience puts out a candle flame with his sword without touching the candle. I had fun.

One Sunday morning I took part in voluntary agricultural work: A highly unproductive activity but sociologically very interesting. You just go, at five in the morning, standing on any corner together with some more voluntary candidates for saving the rural economy of Havana, spending a day out. The truck will show up at around eight, in that time you made acquaintance with the people from your block. There is always someone carrying a guitar or a bongo and you have been singing revolutionary songs to pass time. One or two hours later, packed in the trunk of a lorry – model 1955 of which the last suspension had died in 1960 – you'll discover a potato, yucca, tomato or any vegetable field. After having listened to a speech about revolutionary, voluntary productivity, you harvest potatoes which you put in a bag that will stay there until God knows when. Soon the lunch break is ordered, after which you lay on your back to rest and talk to the revolutionary most simpatica and best looking girl of the good looking revolutionary girls. Around three you get back on the truck because the chauffeur has to be back in Havana for the afternoon ball game. Everybody carries some potatoes, tomatoes or anything edible in their pockets because it is prohibited to bring along bags. That's the way you passed a productive day out, of very questionable efficiency but of great utility for political and moral control. The more you participate, the better you are looked upon by the Party and the Defense Committee of the Revolution (CDR). Maybe even one day they order you to join the Party if you want to keep your kids in school or want a job: it's the best possible organization to belong to. That the potato bags you filled are likely to stand still in that field the next Sunday is the least important thing.

For my general hangout quarters I choose the lobby of the Habana Libre hotel – ancient Hilton and still belonging to the heritage of Paris Hilton - standing on top of the Rampa two blocks from the university. That lobby was the meeting point of many Latin American revolutionaries in Havana. I could say worldwide, because I met adepts of the Quebec independence, French from the Breton liberation movement, Basques from Eta, Italians from the Red Brigades and more Germans from the red army, etc...These world revolutionary hangout character, the "Habana Libre" shared it with another hotel of the same category: "The Riviera" on the Malecon. Everybody belonging to one or another international Castrist revolutionary movement had passed, passes, or will pass in one of these two five stars hotels. Of course escorted and courted by a legion of girls and young females, and the secret services of which many belonged. I mixed with the Quebec revolutionaries, Tupamaros from Uruguay, the Valpalmares from Brasil, the MIR from Chile and I don't know what their name is from: Nicaragua, Argentine, Haiti, Bolivia, Santo Domingo and almost every country. There were some authentic guerilleros who had sequestrated American consuls, ambassadors or industrialists and had attacked military quarters. Some became real friends.

When I went to take the - once in a while working- elevator of my private hotel I passed a very good looking silhouette in a mini skirt, for as far as I could see short haired because a funny cap covered her head, it was not a workers cap although it was of proletarian style. We took the elevator together to find out that they had lodged us on the same floor with rooms one in front of the other. For sure that made the survey easier. She said hello briefly with a smile which illuminated her face and her laughing eyes. Of all possible nationalities she was Belgian, from nothing less but the little town of Waterloo and her name was Paule. This meant that she was from the "other" Belgian ethnic group, the "bad" ones. She had a very noble way of moving which corresponds with the inside, but that I learned later. (From now on in this story I'll often talk in the first person of the plural form, because Paule still is my companion). Without more formalities, we sat on the bed. She was employed by UNESCO in the regional office of this respectable organization.

For a while we looked at the waves breaking over the Malecon with high rising, white spray which reached the upper floors of the houses on the other side of the large avenue. The Havana Malecon with a northern sea is a spectacle that no artistic presentation can equal. Here in front of the seaside I put my arm around her shoulders and we kissed softly, naturally and then passionately, we moved to the bed and made love. I was sure that this room was filled with microphones and cameras but we did not care. We brought peace to our bodies with more passionate love making. Caressing her beautiful body with my right hand, while sustaining my head with the left one and she doing the same, after a long moment she opened her eyes and smiled. I wanted to talk but about what? What do man talk about after an orgasm? (The joke says that fifty percent fall asleep and the other 50% put on their pants and go home). I just wanted that moment to last forever, without stopping my hands and fingers whispering over her breast, belly and legs and finally came up with a rather stupid question:
- Why do women close their eyes when making love?
It was a stupid question but that's all I could come up with. She started to laugh; a franc and clear laugh which also tinkered in her eyes.
- That's what we were taught. It is not decent for women to show too much pleasure.
I was surprised, never thought of it before.
- Is that so? Since when?
She entered the game.
- Since Eve
- Since Eve? That was a long time ago, can you explain?
She put a pillow under her elbow.
- As a catholic you know about the original sin, guilt, and the desire to know? All these things brought to you by a woman?
She said that smiling as if it was a good joke.
- Yes I know that the Adam part of the story is not very glorious. He was just happy to obey and conform himself. The curiosity, the desire to know of what is behind the curtain, disobedience, all this is Eve. That's why the male part of the creation story decided to oppress the other part and declared that the original sin is transmitted through the

132

belly, as said Saint Augustine, and that everything related to sex and pleasure is impure, justifying the combat against the body and all the pleasures it procures. Creating a culture that is based on guild.
She interrupted me:
- That's why all that is left to us, women, is being wife and mother, the women got drowned by legions of all kinds of religious preachers.
She talked with a soft, calm voice as if this was a social conversation about the weather, when to me it was the most intellectual post-orgasmic conversation I will ever experience. This excited me very much. We stayed silent for a long moment leaving our hands resting on each other's body. Limelight had set in and fast running clouds over the malecon speeded up the setting of the night. After some time our hands started again to explore our bodies and some thought adjusted themselves in my brains:
- It is true that in all the sacred writings the female body is doomed, maybe most of all in the writings of Saint Paul who is the most implacable misogyny of our history. In addition there is the dooming of the menstruation because it permits sex not related to reproduction. The family is the only skyline left to the females. Therefore, all the ways and means of procuring pleasure are banned. Homosexuals were brought to be burned alive for procuring pleasures outside the husband-wife pattern. The Jewish Talmud declares that a bachelor is only half a man. I remember the title of a conference presented to the church fathers in the Macon Council in the fourth century: "Controversial dissertation to proof that females are not human beings". Not bad heh!
Sure I was trying to impress her, because I did want with all my will power that this woman, caressing my body and smiling, would stay in my life by all means. She responded:
- You know the Muslim Koran is not bad in condemning and hating woman either. It says in some part that: "The man has the right to labor his wife the same ways he labors his field". In Islamic countries a female testimony is only worth half a man's. Besides that, a sterile female is worth the same thing as a girl coming to marriage without being a virgin, meaning: nothing. For all this it must be that we close our eyes.
- The thing is that you present too much pleasure, desire, rave, and passion, excess and in the end you put into danger male virility and also God. With this cultural luggage it is very possible that we are not ready to understand female sexuality.
I remembered the Liberian "Name calling"
- Just thinking of it, you men also close your eyes, why?

I stayed thinking for some time:
- Probably of shame.....
She laughed out loud and we kissed. We stayed in that room until the following morning. I told the stories of the two girls who wanted to marry in Ivory Coast, the missionaries in Upper Volta, the strange behavior of American youth in sexual matters. We made love again, more passionate and more carefully of the other's pleasure.
In the morning I asked her to translate my courses into Spanish upon which she agreed immediately.

The following Sunday we went together to the voluntary "productive" day out. For the occasion she wore white boots. At first sight it's a funny idea to come to Cuba with boots and a yellow corduroy cap. But it rained that day and I covered myself with mud from top to bottom, she was the only one in the whole bunch who was right. These white boots attracted attention and to know more about them a tall good looking woman came close to ask straight away, as Cubans do, some explanations about the boots and their owner. That's how we met a Cuban couple who still are our dear friends from Havana, Mariana Vidal and her husband Juan. You just can't be more Cuban than they are.

Regardless of the mud and the rain, it was a joyful Sunday. The more Mariana spoke, the quieter we became because when Mariana opens the words pot, nobody can say a word. We didn't harvest anything. I'll never know why (maybe they did not find the field?) the communist party took us to the fields in the Havana outskirts, known as the "green belt" where one thousand and one things are supposed to be cultivated to feed the city. As almost everything in Cuba; the idea was a good one but it does not work; there too they planted coffee that never grew. We finished the afternoon in the apartment of Juan and Marianna on Virtudes in central Havana, drinking coffee and telling stories. Being a university professor impressed a lot our new friends and they wanted to know it all. The more the people are isolated, the more curious they get, which is normal, curiosity is the basic condition of knowledge.

I moved to Miramar and a nice second floor apartment, across the street from the ocean. It must have belonged to the middle-upper class, and as the whole neighborhood, had been confiscated by the government. The rule in Cuba was - and still is – if you leave your house unoccupied for more than six months, or something like it, it becomes property of the people. Meaning: the Nation, the Government, the communist Party and their members and above all of Fidel Castro (who said that he does not own anything, but he can enjoy everything that exists in the whole country). That's the revolutionary conception of real estate: Everything for the collectivity, nothing for the individual. At that time I did not give it a thought and it did not bother me at all. Although I got the feeling, everyday stronger, that I was living in Georges Orwell's animal farm. (The best description of life under Castro socialism ever written, twenty five years before it happened).

Paule moved to a little apartment on a sixth floor in front of the harbor entrance with a view at the Moro castle.

Came the day that I had to take my academic chair at the faculty of Human science, located at the foot of the university hill, behind the stadium and the shooting stand where once in a while I checked that I still had my sharp shooter's talent. I was twenty five years old and very nervous.

Isabelle made the presentations and the translations when necessary. Fifteen students were waiting for me. And what students! To start with, I was the youngest. There came agents from the Ministry of the Interior – the local CIA – ministry of Foreign affairs, Central committee of the communist party – the government above the government- a couple of professors of social science and a representative of the Cuban cultural institute. This latter, a girl, was the only afro-Cuban. Her knowledge of Africa did not go beyond the Santeria and voodoo ceremonies practiced in Regla on the other side of the harbor entrance. She had a hunger for learning that would make me uncomfortable sometimes, ready as she was to surrender soul and body – not bad at all- to learn more about "name calling". These students were of the same extraction as my fellows from the American University in Washington; in some way their Cuban counterparts, which was not a factor that particularly was to tranquilize my nervousness. Half an hour we spent talking about their knowledge of Africa, which was very thin and could be resumed as: the assassination of Patrice Lumumba in Congo and the incursion of Che Guevara in a guerilla tentative in Congo which later would be called Zaire, submitted for decades to the Mobutu Sese Seko dictatorship and today refers to itself as the Democratic Republic of Congo. Of course, they were all Party members and convinced Marxists. Of African sociology they knew nothing.

Looking at the people of Africa and at history only through the theoretical Marxist filter; important things are left aside and errors had to be made. Errors which the Castro government and army were going to commit in their African adventures in: Ethiopia, Angola,

Mozambique and some more. Nobody mentioned the Che Guevara catastrophe in Congo, based on an orthodox Marxist interpretation and accommodated with the Guevara revolutionary theories. The main line of that theory was: If conditions for the revolution do not exist; create them. Meaning create chaos by any means – bombs, assassinations, hold ups, lies etc... So, once chaos is installed on top of the corpses and ruins, the socialist revolution will be built. It is a rather weird theory, headless, but that's what the Argentinean doctor was trying to do in the Congo. It came out being a disaster and el Che came back with his tail between his legs after having left to rot in the Congo bush several Cuban and Congolese corpses.

We passed the second hour with the African basic social organizations: the small polygamous family, the big consanguineous family, the clan, and the tribe consisting of all the clans and their cast. From the first course on, the subject came up of the "Asian production mode" one of the chapters of Marxism in which everything that does not match the basic theory of communism, is thrown in. I understood that if I did not use that filter I would be considered as a counter revolutionary, an enemy of socialism and per consequence a friend of American Imperialism. The communist-castro dialectic is simple.

It was going to cost hard work to remake history, social relations, the tribal economy, in order to match the Marxist filter of class struggle. A filter from which my audience did not want to deviate a millimeter.

Three times a week, I passed 10 minutes of inter-classes in the corridor together with a history professor, member of the central committee of the communist party. That was very pleasant because for ten minutes I was instructed about the latest jokes and gossip from the Central Committee. The type of : What is the difference between capitalist, socialist and communist dialectics? The first one is searching for a black cat in a black room, the second one is looking for a black cat in a black room knowing that the black cat is not there, the third one is searching for a black cat in a black room, knowing that the cat is not there but to exclaim: "I've got it ". Want another one? : Fidel and his brother Raoul are standing on the Moro castle looking at the "balseros" leaving Cuba, some on rubber tires. Fidel turns to his brother saying" If this goes on, we will stay alone, you and me" on which Raoul responds: "You and who?...." True that these gentlemen and a few ladies, who had assured their daily meals, the house and exclusive schools for their children, plus car and chauffeur, had a lot of fun and laughed a lot. Each one of these jokes, told by any common Cuban would have cost him – or her - from 3 to 10 years in prison or in "reeducation camps". About the same price was paid to possess a single dollar bill or a Beatles record, all this being considered a counter revolutionary cultural deviation, and thus, a crime.

The Beatles record criminalization was explained to me in these terms by a Central Committee member: The Beatles' song "A Fool upon a Hill" was looked upon as a mockery of Fidel Castro pronouncing his endless speeches on the university hill. All tyrants are paranoids.

*

Marxism is a religion with an utopist paradise: the communist state. In present times, I compare it very much with Islam for its intolerance, implacability, the intransigence of the followers and the total negation of individual freedom for the benefit of a mythical and theoretical collectivity. I said theoretical because in this egalitarianism, pushing everything downward, there are some who are more equal than the others. To resume: As we are unable to make everybody rich, let's make everybody poor so we are all equal (with the exception of the makers of it all): George Orwell again; but for real.

*

My relations with the revolutionary groups of Latin America warmed up, especially with the Brazilians and the Uruguayans. I liked their free, cynical, critical lifestyle at the edge of anarchism. Up to the point that I became a member of one of the groups who practiced urban guerilla training: spying, clandestine communication networks, surveillance, protection and more. I lived it as a game, a little more serious, but in the end that's what it was; a game. I had fun doing it and after that in endless discussions analyzing and talking about it. We all were hungry for action. The craziest project of one of these movements was to liberate Regis Debray from his Bolivian prison in Cochabamba.

One day, Marie Chantal, whom I called once a week with Paule's dollars help, put forward one of the conditions I had to fulfill before she would come to Havana: A baby carriage. This was a big problem. In all my time in Havana I had seen two. I visited all the possible and impossible stores of Havana, one emptier than the other and inquired in all places. The baby carriage is not part of the domestic revolutionary socialist equipment. I tried to dissuade her, nothing to do

137

about it, when she got something into her head she did not have it in another place. It was a baby carriage or nothing. I was getting ready for this last option, even though I felt bad about that, but this carriage was breaking my morale for weeks, when an elderly man, well dressed, whom I had never seen before, walking down Virtudes came to whisper in my ear that he had one, that it was new, and that it had to be paid for in dollars. This was not an easy condition to fulfill. Many Cubans were put to rot away in jail or in some revolutionary rehabilitation concentration camps for having carried in their pockets a dollar bill. This money, only the government had the right to hold it, just as lobsters. All Cuban lobsters belong to the government; fishing, carrying or eating one gets you to jail. He wanted one hundred dollars for the carriage, which indeed was new, with four wheels and a model that would have made people happy in Canada in the winter. Of course I did not have one hundred dollars. Paule, without a word and a moment of hesitation went into her purse and gave me two fifty dollar bills. That's the way she is: financing a baby carriage to make the wife of her lover happy, fulfilling a capriccio of the wife so she will come to Havana to reunite with him.

I pushed the stupid baby carriage all the way to Miramar and put it in the middle of the completely empty living room. The visit of Marie Chantal and Jan got complicated before it even started.

The Chief of the UNESCO office in Havana and of Paule, a Swiss married to a good looking Venetian woman, whose favorite theme of conversation was the sinking of Venetia into the lagoon (on which she was an expert) one night invited us to dinner in presence of the famous Cuban poet Carlos Puebla. The author of the song: "Comandante Che Guevara" which he sang there for the first time in public. If you have ever been to Havana in the following forty-eight years after that party you'll have heard that song at least four times a day. Away from the ears of the repressive institutions of the revolutionary government and as long as they let him carry on the good life in the diplomatic circles, the national poet did not take the revolution and less the communism – which he called "the socialist recreation" - very seriously. He ended up singing songs which were not al all revolutionary but very double sensed. "La Camisa" was my favorite. We laughed, joked, smoked ridiculously big cigars, drank a lot and made a hole in the cognac reserve of the Swiss and his Venetian beautiful wife.

Just to be provocative - it's a natural tendency, stupidity makes me provocative – I asked the sales assistant in the Havana bookshop if he had "Animal Farm" by George Orwell. I knew he did not, but what the heck? He answered that he was going to check and disappeared through a side door framed on both sides and also on the top by the complete works of Vladimir Illich Lenin in a variety of editions.   I had entered this bookshop just to pass time away. I already knew what there is inside a Cuban bookshop. Besides the Lenin works already mentioned, you'll find the complete speeches of Fidel Castro, the complete works of Karl Marx, some writings by Che Guevara, some booklets from the editions of the "Casa de las Americas", which pretended to be the top of Latin American Literature. Also, some technical treaties such as: Everything about ship propellers, some science and mathematics books, all previous to 1960. Yes, you can get books in Cuba but on the street, sold secretly from under the sleeve and usually photocopied.

Reappearance of the young book assistant with a somewhat angry expression on his face:

- No Sir, we don't have that book and we never will.

More than sorrow there was hate in that voice

- What a pity, why don't you have it?

I wanted the pleasure to last a while.

- Because that's the way it is!

On that he turned his back to me and went to the small table on which there was a pile of dusty looking books. I thanked him with a smile and went back to the also dusty San Lazaro Street. I knew that I owed my salvation to my foreign accent. Otherwise I would be pointed out and maybe interrogated by the political police who would not understand why I wanted to read such a "counter revolutionary" book

*

Looking back at that époque when the world was directed, much more than today, by ideologies, beliefs, ideals and all sorts of chapels, I still don't understand the enormous energy and money the Cuban government invested to erase the individual in benefit of the collectivity, or at least the idea   of   collective interest that the individuals holding power had of that concept.

It is understandable and necessary that to achieve social cohesion and a certain degree of equality of chances, a certain number of individual aspirations or rights have to be controlled or even abandoned. But why did they want all of them? They wanted to regulate and control what you can read, see, eat, hear and in the end what you think. So, the self proclaimed "guides" of the people, the revolution and the fatherland only inspire me suspicion. The almost daily commemorations, seminars and speeches of the " Maximum Leader" "The Supreme Chief", the "Commander " only got me into a state of rebellion, of cynicism, of irony, of black humor; only defense against the absurdity, the tyranny and more stupidities. It's Baudelaire who proclaimed: "Only by and within the individual will real progress (understanding social progress) be achieved"

The masterpiece of individuality is Liberty. This cult to one's person requires the desire of fortification, of discipline, the formulation of a lifestyle and values. Cuban socialism is at the extreme opposite of these values. Here, dialectics and words are turned into deeds for the simple reason that the demagogic promises of dictatorial egalitarianism can never be achieved; what stays are words, and by Jove how they use them! At every moment, for hours, in endless meetings out of which only come words. This fascination, this way of taking words for accomplished deeds belongs very much to the Latin idiosyncrasy. Words of which they make up the most disgraceful lies. The history of various countries shows it to be so.

*

Marie Chantal and Jan, yet a few months old and a very wide awake, laughing and loud child, arrived. I don't like babies especially not at eleven, three and five at night. Marie had come to Cuba to find out in a last attempt, if our couple was workable: it was not, from the first day she touched Cuban soil. Yet, I was not the same and I had problems supporting her frivolous, capricious side, in fact her bourgeois side. She was not interested at all in the social-political laboratory that was Cuba at that time. She had stayed behind. The center of her world was her son, mine was not.

One Sunday I decided to take them to Santa Maria beach, about thirty kilometers east of Havana and on the way back to visit the Moro castle where el Che exercised the office of Minister of the Interior. Don't think that going to a beach is an easy thing to do in Cuba. Public transport is very hard to get, not only to go to the beach but also simply inside the city. Every day, to transport me from Miramar to the University, about four kilometers, it took me usually one hour, most of the time I ended up walking. Besides that, if in any other place in the world animals on their way to the slaughterhouse were transported that way, the transport company would be sued for bad animal treatment. Transporting yourself from one place to another in Havana is close to a battlefield experience. The signs in the buses that said (in French or English, origin of the buses) "48 passengers only" were a big joke. Yes Sir, we in Cuba, can get as many as three times that biomass into a bus. Fortunately, Isabelle was willing to take us in her shaking Russian Lada to the beach and in view of her communist party membership; she also would help us visit the museum.

*

Hard to believe, but here they were: execution orders of supposed counter-revolutionaries signed by Che Guevara. I said "supposed", because without proper trials, in the first months of the entry in Havana, January 1959. As usual, such occasions are often used to settle individual accounts that finally have little to do with the revolution. Terror is the second phase of every revolution whether in France, in Russia or in Cuba.

These executions ordered by Che Guevara obsessed me . All week long I searched for Joao, the historian- ideologue of the Brazilian Valpalmares ; he was around forty and was known to have participated in an attack on a military camp from which they got away with a bunch of arms and munitions. I had no idea how he had managed to come to Cuba; he was a great friend of Roque Dalton: when you saw one, the other was not very far and so it was when finally I met them in the Lobby of the Habana Libre hotel sitting in comfortable leather armchairs around a tea table. I joined the conversation sitting on the back of one of the chairs, they were laughing very much. The conversation was about oral sex. Joao described it with precise details telling how marvelous it was; Roque found it disgusting, too close to the asshole to risk to put his mouth there. His fingers? Yes! but not his tongue. I stayed listening and laughing: my experience in this matter did not allow me to have an opinion. When finally the theme became exhausted; Roque looking at his watch jumped up and ran away. This was great since I wanted to talk to Joao and not to Roque; the Brazilian dark skinned, crowned with bewildered hair looked at me.
- Flamenco, you have something on your mind.

They all called me "el flamenco". His Spanish was tainted with a heavy Portuguese accent, as a matter of fact he just spanished his Portuguese.

- Joao I want to walk.

Talking in the lobby of the Habana Libre is like talking straight into the secret service tape recorder. We left the hotel and walked through the Copelia Park, which has another name but everybody call it the Copelia Park because of a huge ice cream joint standing in the middle. Without talking, we walked to the Victor Hugo park just a few blocks away from the hotel. We had barely made a block when we noticed that two girls were following us. The number of people working for the Cuban security services must be enormous. The Hugo Park is a heaven of peace; green pasture, big trees surrounding a central kiosk and a lot of benches bordering the walk paths all across. Finally we sat on a bench close to the Hugo bust in one of the corners.

- Joao I feel better making my confidences to Victor Hugo than to the state security.

He smiled. Our "escort girls" were sitting on the stairs of the kiosk. I got out a pack of Marlboros fruit of Paule's access to the diplomatic store, and we lit up a cigarette.

- I too, Flamenco, I too, tell me what's on your mind.

Joao had made himself comfortable, stretching his legs almost to the middle of the walk way; inhaling the cigarette smoke he exhaled through the nose.

- Look Joao, some days ago I saw execution orders signed by Che and I do have problems believing what I saw.

Without looking at me he again let escape a huge cloud of cigarette smoke through his nasal holes.

- And why can't you believe what you saw, Flamenco?

- Look Joao, I don't know for you, but for us Europeans, Che is the symbol of the humanist left, of integrity and humanism and for that reason against the death penalty. Signing orders to kill people does not match our humanitarian ideals; it is even against human rights: right?

While I talked Joao had started to smile, the kind of smile you can see on a father's face when he is softened by his son's ingenuity and naivety.

- Flamenco, where have you been living? On the moon? Did you read Che's diaries in the Congo or the diary from Inti Peredo in Bolivia? Are you aware of the bad relations between the heroic warrior and the Bolivian communist party, both of them disputing the leadership of the

142

guerilla? Do you know that Che demanded the Soviets to put their nuclear war power at disposal of the defense of the Cuban revolution and when they refused our hero slapped in the face the soviet ambassador in the middle of a diplomatic reception in Algiers? So, you don't know anything of all this? In the view of what the executions you are talking about are peanuts.

I stayed astonished, no: I did not know any of these stories. After lighting another cigarette and pushing more smoke through his nose he continued:

- The Argentinean wanted a nuclear war only to defend his vision of "the new man" to be built on the ruins of the old world. He did not say with whom he was going to build a new man after a nuclear war. Happily for all of us, the Russians did not follow up on this madness because the construction of "the new man" in Cuba is rather disastrous as you can see.

He said that shaking his head in the direction of the two girls, still sitting on the steps of the kiosk.

- As I see it, this guy reached a degree of psychic sickness that was close to madness. Everybody knew that, in the first place the Cubans, who a short time later, when Che and his guerilla boy scouts were surrounded by the Bolivian dictators army and asked desperately Fidel to get them out of there, the maximum Cuban leader slammed the door in his face, reading publicly the farewell letter that the romantic warrior had left behind. In fact he condemned him to death, closing the door of a comeback to Cuba. I have to say that in the meantime the Soviet Union was feeding the Cubans and helping to keep the revolution more or less alive.

The more Joao talked, the more I looked at my shoes. We stayed silent for a while: a world was falling apart in the Victor Hugo park. Finally I stuttered:

- No, no, I don't know all that.

Joao put his arm around my shoulder

- Listen Flamenco, you are not going to fall in depression are you? Religions are feeding on ignorance, you know that one?

- But then, what Joao?

He took his arm off my shoulder and started practicing making circles with the cigarette smoke while he followed up with his political course.

- Then? Nothing Flamenco, nothing at all. It's a myth and it is working as a myth, that's all. Believing is the dominant factor of myths together with a cult to the marvelous things they create, turning their back on History with a capital H. You know that myths have a verbal capacity that creates what it announces.

- Yes this I know it, I was a seminarist.

He slapped me on the back strongly and started to laugh loudly. At that moment a youngster, who I had been watching out of the corner of my eye for a while, made a move toward us and from under his sweater pulled out a roll of yellow paper containing four cigars with red rings saying "Winston Churchill". Looking anxiously around him to all corners he said:

- Cigars, cheap!

I was saying "no thanks" but Joao interrupted:

- How much?

- Two for a dollar!

- I take the four for a dollar

Out of his pocket he came up with a dollar bill.

- You have dollars?

- Of course I have, I am a foreigner and not held to the currency law.

Both we lit up an enormous Churchill cigar that looked to me as a chair's leg, what kept us silent for a moment.

I knew about how the tobacco revolutionary labor force smuggle, from their workshops, piece by piece and leaf by leaf; in their underwear or their shoes, tobacco and all the stuff one needs to make a cigar; even cigar boxes are smuggled out in detached pieces with the nails and the glue to reconstitute them. I just found out at how low a price they were sold; which did not keep me from smiling at the fact that I was smoking an exclusive "Churchill". Joao broke up my thoughts:

- I feel sorry and compassion when I see the well fed European youth, romantic and generous, wearing the Argentinean's T-shirt, he who besides being a poor military strategist was also a dangerous politician.

- Joao, why all these lies?

- My dear Flamenco and seminary friend, you know that those who steal the heritage make up the myths. Che did not make up his myth, the one who took care of that is a powerful state propaganda service which has its political reasons to do so.

- This sounds very much like the myths created by the roman emperor Constantine and Saint Paul about a crucified Nazarian, many years ago.

- That's exactly what it is, Flamenco, the guy from Nazareth ended up badly, very badly - but not the emperor who created his myth. Beware of myths Flamenco, even if they serve you for some time, never forget that they are myths.

Not being used to cigar smoking I started coughing and needed badly a glass of water.

- Thank you professor, let me offer you a drink of whatever is available in the Hotel.
- Is there nothing in Paule's place?
- Yes, there must be but I am not livingthere.
He looked at me with complicity in his smiling eyes. I was not going to tell him the complicated situation of my "family" life.
Walking back, watching where we put our feet because of the very bad shape of the sidewalks, making a gracious move to let pass an elderly man with two breads under his arm, wrapped up in a Granma newspaper, almost reaching the Copelia park, I held him back by his arm and asked:
- Joao, then what is the difference between Guevara's shootings and the assassination of the poor leftists in Brazil by the dictators,
He looked around to see if nobody was close and almost whispered
- None, flamenco, none at all: they belong to the same category of barbarianism, the same as Raul's hangings.
- What about Raul's hangings?
He looked at me again, smiling:
- So you don't know about Raul's hangings either?
- What am I supposed to know about Raul that I don't know?
- Raul, when in the guerilla in Orient, used to shoot his opponents and everybody he took for a counter revolutionary. This was bad publicity for the revolution so when his brother Fidel ordered him to stop the bloodshed... he just hanged them.
My mouth fell open. I had never heard such a thing. Joao started walking again. I ran after him and shouted:
- This is a joke!
Just turning his head and over his shoulders he shouted:
- Not that much.

*

Back at the Miramar apartment, we both knew that there was no future in our marriage. Five weeks of conflicts, screaming, reproaches had worn us out. So we decided to separate, she would go back to Neuilly with Jan as soon as possible. I signed, without regrets, a letter in which I agreed on the divorce, abandoning my paternal rights. Nevertheless, my soul sank into my shoes when I kissed Jan for the last time in the José Marti airport. Ten years later, we resumed our relationship, wining and dining in Paris cafés.

CHAPTER IV
HAVANA-SANTIAGO DE CHILE-BAMAKO

In the fall of the year 1969, my courses at the University of Havana came to an end. Not because I finished the program, neither because of lack of interest of my students, on the contrary, but for the simple reason that they closed the university because of the great sugar harvest. The whole country closed up. Complete ministries closed their doors. Even the ministry of foreign affairs reduced the civil servants to a ten percent and put a sign on the door "Closed for Zafra". Fidel Castro, the government, the Party central committee, the committees for the defense of the revolution, everybody, had decided that the future of the revolution and the country (which for them is of course the same thing), the access to a decent standard of living, the opening of the doors giving access to the socialist paradise, etc.. depended upon a ten million tons sugar harvest. Of course nobody explained why all of a sudden, ten billion kilos of sugar were going to save the revolution. But a tremendous collective fever embraced the whole country. If you called somebody on the phone, even before saying their name they greeted you with "Los diez millones van". Radio, television, the two newspapers were full of it. Even a popular band called itself the "Van, van". Finishing a conversation or a phone call with someone you did not know too well, for security you would say "Los diez millones van ". Even Carlos Puebla composed a song about it, but from him I suspected a lot of irony.

With my Latin guerilleros friends, who came more and more often to our apartment, mainly because we had access to the diplomatic store, its beverages and foods that had disappeared from the Cuban MINCIN stores long ago, we decided to sign up for cane cutting in an international cane cutters brigade.

We very much enjoyed our Latin friends. Often, always with Paule's help, we organized national food parties, during which discussions about the construction of socialism in their countries never stopped. After all, how to build a good socialism without a good "feijoada" from Brazil or a delicious "ceviche" from Peru? We gained the friendship of the revolutionary poet from El Salvador, Roque Dalton. He talked a lot about writers and poets, arts and philosophy, popular traditions and legends from El Salvador. The heroic deeds of the Salvadorian soviets in the thirties, how the martyrs executed by the dictator and the United Fruit company screamed "Viva Lenin, Viva Stalin" while facing execution.

Roque Dalton was assassinated, years later, by a rival leftist revolutionary group.

My dear friend Roque,
You did not deserve to die in such a stupid way. You were the one who told me that revolutions, like Cronos, eat their own children. There is no doubt that you knew what was going to happen, and for loving life and integrity so much you did not retreat. You assumed our contradictions. I hope that the fatal bullets did not hurt because you despised physical suffering. I wept when I learned your exit from this world. You knew that our utopias were desperate but assumed your responsibilities. Thank you Roque for your laughter, your teaching, your good humor and your brightness.
Jean Pierre

*

The first thing I saw from our International sugar cane cutters camps, was a pile of wood, zinc roof tablets and boxes of nails; all that in an empty space, as big as a football field, bordered on four sides by sugar cane fields. The two Cubans responsible for us and as lost as we were in that green ocean, had a   plan traced on a napkin, of how to build seventy beds in two dormitories, a mess with tables and benches, a kitchen, toilets and showers. Even so, nobody had any idea of where the water was going to come from. Revolutionary fevered enthusiasm took care of the rest.

Cutting sugar cane is entering in a Dante's hell. Thick rubber boots, thick trousers, thick long sleeved shirt closed up to the neck, thick gloves that prevent you from having a good grip on the machete or the mocha and a heavy straw hat: this is the cane cutters uniform for confronting the endless wall of sugar cane under a burning sun which meant that you could fry an egg on the machete blade.

The Hedonist

So, once you are ready, how do you cut sugar cane? Wrap under your left arm as many canes you can hold, with your right arm holding firmly the machete you give a stroke at the bottom of the canes: since the sugar concentration is higher at the bottom than on the top, you cut them almost at the roots, near the earth. Take care not to cut your feet. Then you get up, still holding the canes under your left arm and with a large swinging movement you cut the leaves and the loaf; you deposit the clean canes upon a pile until you think it is about an "arroba". Then, bend again to grip more cane under your left arm and so on and so on, all day long. After ten minutes all your clothes are weighing a ton, acting as a sponge for your sweat. When you don't see anything anymore through the sweat that runs into your eyes and small stars wink in front of you then you stop. Half a meter of cane well cleaned, chewed and chewed gets you back on your feet. It's pure energy; besides, it cleans your throat and relieves the thirst. Don't do that too often because you have to keep up with the two guys cutting at your sides. By the end of the day walking back to the camp is martyrdom, there are no more legs wanting to carry you, neither arms that can move anymore. Even talking becomes too much. Barely taking off your boots you fall on your bed and sleep. At night you'll wake up and go to search something to eat, a cup of water to wash your face, take off your shirt which is hurting your neck because it is rigid with sweat, earth and dust. I saw some pants standing up straight all by them. After three days your body is covered with a layer of a variety of substances, which protect you from the clouds of mosquitoes, and define your particular body smell. Everyone has their own. I was able to tell in the dark that was walking five yards away, just by smelling. I was one of the best macheteros from our camp, including of several camps around. On Sundays, to pay tribute to the Lord, we organized sugar cane cutting competitions with the neighbors. What a way to pass away Sundays! I suppose I lived what the slaves in the Egyptian Pharaohs' salt mines did not live and much less the American slaves in the cotton fields. On the good side: there was always someone to tell a joke, strike a disaccorded guitar or sing a popular song from one of the dozen countries which were represented in my camp.

I have no idea how, neither from where, but one Sunday appeared Paule carrying three rum bottles, a loving smile and eyes like plates when she saw the way we were looking and living. That day I took a shower with soap she had brought along, and we had a walk in the sugar cane fields. Making love in the late afternoon freshness, in a cane field, when not a single leave is moving all over

148

this sugar cane martyred earth, you don't notice the prickle of the leaves, neither the hardness of the bare ground nor the mosquitoes.

Paule became very popular in the International sugar cane cutters brigade. She came back every weekend carrying all the rum she could. We even cut cane together, in couple. But one day she cut up her left leg. Nothing very grave, the self proclaimed Brazilian nurse put a guerilla bandage around her leg, good enough to keep a mark for the rest of her life.

In December, I went back to Havana to settle a visa problem. The university was completely empty, not even a secretary to give me some kind of certificate. However, I managed to get two months prolongation. If there was one thing I did not want to do at that moment, it was to leave Cuba. So we invented a plan: simply we were going to play with immigration as if we were going to get married, presuming that in the months that it would take to get the papers to Cuba – especially the birth certificates which had to come all the way from Belgium – Paule's contract would expire and we would leave together for Latin America. According to our Latin friends and the daily Cuban propaganda we were all convinced that the socialist revolution was on the Latin continent's doorsteps. And we were curious to go and find out for ourselves. That was the plan.

To give it a kick start, we made an appointment with a notary in Old Havana. This was one of the few private notaries left in Havana after ten years of socialist collectivization. The date was December 24, 1969.

An elderly, erect standing man with a respectable belly, white shirt with long sleeves, black trousers and a rather jovial face received us in a notary office from the 1930's. From ceiling to floor all was in precious wood, the walls covered with thick leather covered books among which the complete works of José Marti, the Cuban national poet about whom I'll tell you some more later on. Displaying the complete works of Marti in a leather edition was the distinctive decoration of Cuban bourgeoisie. Leather covered sofas and armchairs – at the end of their useful life- completed that beautiful scene.

After brief presentations, he asked in a soft low baritone voice from which tiredness was not absent:
- So, you want to get married?
- Yes Sir, at least we want to start the procedures, which we suppose are going to be long.

The master in property rights, wholesale and marriages closed his eyes. This lasted so long that I thought he had fallen asleep but finally he said:
- All right, do you have your passports?
We handed him our passports over the very large office desk.
- Excuse me for a moment.
Slowly he extruded himself from his armchair and disappeared through a door at the left I had never noticed because the office was rather dark. A sole small window let pass a weak winter sunbeam that hardly allowed us to distinguish the corners of the room almost completely wrapped in twilight.

Time was getting long, I proposed to Paule to take a walk on the Malecon to see the sun set, but the notary had our passports so we decided to stay.

Finally he reappeared, with our passports in his hands and some more papers he displayed on his desk. Now he was wearing glasses, which I did not notice before. Looking over these metal framed glasses he looked at me with a twinkle of amusement in his eyes, like joking.
- Where are your witnesses?
I didn't get it right away, but Paule did
- What witnesses?
The master of ceremonies turned his head slowly to her:
- You want to get married? Don't you?
-Yes, yes but the procedures…
There was something like a doubt in Paule's voice.
- No, no, everything is all right. If you don't have witnesses allow me to fill in the blanks.
He got up and walked to the street door from which we heard him shouting "Juan come over here and bring Aurelio along" while Paule and I stared incredulously at each other.
- Paule I believe this guy is going to marry us.
I took her hand which she squeezed gently.
- I think so too, but how can he do it?
- That's his problem.
We looked each other in the eyes.
- Do you have any problem with that?
She shook her head and we really started to laugh.
The man of law reappeared together with two gentlemen of whom one was a santero dressed in white from hat, crowned with a real panama from under which some white hair appeared, to shoes. Besides that he was very black with dazzling white teeth two of which at least were

gold plated. He showed us his most beautiful smile and the fortune he was carrying in his mouth. The other one, in his forties, looked like he came out of a carpenter's shop, his shirt and pants full of lumber dust. We presented ourselves and all listened religiously to the wedding act, read slowly and well articulated, by the lawman. We signed, followed in that by the witnesses.

Paule paid the notary who wished us good luck and hoped to see us again "once that the socialist recreation in Cuba is over". She gave something to the witnesses and invited everybody for a drink at our apartment that same evening which was also Christmas Eve.

Still not realizing what had happened, we found ourselves on the street studying our wedding certificate and laughing. Maybe a little nervous.

We just got married for the sake of a visa which eventually they never gave me. The Cuban government did not recognize this marriage celebrated in its own territory for reasons you'll understand later.

Not without difficulty – due to the cancellation of Christmas and New Year festivities – we managed to get together some of our friends, almost all Latin Americans, to celebrate. The Cubans were afraid of being seen at a wedding party while the country was shut down. For sugar cane harvest reasons the government simply cancelled the Christmas and New Year feasts which were put back until the 26 th of July. Tyranny was – and still is – of such dimensions that they could do that.

Regardless, Isabel Monal showed up and did not leave the very little Marxist Santero for the rest of the night: both got hold of a bottle of rum which they religiously emptied between the two of them. The revolutionary delegate of the "Block committee for the defense of the revolution", who lived two floors below, came to inquire what was going on because he had to report daily everything that goes on in the building who received who? Who talked to whom? What did they talk about? What was eaten and how did they get it? All this will be reported and discussed and analyzed in the. "Block revolutionary comity " in order to protect the revolution. What about that?

We invited him and his wife, who showed up half an hour later dressed as a 1930 doll. We put music on, danced and sang boleros. The party spilled from the apartment onto the staircases. The Brazilians made a feijoada with whatever they could get hold of. Roque Dalton recited double sensed poetry.

The Hedonist

Since there is no night public transportation in Havana, those who could not walk to their own homes, stayed to sleep. Isabelle and the Santero had disappeared. Around four in the morning, a drunken peace hung over our place with bodies lying everywhere. An Argentinean couple, wrapped up in a sheet, slept beside our bed on the left side, while on the right side laid Joao under a blanket. In our wedding bed laid Roque Dalton who had made himself very much at ease, snoring loudly. We pushed him and tried to lie beside him as well as possible.

Not only we got married for a visa but we shared our wedding night with Roque Dalton snoring in our bed. This was the most delightful Christmas night of my life.

*

Thirty years later, in 1999, we passed again Christmas and New Year in Havana, guests of our friend Hector Gonzalez in Vedado, three blocks away from the Rampa. This one was the most sinister New Year's Eve we ever spent. Not a soul on the streets, from no window escaped music or laughter; no car blew its horn. We looked at this from the apartment's terrace on the second floor. Hector, with almost a tear in his eyes said. "That's the way we feast presently in Havana, let nobody tell me again that this is a joyful place." He took a sip from his glass of rum: "There is more joy in the poorest quarter of Haiti than in this socialist paradise, shit". We entered and drank ourselves drunk, sadly. Gonzalez was a revolutionary from the first hour and always faithful to his dreams from the time when he was twenty.

*

The next day of this memorable Christmas 1969, we visited Mariana and Juan, who had to sit down to get over the fact that we were married. That year, for them, New Year never came to Cuba. Juan was preparing himself to join, on the next day, a sugar cane camp. What else was there to be done in Cuba in 1969?

Eventually, the government never got to reach the ten million tons of sugar which were supposed to save the Revolution; they got as far as 8.4 million, just one tenth of a point below the CIA forecast. But what a mobilization, what an enthusiasm as long as the zafra lasted! This is an essence of totalitarian dictatorships: keep the people, body and soul, busy, all the time. This was the case with the Roman games, tyrants, of whatever kind or époque; they repeat themselves but rarely innovate anything. They call upon memories, litanies, but not on intelligence: repeating, reciting, praying, this is not thinking. Listening a million times to "Patria o muerte" (The fatherland or death) prevented every Cuban from thinking that he not even had the right to go to an hotel or sit on the beach he wanted to sit on, in his own country. Marching in a thousand anti imperialist demonstrations without knowing anything about nationalizations, without compensation from the Fidel Castro regime keeps you from thinking about individual property rights. Approving when Fidel kills two poor teenagers, who tried to steal a small boat to flee from Cuba, prevents you from asking what is the future of Cuban youth in this regime. Listening every day to endless attacks against capitalism prevents you from evaluating your own exploitation by a savage state-capitalism system. Applauding all the time the figure of Che Guevara, put forward as an example to follow, keeps you from asking who that guy was and how he got killed? And so many more dead ends.

Here are the problems of a tyranny, doubled with a sickening desire to stay in power and be master of everything: land, houses, goods and people (because deciding what can be said and thought is being the owner of the bodies and souls). Watching; half a dozen of young boys - taken for homosexuals - running on the Malecon, crying and screaming in despair and pursued by a bunch of lumpen armed with sticks and led by a couple of bullies from the Cuban communist party – for whom these lumpen are: "the people" - is not funny, neither revolutionary, nor socialist, neither humanitarian, nor is it progress. It's just the will of a dictator to impose his own personal values on all in the most brutal way.

Luckily the documents of my divorce from Marie Chantal, pronounced by a Parisian court, reached Cuba two months after my marriage to Paule, because I was in a flagrant state of administrative polygamy. Actually, I did not care at all. It just gave me an occasion to realize that I married twice in less than twenty months. I never got married again, so far.

*

Taking into account our cultural heritage, the "merger" couple, which we all are invited to accomplish, is the coronation of Judeo-Christian eroticism. When romantically we talk about love, the matching soul, the prince on the white horse, we are supposed to see in this mutual attraction the reason to establish a social contract or often an existential security policy.

When carried by two people, the weight of existence is supposed to look lighter - of course it is an illusion. The conquest of the "blue prince on the white horse" or his female counterpart, inevitably leads to, and produces deception; never will real life withstand a comparison with the ideal life. The will to complete each other always brings the pains of incompletion or partly completion or in a few aspects only. Disappointment and disenchantment always appear when we try to adjust and match our real lives to the imaginary picture, promoted and imposed by the dominant culture of our environment by means of religion, politics, moral and ideological values. Naturally, the family mobilized man and woman with different roles. For the female: to prepare the food, to maintain the fire, wrap the animal hides, spin, make cloth and of course, keeping the offspring. All these activities are sedentary, while their companions hunt, fish, travel and go to war.

Thousands and thousands of years later this, in its essence, has not changed, regardless of the thin layer of cultural varnish trying to cover the basics of social stratification. These divisions will serve for the very first mechanism of state organization that reproduces the natural plan of the species. The nuclear family produces the project of the species according to the celestial order- inventing much later the concept of one God, who is also called "God the Father". As for the father; the ancestors gave him the power to reign over the family: total power as a divine right, invested with the "last word", occupying the highest place in the hierarchy. The family magnifies less love, made a reality between two free people aware of their common project - than the fatal destiny of all living species living on this planet.

The other reason which explains this ascetic codification: the strong will to reduce to nothing the incredibly strong powers of the female. Experience will teach, very early, to the male components of society that, in sexual matters, obeying only to natural laws, the satisfaction of pleasures, impulse, and desire does not make a good match with the natural female aspirations, simply because female pleasure demands to know and relay on cultural factors, body techniques and erotic sensuality. This just is inaccessible to those who satisfy themselves with natural impulses only. For not being able to comprehend female pleasure, the civilization - ours- reduces them to their minimum. How to spread this and impose this behavior code? By way of religious or other beliefs; in a general way, these are excellent mediums and techniques to reduce and to fix the female libido, God's representatives – messiah, apostles, priests, popes, imams, mullahs, ministers, teachers - declare the body as dirty, impure, the desire as guilty, pleasure as sinful and the female definitively guilty and a sinner. Sexuality? Yes! A little bit of it, just what is necessary to procreate but only in the frame of monogamous marriage, where with time passing, the natural call of passion diminishes and disappears. The boredom of repetition, the taming of desire (by definition free and traveling) switches off the libido.

In the family where time is as a priority given to the children and the husband, the female dies and in her place rise the mother and the spouse who consume all of her energy.

This process is successful, by way of social determinism, ideological impositions, moral rules of all types; the servitude becomes voluntary and the victim ends up encountering pleasure in the renouncement of her real self.

Love, sexuality and procreation are three different things. Confusion of these three aspects as only one obliges to love the sexual partner with the objective of procreation. Add that the sexual partner cannot be a passing relationship but an official husband married to a spouse over whom he has exclusive rights and is officially recognized as such.

Today - thanks to science- a small minority of people can program fecundity, which gets us to a revolutionary situation: to live sexuality for the pleasure of it, without the fears of pregnancy and in a second phase, sexuality without love. Which does not means without tenderness, gentleness, feeling, sensuality, eroticism. Not wanting compromises for life does not mean the absence of love or caring sensuality.

The sexual relation is not a insurance contract for a future relationship, but a complete enjoyment of the present, to live the magnificent moment of pleasure, and the orgasmic jubilation. Onfray: "The heavy Eros" of traditional relations adjusts the relationship towards the death impulse, which means: immobilization, fixing, sedentary life, lack of fantasy, endless repetition and rituals. On the contrary, the "light Eros" conducted by the impulse of life wants movement, change, nomadic action, initiative. We will have time enough in the emptiness of our tombs to sacrifice to immobility"

Taking advantage of the moment, the vibration of atoms floating in the air and which define what we call "attraction" or "feeling" and which does not prevent the multiplication of these moments that do, or do not, contribute in time to the construction of a lasting something. A story does not begin with its end. One cannot make a bet on a relation that has to be constructed by movement only. The contract that can result from this movement is not determined durably, possibly renewable but not assured nor binding.

The dominant pattern of marriage relations in our civilization can be resumed in: "nothing- everything- nothing". We exist separated, not knowing of the other's existence, and then we meet and give in to the nature of a relationship. All of a sudden, "the other" whom we barely knew, becomes everything, the measurement of our own existence, the reason for living, the sense of life up to the details. But comes time and all the destruction that goes along with it : "the other" starts being a bother, the one that's boring, tiring, who gets on our nerves, to end up by being the element we have to get out of our life even in a violent way. The one that was "everything" goes back to "nothing", a nothing charged with a certain amount of hatred.

The other possible pattern can be called: "nothing- more - everything" it starts as the previous one, two people don't know of each other's existence. They meet and start building a relationship on the principle of "light Eros". From that day, day after day a positive relation starts to take shape, defining the "more" stage: more pleasure, more expansion, more complicity, more serenity. When this "more" comes to a real total, appears: "everything" which qualifies the relation as complete, and thus can be called, "Love".

The love relations I have lived, and still am living, can be traced with this pattern in a natural way without having been properly defined as does Onfray. One should not contract what one cannot fulfill if one wants to escape from heavy neurosis, melodramas and frustration that end up rotting one's life.

*

I believe it must have been February or maybe March when I turned back to the University where I discovered that I had acquired an assistant-professor. Her name was Tania and she just came back graduated from Lumumba University in Moscow. Small, very thin and dry, with obvious Asian physical characteristics, she had difficulties to smile at me. At first sight I knew why the Ministry of the Interior did not want to grant me a long term visa. My career as a University professor at Havana University was sealed.

It was impossible for me to present the traditional Peul society in the Niger buckle in terms of Marxist class struggle. She could not either, but she took some grave liberties with the truth and reality, ethics, sociology, the tribal structures and moral values so that it matched. Time was coming to prepare suitcases. In the multitude of academic events, I had taken care of making some valuable contacts in the academic world of South America. As the Cuban propaganda made us believe that the socialist revolution in Latin America was just around the corner, we didn't mind going to have a look for ourselves.

But before that, I agreed to integrate an urban planning team which was sent to the southern Pines Island with the mission to make a "socialist" planning for new villages that were planned. It was understood that a "socialist village" ready to host the socialist "new man" had to be, per definition, different from a "capitalist" village.

We landed in a 2,000 hectares ranch with a thousand heads of cattle. Arguing that I had to understand the basic aspirations of the cowboys we wanted to urbanize, I had to be a cowboy myself. A boy's dream from a Flemish village became reality. Saddling horses before daylight in the biting cold air, even before swallowing a burning hot, very sugared coffee. Walking off on a horse back into the prairies, wrapped up in a blanket, with the sun just pointing over the faraway hills; leaving the reins loose on the horse's neck, smelling nature when it wakes with the first sun rays is like no other sunrise. One hour later, we were rounding up cattle to be taken to the tick dip. Making a stop when passing a sugarcane field to cut some sugarcane sticks and chew them as breakfast. Guiding the cattle one by one into the corridor and having them submerged into the bitter smelling bath, makes you feel like you are doing something really useful. All this fulfilled my boy's dream.

In this ranch, as in all the socialist planned economies, there was a Plan to be respected. The one we had to deal with was artificial insemination goals. Not to meet the goals was considered very bad and deserved you setbacks as a good socialist, revolutionary, patriot and more. So, we had to inseminate a determinate number of cows per day. Who decided the number, nobody knew but there was always somebody carrying a small thermos with semen tubes. This was work for the afternoons after the round ups, the baths and the branding of the cattle, but generally we were all day long watching the herd to see if a cow was not mounting another. The cow which is horny is not the one that mounts but the one that lets her to be mounted. That one we lassoed, immobilized, we cleaned her ass and located the sperm capsule. When it was getting late or when we did not feel like it any more, we inseminated everybody, just to meet the daily goal, even bulls. They gave me an artificial inseminator certificate, which I kept proudly for a long time but lost in the plundering of N´Djamena in Chad by Hissein Habré's Goranes wariors conquering the city, many years later.

I went back to Havana, impatient to see Paule.

Thirty years later, back in Cuba, I heard that indeed they had built villages on the Isle of Pines with two story ensembles. It appeared also that nobody wanted to live in these apartments. (Kind of naïve to put cowboys and peasants in apartments, some of them grew chicken and pigs in the bathrooms). Besides, they forgot the central square for gatherings and fiestas and a store.

The security apparatus of the communist Republic did not give us much time. One day, they knocked at the door and took me away to a police station to be jailed (they said retained). All the protests and the laws about the diplomatic status can't stand the will power and arbitrary decisions of the government. I knew that there were few laws respected in Cuba, but I still was surprised that there were so few. One characteristic of a Tyranny is that the word of the tyrants is the law. I was going to be expelled. Fortunately the process was delayed by three days since there was no plane leaving for Mexico earlier (that's where I had chosen to be deported to), which gave me some time to straighten out a couple of things and advise my Latin friends. All of them showed up to say goodbye, silently, surprised and disgusted with the way the Cubans handled the issue.

Just like big criminals or very important persons, I was walked to the stairs of the Cubana de Aviacón aircraft escorted by four military guards.

*

I still believe in social justice, the right to pursue a better life for the greatest number, equality of opportunities and the matter of "each one according to his needs". But to pay for this with the complete abandon of my individual rights: no Sir, that's too high a bill. To live with and within the most outrageous lies because that is convenient to some addicts of power is not my cup of tea. Finally, blindly supporting demagogy, despotism and more lies was not the kind of socialism I wanted. The socialism of Castro, which already was a paranoid dictatorship and was not going to last long before also being murderous, cured me of my uncontrolled youthful enthusiasm.

Structurally unable to produce happiness - here and now – the Castro utopist socialism converted into something like religion. Meaning: seeing happiness, the maximum wellbeing for the maximum number of people, only in a very faraway future, even in a time beyond time. In the name of this fiction, you are asked to sacrifice today, the present and all that is important for the matter of real life. This hypothetical happiness which will come "tomorrow" almost always is the surest way to make life miserable in its expectation. Disgrace and unhappiness are the price to pay to get to an illuminated future with the main idea that the "happiness to come" justifies today's sacrifices. That idea is not new, neither is it revolutionary, but belongs to the most archaic and basic religious postulate.

There, where the main idea should be "Enjoy life here and now without harming anybody nor yourself" they subscribed to the imposture of a life of sacrifices, intellectual and material constraints, a "half life", just to adjust to an ideal the realization of which is highly hypothetical and in all cases maybe for your very far away future descendants.

The Castro-Guevara duo made the Cuban economy go back to the 1956 level, the same for liberty and the death penalty (abandoned in Cuba in 1940 and reestablished by the Castros). The food rationing in Cuba in 1970 amounted to less than the slave food rationing in 1842. The economy, submitted to the capricious will of Fidel (Che gave up in 1965 when he wanted other countries to benefit from his experience as executive of the Cuban National Bank) is a horror tale.

What were the errors? A long, long litany. Want some examples? - The agrarian reform that finished with the agriculture production and the livestock. - The nationalization of commerce and distribution circuits which completely disappeared: the products rot in the field and no way to get them to the meager shops in time. - Capricious industrialization which traduced itself by buying hundreds of factories without the insurance of getting the raw materials. - The urban reform, which finished with the construction industry. - The militarization and the arms race that finished off the financial reserves. - The African wars that emptied the treasury to the last peso and left some hundreds of bodies to rot in Africa. – The "special plans" which finished off everything that escaped from the previous list: Coffee and rice plan (they made Cuba a big importer of these items); Bullfrog plan; Plan hydroponics; Beautiful girl plan (milk); Plan to stock wine all over the country; Lobster plan (it finished with the lobster fisheries); Camembert cheese plan; Banana plan; Mushroom plan; Greenbelt plan; Shrimp plan (consisting of exploiting fishing rights in the Gulf and building white elephant shrimp farms). Etc...etc... In addition to this, the "prestige-propaganda" endless list of festivals, events, Pan American games, scholarships, congresses, the low productivity of state farms, the absence of transportation, the disaster of the centralized plan and so much more ... and you'll understand the reasons of the extreme poverty and low living standards of this once prosperous country. The only real savior before falling into outright misery: The Yankee dollars that the counterrevolutionaries from Miami - officially designated as "gusanos" (worms) - and the rest of the United States are sending to their families.

The complete nationalization of the economy came to create a bureaucratic monster: useless, inefficient and corrupt. I remember one of Castro's speeches in 1970 when he said "In one decade we will bypass the income of every American country, including the United States". In the year 2008 Cuba disputes the last place in this classification with Haiti and Nicaragua.

It is disgusting and shameful to hear the cynical Cuban communist bourgeoisie proclaim that: "What matters is consciousness, material things are not important" when they themselves shop around with credit cards in dollars. It's about the same thing I am hearing from the Mexican bourgeoisie today: "The poor are happy": of course they steal and plunder every possible thing, including the whole country, for not becoming happy as the poor.

*

In these times, early seventies, when you got off the plane in Mexico City coming from Cuba, uniformed Mexican soldiers would take you to a room where a couple of WASP (White-Anglo-Saxon Protestant) looking like civilians would take your picture against a white wall. Front and profile, the type of picture they take of criminals, with the particularity that in this case your crime was descending from a plane coming from Havana. From the Cuban paranoia I fell into to the CIA paranoia. They would also stamp your passport over a double page with huge letters saying "CAME FROM CUBA". With this, you may enter the free world. This comedy was not to the liking of the gentleman in front of me who walked calmly to the WASP holding the Polaroid camera which he grasped and smashed against the wall. The camera exploded in a thousand pieces. The bold elderly, tall man screamed "You don't have the right, bastards" He got applause from all of us. There followed some pushing and screaming in which I escaped from the photograph but not the stamp in my still Belgian passport. From then on, I let myself grow a beard which I still have thirty seven years later. I kind of like my beard. Keeps me from having to rasp my face every morning, instead I just keep it in reasonable shape with scissors once a week. Anyway by now I am afraid of discovering the old man beyond the beard and the mustaches. I might not like him. In a general way I never thought I am an interesting subject for myself, and still less physically.

The second day of my enjoying the free world I went to the Belgian embassy to change my passport. With a contact from the University of Mexico who knew one of the directors of the National Anthropological Museum we organized a conference cycle about African sociology. I got food.

*

In the first phone communications with Paule, I learned that my father had died a week earlier, after a brief convalescence from what was supposed to be cancer. This stranger I never knew, who for three decades had made steel, who worked the 3 shifts, whom I had rarely heard talking and not screaming to my mother, who did not like his life. That man yet will not be seen again, at sometimes impossible hours, mounting his bicycle to pedal to the road where he would climb onto a bus that'll take him to face the mouth of the ovens vomiting the paste that will become steel. There, for eight hours, he would stand facing the monster that vomited liquid steel, while his back was frozen by the cold air that swept through the hangar. Even if the steel factory was about forty kilometers away from the village on a clear night we could see, from the church hill, the sky lightening up with yellow every time the monster vomited. That was where my father was, the man who saw that there was food on the table. Among gases, toxic clouds, smells of sulfur and metal dust, separating impurities from the river of magma with a large metal hook and surveying that the magma went where it was supposed to go.

No, he was not there for fun. Every day of his life he cursed the day that he went to the mill, but kept going. I'll never know why. I had never seen him doing anything else. My mother told me once that in the Nazi war he got a job from the village council guarding the fields to prevent the people from Liege from steeling the crops. There was hunger in the cities. Our house was his life project. In its time it was the most modern home of the whole village with its very pointed, double edged roof and it's very regular and well laid red brick walls and a small five stair terrace in front of the main door, which I never saw open, except to let pass the coffin of my grandmother (who passed away in our house when I was a sergeant in the Belgian army.) It had an average sized living room, a dining room heated by a coal stove and a kitchen with another stove. These two coal stoves were the only heating devices of our home. On the second floor there were three bedrooms. Coming out from under the various blankets in the winter meant getting transpierced, body and soul, by the bitter cold. Getting dressed, running down the stairs to penetrate the well heated kitchen was like getting reborn.

It's probable that this house was the main reason for the very difficult relations between my parents. Must have been that paying the monthly mortgage for thirty-five years was not easy, since we were six to live on my father's salary. I am convinced that for the sake of this house my father did not miss one day at the monster's mouth until he died, one year before retirement. To fail a single payment must not have entered his mind. Debts, before being a matter of money were a matter of honor. When my father came back from the monster, a smell of metal dust filled the room, very different from the agricultural and animal odors that reigned over Heur, the smell dominated by cow shit that characterized the whole village. Especially because the social show off was measured by the height of the piles of manure that every respectable farmer was building on his street front. If social status in Havana was measured by the hugeness of the mansions, in Heur social levels were proportional to the hugeness of the stable dung you displayed on the street. That's why black greasy cow shit was the main perfume of the village. These agricultural perfumes disappeared when my father entered the living room.

In my father's world, tenderness was never shown, neither in words nor in deeds. It is easy for me to remember the few times I saw his eyes with a tender expression letting escape a moment of pride or softness. It happened a few times in the village tavern when I accompanied him in the weekly ceremonies of rooster singing or pigeon racing contests. In this occasion he would buy me a chocolate bar or a soft drink and furtively pass his hand through my hair. A heavy hand that much more often slapped me than caressed my head. It was almost, almost a caress but retained, as if he was afraid of doing or saying something inappropriate. These rare moments became eternal to me but did not have to last more than reasonable. Quickly he would withdraw his hand.

My father did not talk, especially not to say anything futile. He hated words. When I got to the age of the thousand and one questions: Why do birds fly? Why does it rain? Why this earth is gray and that one brown? Why this and why that? He angrily told me to be more silent and when I kept asking he sent me flying. Sure that his plan for me was to take me along some day to the magma vomiting monster of the Belgian steel industry and on Sundays to the village tavern where roosters were singing and pigeons were flying.

The day I took Marie-Chantal to the village because she wanted to meet my parents, he asked me what I was doing. With difficulty, I explained about my school going in America, the African voyage and the Cuban teaching. He asked me gravely if in Africa I had been with black females. I did not answer to avoid a racist discussion. Then he wanted to know what sociology was all about? I tried to be simple but got mixed up in my explanations. Very troubled he looked at me and asked:

- And when are you going to start working?

When I looked at him with his massive body and bald head - I always knew him baldheaded - mounting his bicycle with difficulty, which he had to incline to be able to pass his legs over the saddle, it was difficult to believe that once he was the smartest looking and strongest man of the whole village who climbed thirty five stairs with two bags of fifty kilos of wheat, one on each shoulder. I admired the fatality with which every day he returned to the steel mill. In the winter, when he came back from the mill, almost frozen, with his face turning blue and reviving his feet in a bucket of warm water that my mother had prepared minutes before his arrival, my brains boiled with compassion and anger up to the point of crying. This was the way I learned about the working class condition of the steel industry, the poverty of existence, and the miserable physical and moral conditions.

This is the origin of my rebellion, which in parallel grew with social and political conscience. The facts, before being formulated in a socio-economic framework, taught me the working class condition, the consequent justification of class struggle, the basics of capitalism and the shamelessness of exploitation.

I don't know what I owe to my father, neither how to cancel the debt of my existence? Maybe just by not forgetting, as I am doing now. Telling the story of the lives of those who were exploited, those who were paid a pittance, those who were alienated, those who did not have the conscience, neither the means or the words, or the opportunity to rebel.

Maybe just by being the son of my father: wherever I go, I'll be the son of a steel mill worker. Amongst the bourgeois: those who possess those who were lucky, those who are sure of themselves. In

163

a certain way they are the bosses of my father, responsible for the miserable conditions of life that were imposed upon him and have made that I was, am, and will be a rebel. This is what I owe him. This way my father's life, at least, will not have been in vain, as it might look. Our lives have drifted us apart, so much so that we lived on different planets, strangers to each other.

*

Why we wanted to go to Latin America? I don't know, for nothing, for looks. Maybe we were just aware that there is a lot to learn out there and a lot of world to be seen. Paule had decided, for at least another while, to keep walking along this next bit of road we had decided to march on.

Anyway, I hit the road for Laredo, Texas, to buy a fourth-hand car. Traveling in Mexico with your thumb up is a rare experience. For all kind of people: rich, poor, old, younger, you become ipso facto a possible sexual object. I saved my virginity on that side and got to Laredo with the heavy opinion that in Mexico bisexuality is very much developed.

On the way back, at the wheel of an automatic, blue Chevrolet only ten years old, what had to happen, happened. You don't buy a car for 175 dollars thinking that it's going to take you far. So, it left me stranded about a hundred kilometers south of Monterey but, good girl, she had the class to breakdown just 50 yards away from a gas station and repair shop. Besides this gas station, there was not a soul on the road. Kilometers away, as drawn against a hillside there was a village, but on the road only the solitary gas pumps, and a couple of wooden barracks serving as garage, coffee shop and john.

The repairs required a piece of the motor which had to be bought in Monterrey. The chauffeur of the regular line bus, stopping four times a day, charged himself with the job. I got lodgings on the second floor of the village cantina. This village had run away from a John Ford Hollywood movie. If you want to know how it looked, I recommend just looking up a John Wayne movie where a Mexican village is featured.

The following three days I spent sitting on a chair in front of the coffee shop, my back against the wall, looking at cars and trucks go by. Just like a cow looking at passing trains, but drinking Coca Cola, eating hot peppered hot dogs and smoking.

Here I became a visual witness of the high degree of Mexican imagination and cleverness. From the first day on, I noticed that every time there was a car stopping to fill up, with US plates and going north, the short-legged, bellied master of the gas pump tried to sell a small package wrapped up in a newspaper which he showed to the driver from under his overalls. I understood that that was a package of marijuana...

If the sale had worked out, which it did one out of three times, the guy went to the phone, spoke briefly and turned back to the workshop or came to chat with me. Hours later, a bus coming from Laredo would stop on the other side of the road but nobody would come off or get on. It just stopped and horned. To which my mechanic reacted quickly moving his big ass and short legs with surprising speed towards the bus, from which the driver passed through his driver's window a plastic bag with a small package which I discovered quickly was wrapped up in a newspaper. The second day I understood the circus. The master of the pump had a buddy at the border, maybe in immigration or border police, to whom he signaled the car traveling with the marijuana package. For sure, and not to make a big fuss, the American owner of the package would pay a good bribe and the police kept the package which they simply handed to the chauffeur from the bus who returned it to the gas station. I have no idea how many times a package made the trip to the border, but everybody in that gas station showed good humor and a certain level of wellbeing.

Back in Mexico City, I got lodging in the apartment of Jaime and his lovely wife Margarita. Jaime was a Havana contact; architect, and probably related to the Mexican secret service. Margarita had two single friends, one of whom claimed to be of noble Maya origin. Both were as agreeable as was Margarita and took me several times out to the Zona Rosa which at that time resembled a lot to the Parisian Latin quarter with agreeable cafés and restaurants. Being stupid, inexperienced, imbecile, young and clumsy I missed the occasion to make love to them (not separated but together). Something I will make up for, but many years later, I'll tell you.

By the end of July, Paule, who had known this city in a previous life, joined me. We loaded the Chevrolet, threw a goodbye party and drove off to Yucatan, which was not precisely the shortest way to Santiago de Chile. Bum tourism, that's what it was, free, just going where we thought something worthwhile had to be seen and visited. I remember that to visit the Palenque archeological temples, we had to go to the village and ask for the key from the guardian. (For those who recently went to visit Maya ruins in Yucatan or Chiapas, I just let you imagine). We sympathized with the guardian and a single German archeologist who was trying to find a sense in all these stones. He let us pitch our tent just beside the main temple. I also remember a naked midnight shower in the bath of the virgins (or something like it); to see the small waterfall today, you have to stand in line. The guardian sold us a Smith and Wesson .38 and a box of bullets. Just ahead of our signatures when signing the guest book, was the large signature of Jacqueline Kennedy. I thought that was funny. After having done the round trip of the Yucatan Peninsula and seen a lot more temples and sites, we went back to Palenque and stayed for some more days. We liked the place.

From Guatemala City to Antigua we were stopped at, at least, five army posts: they were looking for guerilleros. Coming to Antigua at sunset, we found cheap lodging in a small hotel just across the street from the main police station. When I locked the car some policeman quite hurriedly closed and locked the huge double, heavy wooden porch. The few people on the street walked fast, keeping themselves close to the grey stone walls. These were not relaxed strolling tourists. We decide to keep the room for that night. Around ten, all of a sudden, shooting started with different types of gun noise and distances, some were like canons. Fear was falling upon us. To calm and cheer up Paule I tried to display my "infantry science", taking guesses at the arms that were being fired. "That's a FAL gun", "this is mortar" and "this is a .50 machine gun". She was very impressed. The shooting diminished after an hour but did not stop completely. Still very worried we finally fell asleep.

On the next day, in front of the cathedral, an old very sympathetic Indian tried to sell us a colorful blanket. We made small talk. All of a sudden the guy said:
- It's a shame we did not meet yesterday, we had a fiesta in San José, and we shot fireworks all night long. Up until today Paule is still laughing at my "infantry science".

The day before we wanted to leave El Salvador, there was a bank robbery, a couple of million dollars. The newspapers carried the news in the following terms: "This robbery was so well executed that surely it must have been done by foreigners". At noon we tried to cross the Honduras border. Never a car was that well disassembled while Paule stayed stoically seated on the .38 colt, dedicated to her reading. There is a blessing for bum travelers.

On the Honduras-Nicaragua border we fell in the "football war". Both border posts had retreated several kilometers. It took hours to cross the no man's land slaloming among the bomb holes. The Pan American highway looked like the Berlin streets in 1945. When we eventually came to the other border, we thought that we had been driving in a circle. The soldiers at that border were the same as the ones we had left hours ago at the other border. Same dress, same height, same color, same guns, same belts with the inscriptions "US ARMY", same helmets, same boots. For those who don't remember: This war broke out after a football game that was not to the liking of one of the parties. It lasted several months. In a memorable "prisoner exchange" the Nicaraguans (or was it the Hondurans?) had emptied their psychiatric hospitals, hung a board around the neck of the victims on which was written "I am Honduran" (Nicaraguan?) and had sent them over the border.

In Costa Rica, we took on board two youngsters – which meant, just some years younger than ourselves- one was a Peruvian and the other Columbian. They had been turned down on the Mexican-US border and were making their way back home. The Peruvian saved our lives when descending the Death Mountain and the brakes of the Chevrolet just decided not to work. Through the open doors we tried to stop the car with our feet; finally I managed to stop it against a soft mud pile on the side of the road. He was a good mechanic and repaired the car several times. They were good and funny companions and we stayed together to the Panama Canal.

In Panama, we camped close to a village where there was going to be a fiesta. We went to see what a fiesta in a god forsaken miserable village looked like. Our companions got into a fight because the Columbian had invited a girl to dance, which was not to the liking of her papa and her brother. Paule cured them from a couple of cut ups with what was left in the first aid box. That night we slept in the car with the gun loaded. On a beach we had a gun slinking contest, instinctive shooting from the hip like John Wayne. I won and Paule came second.

When finally we reached Panama City we were dirty, tired, and pretty bone broken. Here we realized that the Pan American highway came to an end because the American army was using the southern part of Panama as a training ground for the Vietnam War. At least that was what we were told. Our Peruvian companion decided to take a plane to Medellin in Columbia because that is the place with the most beautiful girls of all the Americas. I thought that was an excellent reason to go to Medellin. The Colombian wanted to stay a while in Panama where he got a job as a waiter or something. They were excellent companions, with a great sense of humor, sometimes we laughed our heads off. Hello to you my friends

I don't remember how we met but an elderly American, employee in the Canal Zone, invited us to his place and gave us a guided tour of the Canal Zone. Socially and economically, the American controlled Canal Zone was like any American suburb town. He was a very kind man and probably belonged to the CIA or something like it.

We managed to sell the Chevrolet, the colt, the tent and anything else we could not carry to a young very Chinese looking Panamanian. This allowed us to buy passage on the nicely named "Leonardo da Vinci" Italian cruise ship, which, once passed the canal, gave services all along the Pacific coast as far as Valparaiso. But Valparaiso was, financially speaking, out of reach and also we preferred to do it by road. So, our tickets were to Callao, the harbor of Lima.

Four nights in the comfort of a Transatlantic ship, in a double cabin, with Italian food was just what was needed to recover from three weeks of camping on road sides, car sleeping, and driving. Morally we did not need any recovering, we were doing fine and happy. Paule is a magnificent travel companion; she takes everything on the light side, including the unbearable humidity and the clouds of Panama mosquitoes. She never complained.

We discovered Lima where I had a good contact at the San Marco University. The first question that came to my mind was "why this place stands where it stands?" The sky is always grey, the buildings are grey, the magnificent colonial palaces are grey, the roads are grey everything is grey. We never saw the sun shining in Lima. The peculiar thing about Lima is that when you drive ten miles out of town up into the Andes you are met with a bright shining sun almost all year long. Somewhere there must be an explanation? The Peruvian girls we had met on the Leonardo Da Vinci offered us hospitality in one of the palaces their family owned and which happened to be empty. One dozen of rooms, bathrooms, halls, patios and a huge stairway all marbled, at least four meters high ceilings.

When the phone rang in the entrance hall you had to run forty meters and twenty five stairs to get to it, very cold and very show off. These places were built when the bourgeoisie of Peru still displayed their wealth with stones long before they put their money in the stock exchange. The more marble floors and walls, more columns, bigger stones and larger porches, the higher your social ranking and the more jealous the neighbor. We had already experienced this "who more" in the Vedado quarters of Havana. The rich behave and have the same phantasms all over the world.

One week of African seminar in the San Marco University, a couple of conferences and TV shows, left us enough money to travel to Santiago. At that time - I don't know about today - the easiest thing to teach in Latin America was African social sciences or anything related. General culture about Africa in those regions was very close to zero, hardly anything more than the Tarzan and Jane comic strips. So, it was not difficult to be an expert. We got on the bus, content to leave grey Lima.

*

Yesterday, from Campeche, we sent twenty five thousand fish fingerlings, each weighing 0,89 grams to Culiacan on the Mexican Pacific coast, just on the other side of the country. Like fifty and something hours by truck. I am telling you this because this has never been done before. We are innovating and establishing precedents. The clients? Huge shrimp farmers, who just want to find out that fish growing in their shrimp ponds is maybe a better business than keeping insisting growing shrimp. It has been a while now that shrimp farming has become a difficult money maker, and if it were not for big government subventions most would be bankrupt. This difficult situation of shrimp farming had been predicted to me, fifteen years ago, by Mister de la Pomélie, deputy director of the research station of IFREMER, when he came back from a study trip to Asia. The majority of the Asian shrimp is produced in a cooperative system, where the state sponsored cooperative hands out to the farmers: post larvae, food, sanitary care and buy up the harvest. The producers, farmers also producing rice and vegetables, don't have production costs. Shrimp ponds are left to the care of their wives or children. Shrimp income is just an extra to the family budget. Individually they don't produce much, but there are tens of millions of them. This is how low income class people in the rich countries, blue collars in Milwaukee and Milan can eat shrimp whenever they feel like it. But also that shrimp farming in any other part of the world has become a difficult profit business. For years, I have been telling this story to our Mexican shrimp farmers and government civil servants who sustain the production. Nobody believed it and nobody wanted to pay attention. The monies at stake are too important and political interests too high. They prefer to keep pumping public money into a product that barely has a market. It seems that they don't know what else to do, hoping that the shrimp bonanza will someday return, held up by the treasury. That's what has been going on for nine years now.

I better shut up because I made exactly the same error with my fish farms in France – trying to hold on to a business that was programmed to be doomed. You'll learn more about that later.

One of the aquaculture alternatives to the declining shrimp farming in Mexico- but still not understood by the ex senator in charge - remember him? - Of aquaculture for the government is to change shrimp for fish growing in their already paid for installations. Apart from the company which is buying our fingerlings in Culiacan, nobody has seen the light yet. The rebirth of the Mexican fishing industry depends only on the fact that the Senator is able to see a little farther than his personal immediate interest. One thing I have not seen, in all these years, from a single Mexican politician. A small percentage of the multi billion budget of the fishery and aquaculture ministry – of which nobody really sees where it goes - could set off the process. It has never been productive to leave basic economic sectors, such as agriculture and fisheries, in the hand of politicians. They are simply incapable of seeing any farther than the term they spend in office. In addition to that, the concept of "common interest" does not belong to their vocabulary and we have one of the explanations of why Mexican growth rate, for years, is around 2 % per year while Chile and Brazil turn around 8 % and the Asian emerging countries around 11 %. Poverty and underdevelopment always have reasons; the disgrace just does not fall out from the sky. In this case look to the mediocrity of our politicians. In the meantime we keep being the only sea fish hatchery in the country, struggling to survive, circled by dwarfs of vision and courage.

*

Santiago received us with a chilly winter air; the heights of Lo Barnechea were snowed in, the Mapocho river was carrying ice cubes and the trees of the providence park had cold feet; this was July 1971.

We had not read many papers on the way down from Mexico and were surprised to find out that our entry in Santiago coincided with the election campaign in which the Popular United Front of Allende, the Christian Democrats from Eduardo Frey and the conservatives of Alessandri were contesting. This latter one, Alessandri and his party, was called by the other two "The Mummy" for the age of the candidate and the far right political position of the party. Our Santiago contact, Arancibia, very much engaged with Allende updated us very quickly. The leftist coalition of "Unidad Popular" included everything. From the far left Guevarist MIR youngsters – adepts of armed struggle - to the weakest social-democrats from the socialist party, through the very Stalinist Communist Party of Chile. This supposed for Allende, a very high flying equilibrium exercise and without a security net.

We liked everything about Chileans, their frank, direct, open, critical, ironical, humorous and independent - up to disrespectful - spirit towards their rulers and the establishment. This was refreshing after our social experience of Cuban real-socialism where submission, boot licking and cowardice are the main trends of political and social behavior. Chileans don't take themselves too seriously. The type of seriousness that ends up being pompous is not in their characters. Something like the Jews who also laugh a lot about themselves, which saved them from the many existentialist dramas they had been going through as a people.

Never had seen anything like it. According to their political preference they walked all day long showing one, two or three fingers in the air (each candidate had a number), hooted their cars one two or three times and even posted their preferred number on their doors or balconies or in their shops. When numbers did not match, they smiled and made a movement with their hands to their bottoms, meaning that the other one was going to have to carry a tail. Carrying a tail is losing the election. Difficult to tell and to believe but the day after this famous election, won by Allende, many losers indeed carried a paper or cloth tail to their belts and walked around   all day long with this thing hanging between their buttocks.

How to resist the seduction of such good humor? We were seduced by these people and up to today we are convinced that they are, amongst the Latin American peoples, the most cultivated and socially aware. Something they share with the Uruguayans. These opinions of course are very personal. However the enormous cultural and economical progress of Chile in the past years proves that I am not far from the truth. Where I really got it wrong was with the United Popular front of Allende.

The Hedonist

Between the hooks, for those interested in Chilean idiosyncrasy I recommend heavily to read Isabelle Allende, everything this lady wrote, but especially "My Invented Country".

The first one to get a job in Santiago was Paule. Nothing less than as a translator for the Bishop of Santiago. It was temporary but it paid well. We installed ourselves at the edge of the middle class quarter near Providence Park, on the other side of the University of Chile with only the Mapocho River separating us, in walking distance, from downtown and the Alameda Park. I spent days and nights in that park which was converted into a public tribune of all the political parties. Debating was constant and civilized, although sometimes voices raised - but I never saw things deteriorate into pushing or boxing.

Don't think that this was only a city phenomenon. The first Sunday in Santiago, Arancibia took us up into the Andes, which Santiago is leaning against and where the middleclass have their country homes. In all the villages we passed the peasants, their wives and children, sitting on their doorsteps, stuck up their fingers. Most were three fingers, the Allende number. I got emotional passing by these very modest stone built and palm roofed huts and seeing hope in the eyes of their dwellers.

The two universities of Santiago, the catholic and the Chilean contracted me to give some courses and seminars about my usual sustenance subject: Africa. The University of Chile also gave me a weekly program on their television network which allowed us to accompany our salad diet with cheese and wine.

Democracy is beautiful when it is well understood, but in our entire travels through Latin America this was the only time that we experienced it. Almost every two days, one or the other party organized a demonstration on the same Alameda Avenue. This gave way to newspaper titles the following day: "Yesterday the Social Democrats reached such or such number". The next day of course the other party wanted to do better. The most impressive demonstration I have seen was the one of the Chilean women supporting Salvador Allende Gossens. I have to explain that Gossen written with a C instead of two S, stands for "enjoy" - rather in the sense of orgasm. Their banner stretching all the width of this large avenue read "Mujeres de Chile con Salvador Allende.....gocen" (Women of Chile with Salvador Allende ...enjoy). Here was all the lightness, the humor and the liberty which characterize Chilean women.

172

As far as I could see, the Chilean women are libertine, which means lovers of liberty and of independence. The story circulated, I did not check, that genetically there are many more women in Chile than there are men and that in the Australian colonization times, mainly initiated by English prisoners, full ships of Chilean females were sent there to start a balanced colonization. I don't know if that is the truth, but it is reasonable to believe that this genetic distortion of genders is one of the explanations of the Chilean female spirit of independence and integration. The Chilean female is the contrary of the stereotype of the Latin woman, submissive, dependent, poorly educated and in continuous search for material security, sensual and emotional exclusivity up to the point of sacrificing herself to reach these life goals. "Mothers with big boobs" as wrote Fernanda Familiar, who gives us a picture of these Latin females. The Chilean women as I saw them do not match that picture. But let's stay away from always dangerous generalizations.

*

Libertine, here is the word. To my understanding there is no man or woman on earth, who does nor aspire to be a libertine; autonomous, independent, little preoccupied by order and ideas "à la mode". Especially in our days when all of us are submitted to something or the other. The libertine spirit is the contrary of submission. The true libertine is without a God and without ties which restrain his liberty. He or she are authentic balanced human beings.

Of course, you will recognize the libertine at a glance: he has enemies all over the place. Because the libertine does not want nor accepts ties imposed upon him, nobody likes him. He puts the all powerful individual above the group, the masses, casts, tribes or whatever ties. He does not want the mediocrity of societies, not today's nor yesterdays, even if it looks like they are enlightened. The libertine wants happiness, satisfaction and pleasure: "Here and Now". He searches for an enthusiastic existence and personal happiness as the opposite of a hypothetical collective happiness, always programmed for later. He says out loud what everybody thinks, or would like to say but dares not.

Does that mean that he rejects all moral rules? Of course not, on the contrary. The libertine announces an ethic of replacement. He uses his consciousness in the codification of pleasure, distinguishing a subtle difference between quantity and quality. The libertine as said by La Mettrie, philosopher and medic in the army of Louis XIV,

173

enemy of Voltaire and Rousseau (dixit Onfray), never neglects the other. To him, complete happiness is impossible without the happiness of all. This is the opposite moral to the moral from the sacred books which over the centuries accommodated themselves very well with injustice, ignorance, brutal exploitation and misery of important parts of society, promising a better life - after. For the libertine; satisfaction and happiness cannot be solitary or individual. For him pleasure without conscience undermines the soul. Pleasure of the other and his happiness are so important that his happiness and his pleasure are not possible without pleasure and happiness of "the others".

La Mettrie, again: Sensual pleasure, desire, to want it, solicit it, remember it, realize it, suggest it; is so big that: "Pleasure takes us above ourselves" and liberates us from our miserable and sad condition of mortals. Since anyway we have to die "Enjoy the moments which are left; drink, sing, eat, love those who love us, that their plays and laughter accompany us, that we live all our desires to meet our souls, however short is life, we will have lived it."

A few words about La Mettrie, who took me a long way from the enchantment of Chilean woman. In 1742, in the battle of Flanders, he was struck down by fever, which left him several days unconscious. As a doctor and philosopher, he experimented on himself the demonstration that the soul, the body, thinking, are of material content. Because when the body failed everything stopped and thoughts did not occur anymore. He spent the rest of his days writing about his vision of life and the world that flowed from his experience.

What can the body bring apart from enjoying love? Apart from enjoying everything? In any case; living is the search of happiness, it is wanting to enjoy. This is not good or bad, this is nature. One does not need big demonstrations to prove what pleasure is and what disgust is. The body knows it all.

*

I don't remember what got me from the enchantment of Chilean woman to La Mettrie, if not the search for a way to live in harmony with real human nature. This, of course, is a dangerous generalization, I have already said that all Chilean women are certainly not the way I saw them. Probably, the ones who formed my opinion are a small minority; fortunately I met a few who led me to this opinion.

Soon I'd find out that with a security pretext, the close surroundings of the candidate Allende were monopolized, physically, by the Castro revolutionaries from the leftist revolutionary movement MIR: The most extremist component of all the extremist components of the Popular Union. This will have grave implications in what is to follow.

Allende got elected in a one runoff election among all the candidates, which meant with little more than 38 % of the popular vote. This of course did not diminish our happiness nor the fiesta. We spent almost a whole week dancing cuecas and drinking white wine that besides making me drunk gave me a bloody headache - which did not keep us from doing it all over again, the next day. We were young and marvelous.

In a short time the University of Chile, generally leftist, put itself at the disposal of the Allende government. I wrote myself up in the section "Agrarian Reform" and left Santiago for the South in company of a dozen more "agrarian reformers", towards the region of Bulnes, in Mapuche Indian territory, with the purpose of backing the Ministry of Agrarian reform.

The Hacienda we landed in was a marvel. It consisted of and produced: wheat, corn, a cheese factory, around two hundred Normandy black and white milk cows, a stable with two dozens of horses, among them two Arabians, hectares and hectares of vines and its own registered wine trademark in underground bricked caves, two barns with pigs and another one with a thousand chicken. Almost everything was mechanized. There was a respectable repair shop for the tractors and the two harvesting machines. All this, with the houses for the peons spread in a large circle around the huge mansion of the owners. Better said the "former " owners, because our reform mission was to organize this marvel into a cooperative .

I knew a few things about cows and wheat. The first thing I did, even before finding a place to put my sleeping bag was to get some farm hands out of their houses to milk the cows. The poor animals were loudly mooing as if someone was killing them, chopping them up with a small knife, in front of the stable. Some had their tits hanging almost to the ground. They had not been milked for days. I can't stand animal suffering. By nightfall they were again in the willows and the future cooperative was richer with two thousand liters of milk nobody knew what to do with. The milk collector had not been around since the expropriation of the hacienda by the brave workers exercising their just rights of expropriation.

This was not a much planned agrarian reform. A few days before, the owner of the place went to Bulnes with his family. When he came back the farm hands and workers, armed with some machetes and forks, just had closed the main gate and did not let him in. That's what I was told in the first meeting that evening. As "planning of agrarian reform" that did not look very much to me.

The problem was huge. In the head of the future members of the cooperative, the picture that was playing was not the same as the one that was playing in the head of the agrarian reform government delegates. They waited for us just to split up the property and the farm- from land and animals to tractors and eggs- and everybody back to his own individual business. That's why they did not milk the cows; nobody knew who they belonged to. When the civil servant of the agrarian reform ministry, tried to explain the functioning of a cooperative and all working together to the advantage of all, etc... it was clear that he was talking Chinese: the incomprehension was total. Even if nobody dared to say it clearly, their eyes and faces spoke for them, they were disappointed. In that very loud and noisy founding meeting of the cooperative, it was clear to me that many of these people did not like each other, some almost got into a fight. How to create a cooperative with people who don't like, or even who hate each other? Neither in the first, nor in the second and the following meetings, did anybody agree on anything.

I decided not to be part of this which would go on for days, or so it looked. There were things to do if at least they wanted to hold the whole, magnificent thing together, for example cows and horses. With the foreman, who had stayed on but was on the owner's side, and a few farmhands we milked the cows, threw the milk away and got them back to their pastures. In the afternoons we saddled horses and made long rides all over the hacienda, looking from the hills, over the vineyards which already needed some maintenance. Later on, by sundown we rode to an aldea of four wooden constructions where there were only women and children, to have a couple of glasses of white wine. We did not talk very much but we did appreciate each other's company.

Lenin, Stalin, el Ché and Castro got it dead wrong: socialist planning is no good for production, even less agricultural production. This has been proven in Bulgaria, Poland, Russia, China, Cuba and many other places. The joke became truth. In these times when the soviets started to buy American wheat it said: "The communists are the greatest farmers in the world, they sow in Ukraine and harvest in

Arkansas" or the other one that said: "You establish socialism in the Sahara desert and in a short time you'll be importing sand"

The second weekend I spent "reforming", a sad, melodramatic show happened: the personal belongings of the owners would be sold. There they were, sitting on a dozen chairs: six or seven men and as many women, some elderly, some middle-aged and two younger girls of, I guessed, about twenty, good-looking, their heads and chins up. They talked among themselves in low voice. All of a sudden one of the girls exploded in loud cries and weeping, when a farmhand, looking at his sandals, brought to the middle of the circle a magnificent mare and the small farmers or workers started shouting their bids. The crying girl took refuge in the arms of a gentleman, half grey, with large moustaches, certainly her father. This crying that came from deep inside, cut with sucking as if she searched for air was pathetic. The master of ceremonies who was presiding the public sale raised his voice to announce the bids, although it was not necessary at all, a grave silence had fallen over all the bystanders. Even the boys and girls from the Isabel Parra brigade from the communist party, who had been brought from Santiago for the fiesta, stopped laughing and singing. They turned down the cassette machine from which since they had arrived revolutionary songs, among which the famous "Comandante Che Guevara", "Bella Ciao", and "Adelina" had been played to a point of boredom. An elderly man from among the owners, dressed in the Chilean traditional hacienda owner outfit: black trousers and jacket, boots, white shirt, large black hat and a large cloak, black outside and red inside, walked to the middle of the circle in a very theatrical and majestic way. By that time, there was complete silence. He shouted a number that apparently nobody was to raise. He walked, straight as a lamp pole, to the horse and took the reins, without even looking at the farmhand who kept studying his sandals. He turned around and led the mare to the crying girl who dried her tears with the sleeve of her white blouse and kissed the nose of the mare, who apparently liked that, judging by the head shaking and noises she made. I wanted to applaud, but kept cowardly from doing so, with so many communist brigadiers at my side. The same thing went on with the next piece: an English hunting saddle and gear, which another of the owners bought and offered to the yet almost smiling girl. The audience kept silent. The kind of ashamed silence of those who all of a sudden realize the cruelty, gratuity and lack of humanity of which they were responsible. After that, the ex-owners all stood and walked away from the scenery. The master of

177

ceremonies closed the sales for that day and shouted that he would be there again the next morning at ten.

We, the secondhand revolutionaries, were supposed to meet for a fiesta with barbecue. I searched for my sleeping bag in the dormitory room where we all slept. This "feast" had left me without hunger. I could not convince myself of the necessity of making the bourgeois buy their own personal belongings for the sake of social justice, the prosperity and happiness of the proletarians.

Early next morning, I went to visit the owners' mansion. The garden, or what was left of it, was strewn with all kinds of garbage, cardboard boxes, pieces of wood which one day had been furniture, two half burned mattresses and a huge quantity of empty bottles. I took the bother to read some of the labels: Remy Martin cognac, black label of the walking Johnny, Tennessee Bourbon and of course, champagne Veuve Cliquot. It looked like there had been some heavy parties going on right here. One part of the double porch was missing, so that entering was not violating the law, which I thought was a funny thought in view of the circumstances. Passing the doorstep a huge hall, once a living room, with wooden floor stared at me. There was not much furniture left, beside a three legged chair, two heavy leathered armchairs cut up which showed their cotton fillings and some springs, a massive wooden table, that probably still was there because of its weight and size, showed some machete cuts that had not done it great damage. The rosy-yellow walls were empty, letting clearly visible the squares where the paintings which once decorated the room had hung. The monumental fireplace, with small stone carved benches on each side, was full of papers, cardboard boxes and ashes. The only furniture still standing and untouched, still having all the glass windows intact, was a wall to wall and almost reaching the ceiling, library. I read the titles: books about horses, hunting, wild animals, some geographical ones about exotic places; The British Encyclopedia (must be worth a fortune) and about four meters long of the National Geographic magazines. All the books bound in fine leather with their titles in gold letters. In one corner, about two dozens of sociology work in English by authors I did not know. I took one and went to sit on the edge of a couch, my back turned to the door. It must have been interesting since I had not heard her steps when all of a sudden a female voice broke the silence, just behind me.
- You may take it, they are yours now.
Jumping on my feet I let the book fall to the wooden floor. Turning round, I stood in front of a woman, around thirty, clear eyes, with a

harsh but beautiful face and long black hair falling on her shoulders. She wore a white shirt buttoned up to the neck which she also had exceptionally long and slim but maybe it looked that way because she was highly buttoned up. She repeated with a clear soft voice:

- They are yours now! You can take them.

It took me a moment before I found the right words in English:

- I believe they always will be yours.

Her face showed surprise, I thought that it was just right that she too got a surprise. She answered with a strong Oxford accent. Anyway, very British:

- I already have them inside me; I don't need them anymore.

- Books are life companions; one always needs to have them close by.

I believe that in some place I must have read that.

- Is that so?

Neither of us was prepared for this conversation. She followed up:

- You are not from here are you?

- No, madam, I am not from here, at least not from this country. But who knows, for the other things maybe I am from here.

I said that without taking a breath, fast. This time she was the one who needed time to search for words. The harshness of her face had disappeared to leave an expression of surprise, and almost but not quite, a smile. I thought she started to enjoy this, having fun. I recognized her as the woman I had seen in yesterday's revolutionary show and I had taken for a young girl.

- So, you are a poet?

- No madam I am not a poet, maybe am I romantic, but I am not a poet

- Poets get it wrong, many times.

I did agree with that nodding my head.

- What are you doing here?

The question was direct, clear. After a few moments watching each other, because indeed I had never given it much thought: to be there was just the natural thing for me, I murmured something like:

- I am participating.

I heard in my own voice, hesitation and poor conviction.

- And you read sociology?

- I am a sociologist, with a specialization in African affairs. And you ?

This conversation took place with the armchair between us

- I, too, am a sociologist, with urban specialization.

Both of us fell from surprise into more surprise.

- Our trade does not serve for much, does it?

- Not anymore, this government is taking us towards Castro communism, and there sociologists are not very much needed.
- I was there!
- Where?
- In Cuba.
- So, then you are a Castro agent?

I was getting nervous and tried to smile without much success:
- I don't think so, he threw me out
- Who? Castro?
- Yes, Castro.

We both kept silent, looking at each other. She was what one will call a beautiful woman, agreeable to look at and most of all she turned out to be far from stupid.
- Then what are you doing with them? These thieves who are stealing even my sister's horse! You saw what happened yesterday?
- Yes I was there
- And what do you make of it?
- Pitiful

She came closer and put her hands on the back of the chair. Hands she had very slim and with dark red painted nails.
- Then, why do you participate in this?

Deep inside I was a bit asking myself the same question.
- Because you exploit them, that's what they say

Her face became harsh and angry again. On a louder tone she responded:
- Not true, we give them work.
- Yes, but they have breakfast with a green pepper, an old and hard biscuit and a sip of mate with little herbs.
- They drink it all.

Her face showed that she was not completely convinced of what she was saying. A couple of days later and I will tell you that too, I had a chance to verify that she was not completely wrong. There was a "feeling" starting to grow between us and we both were getting aware of it. With an arm movement I offered the armchair, after a brief hesitation she accepted. She sat at the edge of the armchair, her legs firmly held together the way they teach girls in high society. I sat on the floor in front of her, with my legs crossed as Indians do. All this happened without keeping from looking at each other. At the end she lowered her eyes and let herself go more into the chair. That's when I saw big tears running down her cheeks taking along the black makeup from her eyes, making their way to her chin and falling upon her white blouse, leaving black spots on her breasts that were choking. There is one thing I don't stand: it is seeing people suffer, especially not beautiful women, whom I consider are born to be happy. Holding back a natural desire to take her in my arms and console her with all the things she would allow me to do, I felt stupid not letting things go their natural way. She stammered:

- We are not "momios", we are Christians, we have always treated well the people as the Bible tells us to.

That made it difficult to say something.

- The Bible does not tell it all, even if they pretend that all is there.

- The rest is in Marx?

This put an end to the river of tears that had been rolling down to her chest. Hell, did I desire that woman, with all the hacienda owner and bourgeois manners she displayed. A huge erection was manifesting itself, which I tried to hide closing my legs and putting my arms around them. But that was very uncomfortable.

- Do you know Pablo Neruda?

- Yes, some of it.

That was a lie: I had never read anything from the national Chilean poet.

- It's my favorite

I knew that Neruda, a communist, was a big supporter of the Unidad Popular of Allende, of which later he would be the Ambassador in Paris. A little surprised that the rich Chilean landowners liked Neruda, I kept the conversation going:

- Say something.

She recited a whole poem from Neruda, something about the sea. There I was, listening to, admiring and desiring, with a big erection between my legs, a woman reciting Neruda, daughter of the hacienda owner I was supposed to help expropriate.

She got up and walked to the library from which she took a fine leather covered volume which she handed to me:

- Take this, as a gift. The rest is theft!

I smiled, thinking how the missing paintings and pictures of hunting scenes in the Alps would look on the walls of the farmhands' wooden huts.

The Neruda book she handed was "Canto General". To my great relief, because I did not want this to end, she sat back in the chair. I don't remember how we came to talk about Washington and its monuments, which she knew very well: even the Circle was familiar to her. Then we went to London and the Tate Gallery which I did not know, then back on the Negro rebellion in Los Angeles where they were burning a full neighborhood. We chatted about my African experiences which impressed her very much.

I could not stand it any longer: only two possibilities, either I tried to give into an animal desire for that woman, or I kept sitting on the floor. I got up to sit on the arm of the armchair. Doing so, I touched her arm. I understood that the sexual desire was shared but we did not get any further. Hardly touching my leg, she extracted herself from the chair and walked across the room to get me the three legged chair which she put in front of the armchair. We both smiled and she blushed very heavily, which made her clear eyes shine even more.

I spent the most delightful hours from all my Chilean adventure. Yet with the sun standing high we got interrupted by a discrete cough. As if sitting on a spring, she got up.

- Papa!

The patriarch was standing in the door, his silhouette clearly cut against the bright daylight. There stood the ex-master and owner of all things that belonged to the hacienda; fields, vines, cows, tractors, horses, farmhands living and dead.

- Helena, we are waiting!

The voice was deep, baritone, with a very light, but present, tone of reproach. Of course, she could not carry any other name but Helena. The Helena from Troy could not have been more beautiful.

Her father dressed as I had seen him yesterday, except that he had put his pants in his boots which in livestock language stood for that he owned cattle, came to us without saluting me. I replied with the same courtesy, keeping the book with my two hands closed over my chest.

- You have been crying?

If his voice was soft and deep, the look he gave me was not, there was hate and vengeance in these also clear eyes.

- No papa, no es nada.

In Helena's eyes there was love and admiration.

- Let's go, they are waiting for us to finish the socialist comedy.

He said that with a straight look in my eyes, which I did not lower. I knew that this man, if he could, would kill me. Helena stood close to her father and when I thought that this was the last I was going to see from her, she came back to me. Tending me her hand she sort of whispered.

- Maybe we will meet again, in better times.

Her hands were soft and she squeezed mine slightly. I responded with the same soft, warm tightening.

- Where?

She laughed letting me see for the last time her mouth which I desired so much.

- In Bulnes.
- In Bulnes? You live in Bulnes?

To me all the hacienda owners lived in palaces in exclusive residential areas in Santiago.

- What do you think? This has not come to an end, yet.

She frankly laughed.

- When?
- Friday afternoon in the hotel bar.
- Is there more than one hotel?
- No, none that's worth the name.

In this exchange, we stayed with our hands enlaced. Before breaking the only physical contact we had ever had, she squeezed my hand again softly, before slowly taking her hand out of mine and walked back to her father who kept observing us from the door, without moving.

Here I was again, with a date with a woman whose father would rather have me killed and who was going to assist at the show where their whole world was falling apart.

I did not go to the show where the bourgeoisie had to buy their own personal belongings. Instead, I headed for the stables. Saddled my favorite black stallion and rode away at a savage gallop into the vineyards. I came back by sundown with a devastating hunger and a painful headache. After drying the horse that was sweating, I walked to the fiesta. Yes, this time I was going to eat half of the barbecue even if I had to listen again to the complete revolutionary repertory of Comandante Che Guevara, of Isabella Parra and songs of the Spanish and Cuban revolutions and even "Bella Ciao".

I passed the rest of the week expecting Friday, making sure that the cows were milked and in the afternoons playing football against the farmhand team. This was more a massacre than playing football but I got a kick out of it.

One day, a newborn child died in one of the houses of the farmhands. The small coffin, in fact a carbon box, was displayed in the middle of the room. When the room was filled with people the father and the mother silently danced a cueca with white handkerchiefs around the coffin covered with a white cloth. I was very touched and tears ran over my cheeks and into my beard. I did not try to hide them but let them run. When the cueca finished, the father took the box under his arm and went to bury it behind the house, accompanied with the weeping and screaming of the mother and a few more women. After the last shovel of earth thrown over the grave, the father saddled his horse and rode off to work. A couple of youngsters from my group of land reformers shouted "Viva la Unidad Popular"! This was of extremely bad taste.

Even if is was only about four in the afternoon, the hotel bar in Bulnes, looking much more like a tavern furnished with fine wooden walls, ceiling and floor in pure English pub style, was packed with people of all kinds: ranchers, civil servants and politicians who one can identify, all over the world, by their avoiding, escaping, out of the corner looks. The kind of look that wants to make you believe that they know more than what they say or look like. I found a table with two chairs against the wall. The table to the left was occupied by four uniforms of different styles and colors, all of them wearing mustaches, and two civilians of advanced age. To the right, two middle aged couples, dressed as if they were at mass, talked in a low voice, the woman to the woman and the man to the man. All this looked much more like a German tavern from around Munich than a discreet hotel bar. Much smoke, much noise but not disturbing, ambience of civilized people and straight drinkers respecting the forms.

Regardless of the effort I had made to wear clean pants and an ironed shirt, my sockless feet in my moccasins told all about me. I did not belong to them. Looking around, I was surprised by the number of uniforms there were sitting on different tables who drew my attention even if I didn't know why.

The waiter, short, with a Mapuche face, and dressed with a large apron hanging from his neck reaching his knees, as they wear in the Parisian brasseries, took my order: a beer, which looked like it surprised him. All the tables were covered with bottles of wine, but I was dying for a beer, the first one in a long time. There are things that betray one's origins.

It was still not very clear what the heck I was doing there. For a while I observed the tables. The most silent ones where no talking was done or in very low voice, was the ones with the uniforms seated around them. The familiarity of the military with the civilians all of a sudden appeared strange. Usually, in all parts of the world the uniforms go together. These are people who march at the same step; know how to obey orders, heads in which everything is square and simple: black or white, good or bad, for or against the rules. There is little place for grey or half tones in a military brain. That's why they feel good together. Familiarity with civilians –the inferior race- is very rare and when it happens is reserved for the very high grades.

On some tables chess was played, on others cards, almost everybody smoked, which awakened my desire. Along with my second beer I ordered a pack of Marlboro's.

Maybe an hour later, I saw her making her entrance, together with her sister, the sentimental one, which bothered me. When I have a date I don't like chaperons. They came direct to my table, shaking hands here and there with some gentlemen who stood at her passing by. It was not exactly Marilyn Monroe descending the great stairway, but still it was something like it. I stood and, taking advantage when she stretched out her hand, made a discrete, fast but warm hand kiss which provoked surprise and laughter. Her sister blushed like a cooked shrimp. The ice was broken. We stood some time in introductions and civilities. Her sister was named Orfea, must be that her father, who wished to kill me at the first opportunity, knew about Greek mythology. Half the tavern was looking at us, some with their mouths wide open. Finally, the Mapuche waiter brought us a chair.

- And how is our hacienda? Helena asked when barely seated.

If I had surprised her with the hand kiss, she surprised me opening fire as if I were a vulgar informer.

- I don't know, it seems that there are some problems getting the cooperative going.

- Of course, the majority of the farmhands and employees are on our side. You saw their faces at the sale?

- I don't know. I didn't notice.

- Oh, yes they are. We know everything that is going on, including that you milk the cows and keep them from dying.

This made me laugh but I did not feel like making a comment.

There was a silence, while the Mapuche servant put two glasses of Martini with ice on the table.

- My God, how hot it is here.

She unbuttoned her blouse, two halves of beautiful, well formed breasts appeared. Instinctively I started to phantasm, seeing myself caressing and kissing. Helena knew how to talk to men.

- My dear Jean Pierre, this is not going to go very far.

The tone was firm, sure, no questioning was allowed.

- Why are you so sure? I dared

- This comedy is completely out of tone with the character of our people whom I know, believe me.

- Then what?

She lifted her glass as for saying cheers with the little finger up in the air and took a sip; her sister   followed the movement. Judging by

Orfea´s eyes she was enjoying the verbal ping pong that was going on. Delicately, she put her glass back on the table and replied:

- We are going to take it all back. Allende is not a bad guy, he is going to resign, in the best of cases he will call for new elections, which we are going to win.

So that was the program, she kept talking:

- Fidel Castro is coming to Santiago next week; this is going to speed up collectivization, which nobody wants around here, not even the socialists.

I thought she was right. Softly I objected:

- Allende was elected.

- Yes with something more than thirty five percent and he is behaving as if it were eighty.

I smelled her light perfume with something like Jasmine in it and studied her breasts, which provoked a soft delicious, warm erection. She must have noticed it because she lightly blushed, but acted as if nothing was happening. I smiled   thinking that maybe she was pleased to see that every time we met I had a rosary of erections.

- When the moment will come, I hope you will be magnanimous.

She did not reply and took another sip from her martini, always with the little finger up.

- Let's take a break Jean Pierre. I brought Orfea along because I wanted her to hear about Africa.

She smiled as if she knew what I just had been thinking.

The stories about this other civilization, really other in its basic values, its behavior, rules, moral values and impossible to grasp customs, had impressed her. The stories about the two girls getting married in Ivory Coast and the Liberian "name calling" as well as the social role and value of the marriage dowry, the mother-in-law avoidance and more, fascinated them and we laughed goodheartedly.

Looking with surprise at us, some customers of the neighboring tables brought along their chairs to listen. They generously provided me with beer. Never had I had an improvised audience of such good humor. I had to tell the "name calling" story over and over which made them laugh loud.

A long time ago the night had eaten the afternoon. Helena asked a couple if they could take me to the hacienda. Fifteen kilometers in the car between Ofelia and Helena, holding her hand with her head on my shoulder was a great moment, still remembered.

The middle-aged gentleman who served as driver leaving the motor running said: Up to here. Helena stepped out of the car with me. We kissed with passion our bodies searching each other. Without

shame I felt the ejaculation and my spermatozoids searching their way to my left knee, which was not the good natural way. But so what? She was aware of what was going on in my pants and smiled, whispering to my ear: "Good luck with your life". A tear was running down her cheek. I stuttered: "Good luck with your life too" also with tears running into my beard.
- You are a good man.
- You are a good woman, don't get lost.
In the headlights of the car, I passed through the wired fence and started walking waving for the last time to the silhouette that stood behind the open car door and who also had her arm up.
This was a love that never was.
I walked the two kilometers of dusty road with the Southern Cross in front of me, along a huge pool where thousands of frogs were making fun of me.

*

Campeche, 19 th September 2007

Dear Helena,
Thirty seven years have gone by since we met. I suppose that you recuperated the Hacienda and Orfea her horse. I hope that you have had a good life and that you continued to be preoccupied for the others as you showed me you were. I hope too that you were loved very much and that you had all the lovers you desired because one has to live completely his desires and his loves. I hope too that the Stalinist intermezzo in Chili did not leave you with wounds or harshness but that you have gained from that experience the wisdom, which our daily preoccupations and routine often make us forget, that not everybody is living the way we do; something that fools too often forget, until it falls on their heads. The poor who cannot stand any longer their poverty do not have many ways to let us know that they want to be accounted for. They don't write in the newspapers and don't have TV stations programs. I am sure that you discovered that beside you oppressed people live, unhappy people who have been treated with injustice. Whether that injustice is divine or human does not change the matter.
Finall, I hope that you lived every day completely and that you passed without harm to your soul the black years of the Pinochet dictatorship that did not have any compassion with the poets who made mistakes. Even so, that it is no excuse: our youth was our youth.

The Hedonist

On what I have been reading recently, the Chileans are doing well :
The country grows more than any other in the Americas, even so that
you elected for President two times a socialist and even an agnostic
woman who keeps herself of becoming an extremist (what Allende did
not manage to do).
In 1985 I was offered a job in Chili in the Mapuche region. I did not
take it because I was afraid to meet you, which of course would have
been inevitable. Things among us are good the way they are.
Thank you for having been my greatest love that never was.
Good luck with your life.

Jean Pierre

*

Waking up in the morning, I went to see the head of our expropriation
team, or agrarian reform team, whichever you like, to tell him that the
next Monday I would go back to Santiago. He only shook his head to
let me know that it was ok. Even though I was under an enormous
nostalgic desire to see Paule, I did not want to miss the fiesta in a
small dwelling about a couple of hours on horseback from the
hacienda, to which the headman had invited me.

Dressed up like a real Chilean ranch owner: large manta, boots
and hand sized silver spurs, woolen gloves and a large brim black
sombrero: all this was lent to me by the headman and belonged to
the real owner, the one who wanted to kill me, and kept in a trunk
under the headman's bed. I felt like a real hacienda owner. We
pushed the horses into gallop in the valleys and dismounted and
walked the steep hills.

That village was not a village, only a dusty street with a couple
of dozens of wooden two-room houses on each side, looking more
like mountain refuges. At the end after the last house, stood a four
pole structure with a red plastic roof on which was written Coca Cola
with the characteristic letters of that beverage. In the entire fiesta I did
not see a single bottle of Coca Cola. We left the horses, the mantas
and the spurs to keep at one of the houses of someone familiar to my
companion. We just got there in time to see the last steps of a
procession. Four men carrying on their shoulders a board on which
stood the statue of a saint – I don't remember which one- the carriers
must have been thinking of something else because the saint almost
finished in the drain along the road. He was followed by six musicians
playing drums, trumpets and one accordion, a dozen children and two

dozen women dressed in traditional Mapuche outfits, very colorful and beautiful with their heavy silverwork collars and chest pieces, made up the procession. We took off our hats and put one knee to the ground when the saint passed. The women prayed Ave Marias. I did not see a priest.

Barely the saint put into the chapel, which distinguished itself from the other structures thanks to a wooden cross planted besides the door, the horses races started; two at a time, in a straight line, right on the dusty road. There were races of 100 and 200 meters. On the porch of one house, two very large representatives of the female gender dispensed white wine, not in glasses but in a one liter cardboard buckets, also tortas and bread with roasted meat, or greasy sheep bowels with onions and green peppers. I tried one of each. One finished off my throat, the other one, my stomach. Tired that everybody I crossed offered me to drink from his bucket and also of feigning to drink while all I did was just wet my lips, I retreated to a small elevation to see the horse's races from above. Since I was not betting, they did not really interest me, but some were spectacular and some horses ended up in the ditch.

It must have been around three in the afternoon when the musicians started to play under the red Coca Cola tent. At that time I already had a reasonable headache from the white wine I don't hold very well. Dancing started. Up until then I had not seen a single woman less than forty years old. I don't know where they came from but yes, there also were girls in this place, heavy, short, with long black hair framing expressionless faces, no smiles. I even found them looking afraid and grave as if they were doing the most serious thing of their whole life. I got bored fast and returned to the races.

The public had already diminished, they had fallen, some in the ditches, some between the houses and some just at the edge of the road. This started to look like a battlefield after the battle, with corpses of the fallen scattered all over. Some had fallen one on top of the other like couples in love. As you know, I had been seeing some pretty heavy drinking in my short life: in Liberia, Nigeria, Germany, Antwerp, Heur and other places, but something like this, never. People just drank till they fell and where they fell they stayed, until recovering a semblance of consciousness by way of the bitter cold or when a partner, a little less drunk than they were, drew them over their horse's saddle. I felt better when the overseer came to sit by my side. I offered my wine bucket which he declined.

- Thanks, we have some road to ride.

He did not completely finish his sentence when from under the Coca Cola tent came a horrendous scream, followed by more shouting and screaming of which I did not understand a word. A bunch of people ran away from under the red tent. A young boy running on the dust road screamed something to my partner from which I understood that somebody had knifed somebody else for dancing with the, apparently, wrong girl which did not please the murderer. My partner got on his feet.

- Lets go!

On which he took off to the place where we had left our horses and spurs. Because of the, I don't know how many, liters of white wine making waves in my stomach, I had difficulty in keeping up with him. In less time than it takes to tell it, we collected our mantas and spurs, saddled the horses and galloped toward a bunch of trees which we reached when the last sunrays disappeared behind the hills putting the small bush in the dark. We stopped to adjust the saddles and put on our mantas and spurs.

- What happened?
- A boy knifed another for a matter of skirts. It often happens.
- I know, but why are we on the run?

He gave me a paternalistic look, with some compassion in his eyes.

- Because of the police
- I haven't seen any police.
- They will be here soon, and in a very bad mood. Anybody still there is going to be treated as if they were assassins or witnesses: the treatment for both is the same.

He laughed at his own joke.

- And why are we not going on the road?
- That's where the police will come from. When it gets dark we will return to the road.

We mounted and from vineyard through vineyard and wood through wood watching carefully for branches, leaving the reins loose on the horses' necks. The half clouded sky of the afternoon had given way to a splendid densely stars sown firmament. Such splendor resulted in my taking some branches straight in the face. When finally we returned to the road, the horses went by themselves. The wine and the excitement had got the best of me and I felt tiredness creeping over my body. Getting to ride by the side of my partner I heard that he was snoring, he knew how to stay straight in the saddle, sleeping. I still had a lot to learn to be a real cowboy. The clothes do not make the man! An African proverb says: "The piece of wood can drift for a hundred years in the river; it will never become a crocodile".

Two events welcomed me in Santiago: The first one was the official visit of Fidel Castro to Chile and the second one was the daily demonstration of "empty pots and pans". This latter was made up of middle class housewives, and their maids, beating pots with sticks and spoons, making a very loud concert in the central streets of downtown Santiago. Paule told me that the supply of food had considerably declined, that there were queues at every shop and that prices were sky rocketing; that public transport was continuously striking and more. It looked like the socialist management of shops was not any better that its agrarian reform.

The Cuban delegation brought in its luggage professor Isabelle Monal with whom we passed an almost complete night drinking wine and trying not to talk politics, which was impossible. It seemed to me that the communist governments in their practice and results looked very much like the military dictatorships, even if speeches and intentions are opposite. At that, she called me "petit bourgeois". When I told her that in reality the agrarian reform did not come out as expected, she almost treated me as a CIA agent and tried to convince me that more than ever the armed guerilla was the only way to tumble the capitalist system. Popular polls, elections, parliamentary systems were simply pushed off the table. When I tried to remind her that Fidel Castro had promised free elections six months after he came to power by arms, and that he never lived up to that promise, she eventually labeled me as plain counter revolutionary. A dialogue of the deaf, without interest, in which disqualifying the other and calling him all the names in the book, stood for argumentation: a tactic of dialectics, very well known and used by dictators and fanatics. At that time, and ever since, the Cuban establishment had left the ground and taken off from the reality airport. Their realities had become whatever the dictator said. "What's the time?", "Whatever time you say, chief".

*

Even so early as eleven in the morning, the wine bar of the Alameda Avenue, at a couple of blocks from the Moneda presidential palace, was almost full. As it was Saturday, this is very usual in Santiago. Aranciabia, my date, was not in a good mood at all, he just finished to explain to me how the social democrats, to whom he belonged, component of the Popular Union government were losing ground and fighting the retro guard battles against the assaults of the

191

more radical and leftist movements of the Allende government. He did not like the situation at all and this kept him very preoccupied.

I knew Arancibia since Cuba, we liked each other at first sight, and even so that, in Habana he never had pronounced a single word which was not related to a joke, a story or a banality. He was a chest champion; I had seen him play a multiple game all alone against twenty counterparts, playing while walking along the tables. He won them all. He also was a mathematician and as said, a leading member of the social democrats in Chile.

- It's crazy to believe that we Chileans are going to accept the kind of life that Castro imposes on the Cubans by way of repression and arms. It's crazy I am telling you!

He took his wine glass and almost emptied it, putting it back on the table with a movement of disgust; I thought he was going to crush it.

- Do you realize with what kind of rhetoric Castro keeps the revolution alive? All the manipulations and tricks, with poor simplistic arguments are there, as if he was selling detergent soap, inventing all the time external and internal enemies - and if he does not find them he makes them up. We don't want that!

At this hour, coffee is all I can hold so I slurped my cup before trying to reply something to keep him calm.

- Don't bother, you know and we all know that the Caribbean building will tumble from its own weight.

- Sure I do, but when? After having sacrificed how many generations? We all know that socialism, the Cuban way, is going to be in history only a parenthesis between savage capitalism and liberal capitalism. But I don't want to be held accounted for the repression and the scarcity of everything, only to see if my utopias are going to work.

A waiter filled up his glass with chilled white wine and my somewhat stupid coffee cup. This did not stop him.

- The Cuban socialism is a religious, platonic type construction, they believe what they say and create realities that don't exist.

I thought I had to say something because the neighboring tables started to look at us. Taking advantage that he half emptied his glass I jumped on the occasion:

- With the few things I have seen from Chile I don't believe that that is going to stick; you are more pragmatic than the Caribbean pachanga dancers.

He looked up from his glass and fixed me with his clear eyes.

- I think so too, but what the price is and who is going to pay?

I felt uncomfortable having such an intense conversation, both of us sitting on the edge of our wooden chairs, elbows on the table, trying to get as close to each other as the table allowed us to do, so I let my buttocks glide to the back of the chair and took a long breath. The wine bar had become completely full, even with people waiting on the door, most customers were couples, rather young couples who drank white wine while holding hands over the table and mostly looking each other in the eyes, very romantic, very Latin. It seemed that our table was the only one where bad mood reigned. All the tables around us were occupied, so it seemed impossible to follow up with this conversation.

- Professor, do you know the difference between the socialist, the communist and the Castro dialectics?

First time a smile painted on his face. As I knew him, a good story or joke would get his good spirits back.

- No, but you are going to tell me, no?

- Well: socialist dialectic is like searching for a black cat in a dark room; communist dialectics is searching for a black cat in a dark room knowing that the black cat is not there and Castro dialectics is searching for a black cat in a dark room, knowing that the black cat is not there but screaming "I got it ".

Passed a few seconds before the respectable mathematician let go a loud, very loud laugh, so loud that the whole place fell silent and looked at us. When he finished wiping the tears running down his cheeks and into his beard where they disappeared as a river running into an underground cave, he came closer and whispered:

- Do you have time tomorrow, Sunday?

- Yes, I do!

- Come along to visit an old friend in the country, I pick you up at ten, it's only a one hour drive.

He got up, left some money on the table and we walked into the fresh air. At the far, far end of the Alameda avenue stand the first mountains of the Andes, most of the time covered with snow, as if it was their faith to wear a night cap day and night. Of course, the Alameda Avenue is mostly windy and fresh. On the sidewalk we said goodbye with a lot of embracing and back tapping, the Latin way. Arancibia kept laughing; the dialectic story had put him in a great mood.

Just a little bit after eleven, the mathematician turned the key of his car and the motor stopped not without having back kicked a couple of times, in front of an isolated hacienda in the Mapocho Valley. For almost an hour we had been driving through fields and more flat fields of different crops and some villages where complete families, on chairs and even on couches, sat in front of their door, drinking wine or slurping maté. On the road my friend had talked me about our destination: an elderly man, Latinist, something like the brain trust of the Chilean social democracy, who lived alone with two female servants in an huge hacienda which, when I saw it, impressed by its solitude in the midst of fertile fields, surrounded with huge trees that made it invisible from distance and golf court cut lawns. Without a pound of fat, tall, erect in a three piece grey suit and abundant grey hair falling half neck, holding a fine walk stick with what I presumed was an ivory pommel; the outstanding garn was a black manta loosely hanging over his shoulders. Salutations and introductions were friendly, with looks straight in the eyes: the old man, at once, was evaluating and measuring me. As expected, his living room was walled from floor to ceiling with book shelves, some behind glass doors, all around a huge fireplace in which trunks were glittering. Four comfortable armchairs surrounded a tea table in front. A soft light, because of the cloudy day, filtered through three huge arched windows. Unmistakably this was a philosophers cave. I thought that if one day I would become a philosopher, this was the place I wanted to live in: everything talked about intelligence and equilibrium.

Barely seated, in a simple natural way the host questioned me. He wanted to know where I came from. For not leaving doubts and as briefly as I could I told him the stories about the seminar, Africa, The American University, May ´68 in Paris, Cuba up to the agrarian reform in Bulnes. Doing so, I did realize for the first time that, yes, there was already something to tell and that the story must have been cheerful because at different times my listeners laughed and smiled a lot. All this was done sipping maté, a heavily overweighed aged woman, dressed in traditional Mapuche wear, with her dress sweeping the carpets and a long hair braid falling on her hips (if hips there were under the multiple colored cloth layers) filled now and then with boiling water. I don't like maté much, it is bitter but is believed to do a lot of good to your intestines, even if at that time mine were doing great. After some twenty minutes of talking I let myself fall to the back of the armchair. The host rang a small hand bell, which I had not seen before and had the magic to make appear the Mapuche woman carrying a silver plate on which stood a Bourbon bottle, and three glasses. Yes, now we were cooking.
- So you did pass an intense religious experience?
The tone was soft and nothing inquisitive.
- Oh, yes, and since then I spend a lot of time verifying and relearning.

194

- That's the way real life goes: you learn, you question and then you relearn.
- It takes a lot of time but those who don't relearn have not learned.
- That's the way it is young man. Religion since the Greeks was defined as: "blind faith in whatever the chief says or the dogma stipulates" Lucrecio defined the concept saying that the religions are born from the lack of culture and knowledge. The believer satisfies himself with faith because he is ignorant, because it is the easy way to make sense of anything. Faith does not need thinking, proofs or to be sustained, it stands and holds up all by itself; that's also why we can believe in anything - and most people do. He also said that the sacrifices to the divinities, the myths and the illusions proceed from the lack of information and comprehension of nature. Weakness, fears, anguish are the things that fill up heaven. Reason, intelligence, knowledge empty it. When the philosopher is at work in each of us, the priest backs up.

I never had heard about the guy Lucrecio, but that sounded as logic and common sense as it could be. Arancibia started to act as our waiter and served us a half glass of Bourbon, which I took on the rocks and them straight. Our host drew his manta over his legs and staring at the red trunks followed up as if we were not there.

- Lucrecio was not the only one to question the Gods, Leucipe, centuries before, already said that the Gods should leave their space to mankind; there was also Democrite, Aristipe, Diogene, Epicure, Philodeme of Gardana and many more who taught the same thing. But we know little about them; the work of Plato, Christianity and San Jerome, who was particularly active to erase the Greek and Roman philosophers, had passed and erased everything they could get their hands on. He made a pause, so I dared:
- What was going on in other places besides Greece and Rome?

Without looking up, fixing the fire in which now and then he moved a trunk with his stick the end of which. I noticed, was wrapped up in a metal sheet.

- Sure, in other places to a lot of thinking was going on, Working brains are not a monopole of the Europeans, at the contrary: in Babylon, China, India and other places the Greeks considered as barbarians, the same tendencies of thoughts were going on. I talk about Lucrecio because he belongs to our civilization, nothing else.

He stopped and gripped his glass. Arancibia and I stood up to make our glasses touch; their sound told me that this was first class crystal. I expected a toast, something like: "To the Popular Union "or "To Allende" but nobody said anything. We irrigated our throats in silence. Since I was the youngest I considered that it was my duty to keep the fire burning, so I put two trunks over the almost burnt ones which immediately started to send red and white sprinkles through the chimney as if it was topped by a big aspirator. The master of the Hacienda and of such profound philosophic thinking had not moved from his chair, and putting his glass on the small table he kept talking to my great delight.

- To deny reality, usually not pleasant, and substitute it with theoretic constructions and fantasies, is an old story. Plato, alumni of Socrates invented the concept. Since then, all the monotheist religions have adopted it and it became the source of inspiration of Paul of Tarse, the worst psychopath case of Jewish history, which counts with quite a few psychopaths, and so the platonic concept entered Christianity.

I ventured:

- I have heard a lot about Plato and Saint Paul, but what do they say exactly?

He turned his head to me and I was surprised with the livelihood in his eyes, yes, he was having fun.

- Its simple, Plato says that what you see, touch, feel, the real things; are not real. The true reality is not visible but is in the ideas, the concepts, the ideals and the magnificent things your brain produces. The Plato philosophy includes: the immaterial soul, hatred of life here below, and taste for the life after life in a Paradise, suffering as an essential way to salvation and the hatred of pleasures in particular the pleasures provided by woman. The opposite of Plato is: wanting to be happy on earth while you are alive, here and now, and not in an hypothetical paradise painted as a children's tale. The antitheses of Plato are reality; live while you are alive and the material as sole reality.

- So, Plato is the origin of the values and beliefs of our civilization?

- Yes, probably true.

- How to resist this imposture in which all are participating?

He took a long breath and without quitting my eyes:

- Diminishing the anguishes and the fears of existence. Domesticating death with an active therapy of living it up here and now. Living more intensely, so that the end of it will be less dramatic. Building solutions with mankind and the world, refusing to make suffering a way of individual salvation; cultivating pleasure and searching for it; composing with your body and the pleasures it procures. Actually, the counter project of Plato is the simple pleasure of existence; a project very much of actuality, now and forever.

I still did not understand very well why Arancibia had brought me to this Hacienda, but I will be grateful to him as long as I live. We took another Bourbon Arancibia had served without interrupting and turning towards him, the Chilean philosopher said:

- You know that Platonism is also present in the surrounding of our President. The boys and girls of the extreme left who are filling up his immediate surrounding: the MIR, the communists, the intellectuals a la mode and the other vanguard brigades of all the revolutionary chapels are isolating and disconnecting Allende from reality. A man who is basically a humanist and a social democrat and we, the parliamentarian socialists have not a chance to make our point but yes, we will pay the bills of the disaster to come.

He turned away from Arancibia who gave me a signal to leave the room. I walked into the chilly grey air to make a solitary walk around the park surrounding the Hacienda; found a wooden bench under a huge maple tree; lighted up a cigarette to watch the blue smoke mingle with the low grey sky. I felt good, completely satisfied to better understand the why and how's of things and of my own life, feeling by instinct that there is no real happiness possible in ignorance and without understanding and that this understanding and wisdom is infinite. It was well into the afternoon when Arancibia came out. We said goodbye the Latin way and kept looking and waving at the slim silhouette leaning on his walk stick, who kept waving his arm in the air when we drove away. I never knew his name.

The Fidel Castro visit came to an end. It is during this visit that Fidel Castro gave Allende the gold plated Russian Kalashnikov, Salvador would die with about a couple of years later, and that were agreed upon the huge shipments of arms that Cuba was going to send to Chile. These arms were not sent to the Chilean army but were meant to arm the syndicates, the communist party and all kinds of leftist revolutionary movements. It could be that the unloading of these armaments in the Valparaiso harbor, under the nose of the Chilean fleet, is one of the provocations which were the drop that made overflow the patience of the military. As Allende himself said "we are heading towards a civil war", this did not leave much space for any other solution. Civil war is the cornerstone of the Guevarist strategy for establishing the reign of socialism.

The Hedonist

When I went to the great meeting at the University of Chile campus, of all the parties and movements of the Chilean left who from far or near had something to do with agriculture; the problem of a possible military coup or uprising had been resolved. Feeling that his thirty and something percent of the popular vote was not enough to establish the socialist paradise, Allende had resolved the problem by way of a government decree which stated "The Chilean army respects the constitution". Surprisingly, in such a short time, the government of the Popular Union was already in an advanced stage of Platonism, applying what Joseph Stalin said: "When reality does not match our ideology, we suppress reality".

As in the students meeting in the Odeon theatre in Paris in 1968, everybody was talking, shouting at the same time. Everybody wanted to be the chief and the chiefs disputed among themselves to see who was going to make the most revolutionary statement. The subject of the agrarian reform was hardly touched to leave space for statements of general political nature. As good Platonists and at this level of general politics, the Stalinist dialectic is very strong. These masters of political orientations despise technical, practical, scientific, workable considerations which generally they consider of lower and less noble value. These items are considered good for the lower level technicians, not dignified enough for them. Their theme is: ideology, politics and purity in revolutionary orientations.

There were several Cubans – most of them very brown or black - probably forgotten from the Castro suitcases, who conscientiously took notes.

One representative of the famous communist youth brigades "Parra" finally got a semblance of order, pronouncing a speech in which the armed struggle was recognized as the only way to establish true socialism and the heroic constitutional sense of the Chilean army etc... At the end he asked if someone had a question.

As I was in a good spirits, I raised my hand and standing up, asked:
- What will happen if the army does not respect the constitution?
It seemed to me that that was a good question taking into account the Bulnes experience where the military and the oligarchy obviously behaved like chalk and cheese. The revolutionaries around me were silent. The speaker asked to repeat the question. Clearing my throat, articulating as a BBC speaker, pronouncing slowly every syllable:
- What will happen if the army turns out to be not as respectful of the constitution as we believe it is?

Apparently nobody had ever thought of that possibility. In my vicinity the space was emptying as if I had some contagious disease. Silence gained half of the theater, and then came the response:
- There is a foreign comrade here, I don't know where he comes from, who is trying to split up and divide us and our socialist revolution.
I don't remember everything but I was accused in public of being a CIA agent, paid by the oligarchy and the Chilean reactionaries, and some more. Some of my neighbors started pointing fingers at me and shouted names in which appeared my mother. Then they started to push me to the exit, hitting me wherever they could reach me. Fortunately some girls from MIR recognized me and tried to protect me pushing me further to the door. I did not ask for more: only to get out of there. Once outside I flew down the few stairs and ran all I could run from the campus. If it had not been for these MIR girls, I would have been lynched on the first lamppost they could find. When out of reach, I felt an immense sadness and sorrow, I cried in anger, feeling that this was the final act of our contribution to the construction of Chilean socialism.

*

Years later, in the eighties, I crossed my main accuser in this famous assembly, on the Louvre bridge in Paris. We recognized each other and saluted. He had saved his butt and was a guardian at the Louvre Museum in the section of Flemish painters, while so many good friends and buddies had paid the fires of their youth with prison, violation and torture, were thrown out of airplanes and helicopters or buried alive in the concentration camps of the Pinochet dictatorial regime.
It is difficult to be merciful with the great imbeciles who, in a certain way, are responsible of the bloodshed and death of those who blindly believed what imbeciles, like him, proclaimed as certain and real.

*

When I told Paule what had happened, we knew that it was the end of our Chilean story. Two weeks later we climbed into a bus that crosses the Andes to Mendoza, Argentine and further to Rosario, from where, after having traveled for two days without leaving sunflower fields, on a fresh early morning we disembarked in Buenos Aires

The Hedonist

In my backpack, hidden in a double bottom were several letters and notes from the leftist opposition from Argentine, Uruguay and Brazil who with the coming to power of Allende in Chile had made their headquarters in Santiago for their struggle against the Latin American military dictators. Some of them I had known in Cuba. The people who are on the move live on a micro-planet.

An ex-colleague of Paule, from the time she was working for the United Nations in New York offered us hospitality. The people of Buenos Aires were very suspicious, secrete and there were soldiers all over the place. The friends of our hostess refused to talk about anything else but the weather, the incredibly high prices of the "asado" and the beauty of Paris. When they talked about such or such who had been taken from his home by soldiers at four in the morning and had disappeared, they whispered.

Soon, I got accustomed to the high opinion the "Porteños" (inhabitants of Buenos Aires) have of themselves. The joke that they commit suicide by shooting a pistol thirty centimeters above their head, in their superiority complex, is almost true. That they will climb the nearby hill just to look at the city to see how the place looks like when they are not there, is true too. It seemed to me that they imagined that they were living in London but wanted to live in Paris. Almost all of them held two jobs: One to pay for living and one to pay for the psychiatrist.

In these conditions, it would have been crazy to distribute the mail I brought from Santiago, just going around knocking on doors. So I opened the letters and selected what could be sent through the regular mail and what politically speaking would bring problems to the addressee. The girlfriends, mothers and wives of the revolutionaries hidden in Chile, will forgive me: they only received love letters. The rest I burned in the small garden of our hostess.. They will have to forgive me for this cowardice, but it was not really the moment (it never is) for the political police of the local dictators to discover we were the postmen for the revolutionary opposition. In the best of cases they would have thrown us in jail with some torturing, in the worst case they would have thrown us out of a high flying helicopter or plane over the blue ocean. Some of these letters plainly and simply talked about arms and hold ups. I felt honored by the confidence they had put in me, but the repression of the Argentina dictators was no joke. Two Europeans, coming from Chile, did not pass unnoticed in the colonels' Argentina.

A couple of weeks later we climbed on board of the transatlantic Michelangelo. An Italian line cruiser as its name indicates, sailing to Europe with stopovers in Montevideo, Rio de Janeiro, Recife, Lisbon, Barcelona and Cannes. This was the second time I was crossing the Atlantic on a cruiser, but this time with a fully paid ticket, even if the ticked was second class - the third class did not exist anymore.

It is still crystal clear in my memory: the very slow entrance of the Michelangelo into the Rio de Janeiro bay in a misty early morning, the "sugar cone" rising out of the mist as if it were the praetorian guardian of the city. We clung to each other on the floor of the highest place attainable of the upper deck, wrapped up in blankets letting ourselves be consumed by the spectacle of a new day rising over Rio and the first sunrays lighting up the sugar cone and the bay. It's something unforgettable.

The Rio stopover lasted three days and we decided to spend two nights ashore. Getting off the ship later on with our backpacks over our shoulders, I noticed the presence of a man with a straw hat, white moustaches in a brown face, an impeccable white shirt and also impeccable black tie reaching his also white trousers which half covered his white shoes. He looked at us in a straight way, with an agreeable smile. At first, I thought that he was a contact of the Valpalmares revolutionary movement for which I was carrying mail. (I also had, stored in the back of my brain, verbal messages, learned by heart to transmit.) I had good friends from Valpalmares, first known in Havana and later in Santiago, but something inside told me not to reveal the passwords to this guy, and to be on guard. The individual followed us. When we took the bus, he did too. He sat three rows behind us. When we got off the bus he also got off. All the time we walked in the historical quarter, I noticed him a dozen meters behind; when we stopped, he did; when we entered a café he stayed on the doorstep. That carioca was getting on my nerves.

I thought to get rid of him entering a small hotel. We wanted to take a shower and make love. When we came out, hours later, he was sitting in the lobby. This was not a Valpalmares contact but he looked very much like an agent from the Brazilian secret police, in charge of surveying each step we made. I walked over to him and with my most friendly smile invited him for a coffee which, surprisingly, he accepted with a large smile. I even asked him to take us to a good coffee joint, but that was nonsense, in Rio all are excellent. We walked a couple of blocks with this Sherlock Holmes from the Brazilian dictators who did not stop telling us about the marvels of the city, the things I had to look out for, where the best beaches were and how to get there and the magnificence of its churches. I thought that the Brazilian government must have had a high opinion of us for giving us a private tourist guide. He was a nice man, very sociable, soft, serviceable, delicate, and sympathetic. A few times I surprised him with a cold expression in his eyes and a very fine, stiff, mouth line. He probably was a delicate torturer.

We drank coffee and cachaça. We talked about our travels from Mexico- without mentioning Cuba or Chile – to Argentina although I was sure he knew it all. There we were, collaborators of the Valpalmares revolutionary movement and also of the Tupamaros of Uruguay and others, sipping coffee and cachaça, joking and laughing with a secret agent from the Brazilian dictatorship, but what could I do? Better do nothing and erase from my brain as soon as possible the memorized messages. We walked around some more, had more coffees and cachaça and took the bus back to the hotel, where he entered with us and bending over the counter talked to the receptionist, who started to give us dirty looks. I did not get anything of what was being said, but guessed that at our slightest movement at night or phone calls, this fat man was going to call our secret agent or any other one like him.

Pushing the door next day, I expected him to be there, but instead there was another guy, younger and less easygoing. He just contented himself walking a dozen steps behind us and on the beach sat on the sand almost beside Paule. At least we were assured that nobody was going to steal our clothes while we bathed.

Regretfully, I got rid of all the mail I was still carrying, dispersing them over the Atlantic Ocean. I had read them all and none was of a nature to change the history of Latin America.

*

The crossing of the Atlantic was a feast of dolce farniente. Five full days of eating, making love, sleeping, playing cards, making love, eating, reading, making love, swimming in the pool, participating in stupid deck games, making love.......I remember that I won a disguise contest, dressed as a gaucho with the souvenirs I had brought along: a Chilean cap, the wide bordered hat, my beautiful silver spurs from Bulnes. I won the contest; this gained me the friendship of an Argentinean middle aged woman, good looking, not very tall, blue eyes and a vivid spirit. She was Jewish and had that people's great sense of humor. She laughed a lot behind the back of the young Italian officer whom she had made her lover for the cruise and talked with surprising freedom of her sexual relations with that Italian, which she did not like too much because he went "to the cave". I had difficulty in getting it because at that time of my sexual life, I was still thinking that the tongue is the organ you kiss, talk and eat with.

*

Israel... my sons and other readers: I regret very much to tell you that I don't think neither I, nor you, will see the end of that struggle among Abraham's offspring that sometimes degenerates into straight out war between Middle East Semites. As said the humorist Guy Bedos: "Here there are too many great actors for the same play. Abraham, Jesus and Muhammad all want the main role. How do you want that to work? One is an infanticide, the other one a psychopath who takes himself for God's son and the third one went to heaven seated on a white horse! Why not on a pink elephant? Don't you think that here we are in the presence of heavy dope? And just thinking that the fan-clubs of these three individuals, not very normal, keep killing themselves since centuries: it's enough to lose your faith"

If the major problem of Ramses II, great among the great Egyptian Pharaohs, was Palestine we can be sure that the problem is not going to be settled tomorrow.

For what reason the three monotheist religions, two of which want to conquer the world with the catastrophic consequences we know, were all born in this very small region?

Why here, of all possible places in the whole world, intelligence got separated from reason? Why in this small piece of world geography reason renounced its powers, losing its advantages putting itself at the level of irrational faith, and religions were created? Why in a period of a few thousand years the three sacred books were written? (The first Torah verses about one thousand BC and the Talmud during the Babylonian exile in 500 BC. The four evangels around 300 AC and the actual version of the Koran around one thousand of our era)

The dates are not certain, because none of these books has an author but many who, over the centuries modified, added, erased and adapted according to dominant political interest and the "politically correct" of the moment. It does not really matter. What is important is to notice that it is the Jews who invented the concept of monotheism (inspired by the Egyptian solar cult). And why did they do that? Simple: just to make possible the very survival of that small people, giving them a value of cohesion and existence. The mythology invented by them, permitting the creation of a warrior God, bloodthirsty, vindictive, aggressive, war chief, is very useful to mobilize the enthusiasm of a people without land. The myth of the people elected by God, founded the existence of a nation with a destiny.

It's interesting to count the pages of the foundations of our civilization: the Old Testament counts around three thousand five hundred; the New Testament around nine hundred and the Koran seven hundred and fifty. In about five thousand pages all, and the contrary of all, is said.

In each of these books, contradictions are abundant. When something is affirmed, immediately after the contrary is also affirmed. In such a way that everything can be used by everyone. Everyone encounters in these books what is convenient: Justification of an all out war of extermination or a call to universal peace. A misogynist wants to prove the inferiority of women? A believer, his hatred of the Palestinians? All the justifications needed are there. Hitler founded his extermination of the Jewish people on the parables of Jesus chasing the merchants from the temple, while Martin Luther King found justification for non-violence in the same book. The state of Israel finds its justification for colonizing Palestine. The Muslims find justification, waving the Koran, to throw them into the sea and exterminate them.

Yahweh gave Moses the famous Fifth Amendment "Thou shall not kill ". When God speaks, he speaks in a simple way of primary school teaching: simple future. This does not give any space for discussions. This establishes a program of non-violence, peace, love, pardon, tolerance. There is no space for: war, violence, armies, death penalty, the crusades, the inquisition, the atomic bomb, assassination, bonfires. All these things however are practiced by believers and defenders of the Bible. Why do they do this? Most likely because the same Yahweh, some pages later, justifies that the Jews exterminate a few populations he designates by name and forename: The Hittites, the Canaanites, the Jezubites, the Invites and the Permisites. All those people were also living in Palestine. Yahweh, who likes details, also tells them how to do it: "You will destroy their altars, their monuments and you will kill them". The vocabulary includes words like: destroy, burn, dispose; actually total war. In the case of Jericho and the Canaanites, Yahweh justifies the massacre of all that lives: men, women, children, sheep, goats, oxen, donkeys etc... (The text says: "small animals"). Everything has to be passed by the sword. The conquest of Canaan and the taking of Jericho are at the expense of all

living things. This way the Jews, by order of Yahweh, have the privilege of committing the first genocide of human history.
What to think? Where is: "Thou shall not kill"?

What has this small piece of earth to it that makes it so prolific in metaphysics that millions of people only swear in its name? It is arid, great regions of unfertile land from which it is difficult to extract a living, cut up by small barely fertile valleys. In one word: a desert. Moses, Jesus and Mohamed are sand pilgrims. The desert is a space of truth: either you survive or you die, you don't have the alternative of green valleys, rich pastures and forests; it is a place of constant combat against nature in order to survive. Rights or prohibition to pasture extend or diminish life. Renan in his "History of Israel" and also Regis Debray in "The road of God" write that the desert is monotheist. This is the ecosystem in which monotheism was created. Contrary to the forest and temperate regions where the fantastic and the mysterious are related to nature, tales of animals, flowers and trees, abundance and softness. Here nobody invented a God that stopped the march of the sun so that his followers have more daylight to exterminate   the last man, woman and child, as they believe it was the case in the conquest of Jericho.

A couple of thousand years later, the American Negroes invented a beautiful gospel about the walls of Jericho tumbling down. I hope they did not know what this all was about. To me, it sounds like making a nice song about a Nazi extermination camp or the tumbling of the twin towers in New York.

It's likely that God likes a hostile nature with extreme temperatures, rocks, sand and moonlike landscapes, for having something "inhuman", where it is easier to imagine and accept a "supreme and absolute chief" who proclaims "You shall be faithful to me and I will protect you". This is the God of monotheism who arose in the desert. In the same way – the desert - it is also explainable that the monotheisms seek perpetual expansionism as a prolongation of pastoral nomads. To exist is to march. For Regis Debray the desert is the most implacable enemy of pluralism, saying that the desert is a "spiritual boiler and a cultural suffocated". The fanatics of this God made their homes in: Saudi Arabia, Palestine, Iran, Afghanistan and Iraq or in the Arizona desert: all of them negative spaces which suppose an effort of purification and expansion.

*

I went back to Europe on a cruiser with a new companion, married to get a visa which finally I did not get. But what a great fortune that was. Do I have to thank the Cuban praetorians of the longest dictatorship in the world? I wonder.

CHAPTER V
BAMAKO- BAGIMONT -PARIS

I am not going to say very much about the Parisian junction between Santiago de Chile and Bamako, Mali. Because there is not much to say besides that I learned to ski and appreciate the majesty of the Alps in company of a new friend: Chantal who taught me all this and still is a dear friend of our couple.

*

Yes Madam, yes Sir, besides my somewhat advanced age and my half century of smoking like a sugar cane mill chimney – a thing that I am permanently trying to give up – I still walk on the floating cages like a young man, which fills me with pride when helping or looking at some of these youngsters, forty years younger, crawling on their hands and knees like pre- Cro Magnons. (I have my small prides as you have). There are one hundred and fifty thousand small fish - fingerlings we call them - swimming and charged with all our hopes that one day they will make us live a decent life - or even a little better one. This is a piece of hope I have been carrying now for twenty years of which nine in Mexico, sharing it with my friends, who also got stricken by my fish culture fever: Willy, Patou, Patrick and in a lesser way Paule. Paule never really got passionate about my trade. I don't know why? Maybe since the time we lived in Chad where we had chickens and she fed them. From the moment she begun to take care of these chickens, they started to lose their feathers and soon were completely naked. To my judgment this was a nice thing, shortening the way to convert them into fried chicken. But Paule was disgusted

206

and decided that she brought bad luck to animals. I don't know. We all have our irrationalities.

I made this short escape to the fish farm because today we got the results of the fish count and I wanted to share it with you.

*

Thanks to Paule who returned to the UNESCO, one day we boarded a plane to Bamako, Mali where she had got a job for this very respectable and very bureaucratic organization. I accompanied as a half-spouse, lover and companion, which entitled me to a flashy diplomatic passport of the United Nations Organization. Nothing less.

We hardly ever know why a city is where it is: A crossroad? the caprice of a conqueror? More simply, the place where the head of the conquering army got struck with malaria or syphilis and a provisional camp became a permanent settlement? The village from where a warlord originated? I presumed that Bamako was the ancient capital of the powerful Bambara tribe, but I was wrong, the capital of the Bambaras is Segou, a couple of hundred miles to the north. In the case of Bamako, it is even more mysterious since the Niger River bordering the city is not navigable from here but only after the cataracts of Koulikoro, 30 miles to the north.

The Niger River gives life to almost the whole of West Africa. From Guinea, not far from the ocean it turns its back on the Atlantic and runs inland to irrigate with a splendid curb, five arid Sahel countries, to finally loose itself in the Gulf of Guinea, in Nigeria, in an enormous fertile and oil rich delta. This queen of rivers runs for about three thousand miles: Guinea, Mali, and Niger, the border of Benin and into Nigeria which it crosses from Northwest to Southeast.

So why is Bamako where it is? I go for the explication that the head of the column of the colonial conquest army got a malaria attack here or that he fell in love with a Bambara beauty who transmitted him the "hot piss", a very common venereal disease in these parts and very painful for white people who don't have the natural immunities of the Africans. That the treatment administrated by the army's veterinarian did not work well and that the provisional camp became a permanent settlement. It could have been that simple.

I have to specify that the French colonial expeditions had sometimes a doctor attached to them, but always a vet who acted as medic for all mammals with two or four legs. The vets also were in charge of inspecting the brothels that always followed every army. (These are the war rules established by Napoleon.)

We maybe have to take into account, in the Bamako case, a possible strategic reason of military nature for its establishment. The city is squeezed between the river and a couple of steep hills from which one can control the whole city. On top of these hills stand the former colonial governor's palace – today the presidency - a couple of important ministries and army barracks and a little farther a military hospital with the beautiful name of "G Point". With a few canons and guns you can control the whole city up to the unique bridge that crosses the river. The students from the local university call this hill "The hill of power" in opposition to another hill, across the river, on which the university is laid out, and that is called "the hill of knowledge".

Three or four paved streets bordered by shops, most of them belonging to the Lebanese colony who followed very closely the colonial French armies at the same time as the Franciscan fathers, Dominicans et some Jesuits, as is the general strategy of all colonial conquests: army, priests, and shopkeepers. In some rare cases the fourth element, the colonialist settlers followed, but this is not the case – or very little – in French West Africa.

I already made a description of a colonial metropolis in the case of Ouagadoudou of which Bamako is the sister-city, except for the river. The Bambara population is Islamic in the African Islamic style, regardless of the beautiful cathedral and some very exclusive catholic schools, where the offspring of the Islamic elite also study.

Paule was the coordinator of a higher education scientific program and I had free time. This permitted me to jump with my two feet into sociology and ethnology without having to worry about conveniences in style in the white community of "small whites" as they call the human fauna who keeps trying to make a living and sometimes a fortune in all types of occupations: schoolteachers, butchers, restaurant owners, bakers, shopkeepers, embassy employees and civil servants of international cooperation, "experts" in all kinds of things. The "big white man" is the French ambassador – ex colonial power – and some, but not all, ambassadors of European countries and North America. The latter, is the representative of the two American continents, which does not mean that he would take care of a possible Guatemalan lost in Mali. Continental solidarity of the Americas has its limits.

*

Hervé: to start our Malian journey, I am going to tell your story, which of course is also our family story.

I convinced Paule to lend herself to a contemplation of the white community and some Malians, convincing her that from a sociological viewpoint it should be an interesting experience. Of course, the best ethno-sociological contemplation of this community was at the cathedral after Sunday mass. The best observation spot was the terrace of the café in front of the cathedral "Chez Émile". We got there a bit early, the "Ite missa est" had not been pronounced yet. Walking around the beautiful construction with indefinite architectural style, we noticed a poster, handwritten and pinned to the porch. "We call upon the members of the Christian community who have a spare room for students. Please contact Father Paul." Eager to show off as an experienced Africanist, I said to Paule:
- You've seen the houses they have. I bet you that none of those Christians has proposed to shelter black students.
- I don't believe you. Most of them have houses for twelve kids.
- We'll see.
From the terrace of "Chez Émile" we observed the parade of the catholic community of Bamako, in which dominated by far the "white" skin color dressed up in the latest fashion. Small groups of people gathered on the back of the dozen steps that led to the porch. The white community in the African capitals is not a real "community" for having little in common one with the other. It's more like a kind of tribe divided into sub-tribes and clans: The embassy servants according to their grades and hierarchy; the shopkeepers; the schoolteachers; the development aid people according their specialty: the agriculturists don't mix with the livestock specialists; the clan of the engineers, the entrepreneurs etc...All these clans don't mix, they receive among themselves, they party among themselves and they drink and seduce among themselves, each one in his ghetto.

When there was nobody left on top of the steps except a father with a white skull cap, and a rope around his waist, Dominican style, we moved towards him.
- Good morning, father.
He had carbon black eyes, almost closed, reflecting something like irony. He looked me over from top to bottom. We shook hands and said our names. I followed up:
-Concerning your ad, father, we'd like to know if you have had many replies?

The Hedonist

He looked back at the poster and said:
- No, indeed I have not, you are the first ones.

Two days later a tall girl with a somewhat heavy body, very black, wrapped up in a flower printed cloth and blouse of the same material knocked at our door. At her feet lay a small bundle of clothes. Béatrice Sawadogo just entered in our life.

Here is her story: She belongs to the Mossi tribe from Burkina Faso, then Upper Volta and was born in a small village in the Niger bend in Mali. More precisely in what was called in colonial times "l'Office du Niger" an enormous agricultural irrigation project which was supposed to feed the whole of French West Africa and beyond. What is a catholic Mossi village doing in the middle of Islamic Peul territory in Mali? Simple: The best agricultural lands of the whole of West Africa are those encircled by the Niger river bend which consists of vast swamps and low surface water reserves. The "Office du Niger" was the most ambitious agricultural project of the French colonial period. Problem: This vast region is the territory of the powerful Peul or Fulani herdsmen who in their basic cultural values hold that it is beneath their status and dignity to bend to cultivate the earth. Agriculture is considered a slave work to be done by other tribes just good enough to be slave-raided. The Peuls, as do many herdsmen, are convinced that God gave them the cattle trade to be above all other creatures.

The solution? Easy: import Mossi peasants from Upper Volta and establish them in the Peul territory. This is nothing big, since the dozens of countries now forming West Africa all belonged to the same colonial power, called "The Territories of French West Africa".

This is the story that explains how Beatrice; Mossi, peasant and catholic, was born in cattle and Muslim territory. Let's go on with the story: This young lady was recruited by a French missionary to become a nun and that's why she was sent to a nun's school in Bamako. Now you also know how she landed in the capital.

To become a nun for an African girl is to enter in servitude for life, servitude to the priest, maybe a bishop, some school or a hospital. It implies: renouncing to your sexual life - which probably got resumed with some violations by some priest and masturbation - renouncing from your love life and your reproduction capacities. What else? Oh, yes of course, the whole for free, in exchange for lodging and food, this latter item often tasteless and scarce. Also of course, I almost forgot, constantly under supervision and spied upon, with the obligation to pray or sing psalms all the time you have to your own. With this, your life as a thinking being also ends.

It happens that your mother, Béatrice, after some time as an apprentice nun, came to the conclusion that she did not like that life and its perspectives. So she quit, upon which the already certified nuns threw her into the street. Having failed as an apprentice nun was not a good condition to return to the Mossi village in the Niger buckle on the one hand. On the other hand, having looked, even as into a mirror, at city life in the capital she found that living there was more interesting than in a peasants' village with no electricity, no cinemas, no running water and so much more; where her future was to cut wood, carry water, make food, work in the fields, get screamed at, get slapped and get pregnant almost every year. This was probably not the kind of life she wanted. On the streets of Bamako she quickly fell into misery until eventually father Paul took pity; got her lodging in our house and signed her up in a school to become a teacher. All this because I wanted to show off to Paule about my African sociological knowledge.

Beatrrice installed herself in one of our spare rooms, sometimes took her meals with us but only when Jacob, our servant-cook, did not serve. At first, I did not pay attention to the kind of relationship between the two Malians who lived with us, but soon learned that under no circumstances Jacob was going to serve her when she sat at the dinner table with us. A Bambara, cook and servant of whites, was not going to fall into the disgrace of serving a Mossi girl, an inferior race, caught off the street. I am not going to enter the psycho-sociological relations between tribes and populations of Mali, although there would be a lot to say about it.

*

I am writing this on the 31st of December of the year 2007 in the only integrated sea farm of the Mexican Republic. (I already said that, but since I am proud of it, I repeat it). I have to specify that this title I carry for ten years now. I owe it mainly to the incorrigible stupidity of civil servants - state and federal- who did not bother to make out of aquaculture a new industry and a development factor for Mexico. Regardless of the fact that all the objective data to do so are in place: technologies, sides, proven experience, market, know how, etc...

I am preparing to spend new year's night as I spent Christmas night last week: Christmas, New Year, Easter and a couple of civil holidays have been my guard nights for now over twenty years, for the simple reason that I don't have the guts to ask anybody to spend these feast nights looking after fish and keeping the installations running. The spirit of the winter solstice is not completely absent from my environment and spirit so three China-made garlands are hanging from a banana tree and two more from a coconut tree. To keep away from a possible nostalgia attack for snow, cold outside and heat inside, I made a wood fire and installed myself comfortably in a beach chair admiring the fascinating spectacle of the universe, listening to good old jazz from New Orleans or from the Chicago period. For keeping life simple, in a short while I'll fry a couple of eggs and bacon with bread, butter, coffee and a couple of "grogs" (juice of one lemon, one coffee spoon of sugar, at least two fingers of rum, fill up with boiling water and stir). Grogs are good for any kind of illness, even for nostalgia. If tiredness does not put me to sleep, I'll open a small bottle of Champagne and toast with the dogs at midnight.

Little by little, this ritual of New year's eve celebration made me allergic to the obligatory feasts on fixed dates, these assemblies where one is obliged to look happy and laugh even if you hear the same joke for the twenty-fifth time told by your brother in law or the stories about your aunt's leg ache. On these occasions you have to distribute kisses to perfectly ugly, often stupid, fat women who have absolutely nothing interesting to say apart from the stories of their offspring, their illnesses and back pains. Where you have to exchange gifts that cost you two weeks salary just to find out that the books you gave them last year have not been read. No thanks. With Winky – the stupidest dog in Mexico, who cannot lift his hind leg to piss without falling – Blacky- who is completely white, of course – and Pirata – who has a black patch over her left eye, we are doing fine. I bought them a chicken, because it is New Year's Eve for everybody, and a generous serving of bacon. No, I am not going to give them Champagne, one must not exaggerate.

Even if I wanted to go to sleep early it would be impossible: three hundred yards to the right and another two hundred to the left the fishermen's houses will overflow with ranchero music, as loud as if they were at the Yankee Stadium, together with hundreds of firecrackers exploding all night long. Peace and silence are not part of these nights.

Today I paid the fortnight salary plus the New Year premium; I had to borrow money to meet my obligations. The year 2007 was disastrous. I don't want another one like that, neither for me nor for the country.

Mexico keeps conscientiously cultivating its under development. They say that the country grew at a rate of 2 % - nobody believes it, what we do believe because it exists in front of our noses, is that there is over 40 % of the population living in poverty or extreme poverty. Big corruption keeps galloping. Sometimes I think that there is not a single honest man or woman in this country. That of course is much exaggerated, since I have friends. Everything that has a far or close relation to the state is cheating and lying. The education levels are the lowest of the OCDE countries, which does not prevent the teachers' syndicate from imposing a school calendar of only 115 half-days of real presence on their jobs. (Remember that one hundred and seventeen thousand -117,000, just to make sure that you read right- teachers are on the public payrolls of schools that just don't exist, as already mentioned). This way, we can be sure that the future of Mexico as a prosperous state is far beyond our generation and the one that follows.

The honorable representatives of the Mexican people, for the New Year, just split among their honorable members all the money that has not been spent in the year: 24 million dollars. If that is not stealing, I ask you what it is? The Supreme Court cleared of all charges a governor who jailed a reporter for having proved that he is involved in a pedophile web. Mexican justice remains a joke. This does not prevent our supreme judges being the best paid in the world.

At the local level: our governor spent three million dollars for a monument that nobody knows what to make of, and another four million to bring the "Il Divo Boys" to town for a concert, announcing that next year he will bring Andrea Bocelli, the Italian tenor for another five million dollars, just because he and his wife like them. Only ten thousand people could attend, (out of the 750.000 that the state counts with), of whom six are his employees and friends, the other four were from the Mexican Il Divo fan club. No television transmission was allowed. If we put the three together we have enough to build 1.400 houses for the people living in cardboard and wooden huts with mud floors.

Add to this report " Mexico" that today the local bishop qualified as sins: Eating the twelve grapes at midnight (a Spanish heritage), sweep the dust outside to keep away bad luck, wearing colored underwear – favorable for fortune in the coming year-, walk around the block with a suitcase- to have a chance to travel. All sins of superstition, said the bishop. Maybe there are some more things that are sins which the bishop completely forgot? Like: stealing the public budget, lying on public spending, promoting injustice, cheating the people, making promises that are not kept, etc.

On the matter of superstition the Catholic Church, since its very beginning, has few lessons to give. The founder of that church, the roman emperor Constantine, like many tyrants was incapable of providing for his succession. At his death he left an empty period which destabilized high clerics from the state in such a way that during three months – from may 22 to September 9 of the year 377 – all the ministers (civil, military and religious) had to read their daily reports to his exposed body. On the matter of superstition I think nobody can do better. To believe that a dead body still exercises power was a lousy superstitious trick.

There goes Mexico by the end of 2007 and 2008 does not look any different. The inertia of this country is legendary, due to the general dishonesty and white collar bandits living in corruption and lies, Mexican underdevelopment is doing well and before being economic it is moral. It will take time to make a modern nation of this mess.

I better go back to my story, I am getting mad again and being mad is not a good way to start a New Year. Even though this feast is not important anymore, I do give a thought to the fact that millions of years ago, homo sapiens became aware of the cycles of nature and started to remember that mother nature was accomplishing a time period. Of this, yes, I do want to remember this night partying my way: giving an opportunity to others to party their way and to their taste.

*

Hanging around in the Bamako coffee shops tired me soon, even if I got acquainted with several picturesque personalities, like that Algerian consul who never got tired of telling me the story of his deep emotion when he shook hands with Che Guevara in Algeria or this French architect who specialized in erotic comics he was selling to a French editor.

I don't remember how, but one day I met the vet Boubakar Sy, ex alumni of the tropical veterinarian school of Maisons Alfort in the Parisian suburbs. Because we were both leftist we sympathized: my passage through the student revolt in Paris in May 1968, and especially through Cuba, gave me some credentials as a patented leftist. As he was someone in the government on the side of the ministry of livestock, he proposed me to be interpreter and companion to an American agent from USAID for an evaluation trip to Nara, not far from the Mauritanian border in the heart of the Malian Sahel zone. This is what I wanted.

The mission of Jack Reynolds consisted, that's what I understood, of making an evaluation of the size of the drought disaster that was striking all the Sahel country. The drought, said the Malian government, had killed half of the livestock and spread starvation through the region. Jack would proceed by sampling, and the sample was the region of Moorish and Fulani tribesmen of Nara. He took his mission very seriously and had the means to do so, which mainly consisted of two land rover jeeps; one to carry our august persons, plus a driver, the Malian counterpart in the person of a young vet - unfortunately from the Bambara tribe: this implied that we had to bring along two interpreters, one Moorish and one Peul. The other jeep carried the gasoline, the domestic equipment, four heavy metal boards to serve in case we got stuck in the sand, boxes and boxes of sterilized water, jerry cans with water to wash and the cook. It looked as we were up for a high class picnic. (Many years later I'll organize myself the same way for about the same purpose in Chad, but not for 10 days: for 18 months).

After one hour of bouncing on a dusty lateritic road full of holes, the track disappeared to divide into a multitude of tire tracks which every traveler in the Sahel makes to his liking, in such a way that I believe that the road to Nara must be over two kilometers wide. Jack was nervous all day trying continuously to consult the compass-Special Forces type. Apart from his unmistakable "marine" look, with high boots, short, jacket and hat of the army of his country, he was a very sociable and sympathetic man, expressing himself softly. He must have been around forty, brown eyes and a straightforward, frank expression on his face. He was from Indiana but lived in Washington, DC. We liked each other straight away. He loved hearing that we had so many places we knew in common, he even knew the German tavern on Wisconsin Avenue where I used to hang out when I was a student at American U. and once he had lunch at the Jockey Club where I had been a waiter. All this reassured him for being on known ground.

He had made a rule that every hour and thirty minutes, we make a stop. This was a very wise decision; the land rover jeeps have the particularity of having a very tight suspension, which means that every small stone on the road gets straight into your column. I just let you imagine how our backs felt on this "no road" in free range country, even if our driver Isidore was excellent. On these stops, while the drivers checked the engines - another Jack rule- the cook in no time made us a cup of coffee on his camping gas stove.

I was thus pretty full of coffee and sugar when we crossed our first Moor nomads. They appeared by surprise about thirty meters ahead on the left, coming out from after the curtain of acacias, apparently from nowhere and going apparently nowhere too. The first camel we saw carried a canopy under which a veiled woman from under her black cloth let us see her eyes only. I saw the man walking on the other side of the camel he held with a rope. He was wearing a black turban on his head, half-hiding his face, a sky blue toga from under which appeared black pants down to his ankles. On the shoulder, held by a rope, hung a holster with a sword and around his waist stuck a very respectable dagger. There followed another camel, attached to the tail of the first one, loaded with long rolls of straw woven carpets and long poles. All this made up the tents. Fifty meters behind, a bunch of donkeys loaded with everything else: pots and pans, bags of millet, some cardboard boxes of who knows what. Well, everything needed to survive in the Sahel. A young boy, and children dressed in what looked like burlap bags with a hole for the head and held with a rope, walked with the donkeys. I learned from the Moor interpreter that is was not usual to find these people so far south, which indicated that there must be problems of pasture in their normal zone and   the story about the drought was real. They looked like they just ran away from a Bible page, Old Testament: low grey sky, hot air, bushes full of thorns, little yellow sun, dried pasture. I imagined the landscapes of Judea and Samaria. A place where the sun burns the brains, dries up the body, hardens the soul and gives expectations of paradises where pastures are green, where clean water flows generously in rivers that never dry, where the air is soft and food abundant, tasty and varied. I understand why the sacred books give descriptions of paradises that only can surge in brains burned by the sun.
(We could just add to this paradise description that the good book says that women are at your disposal, forever young - and stay virgin regardless)

We stopped to let pass this caravan of a Moor family in transhumance, of which we still had not seen the first goat. Behind, far behind, would come the herd of cows, sheep and goats, more donkeys and maybe a few more camels and even a horse or two. As nobody saluted anybody, the vanguard of this family kept going, superb, ignoring us, and not even judging us worth looking at. Of course, they knew about us because of the motor noise, but I guess they just had decided to ignore us, following their mysterious path. In a few minutes they disappeared as they had shown up, behind the curtain of acacias. Jack, excited as a first day school kid, had spent two complete 36 frame film on them.

It's only at the third encounter, three hours and two more coffees later, that we succeeded in having a dialogue, when a man carrying a slave trade gun, all of a sudden came out of a bush a few meters in front of the jeep. Jack ordered to stop and asked the Moorish interpreter to go and see if this Moor was willing to talk. We witnessed that our interpreter bowed deeply and was considerably blacker than the herdsman, which indicated that he belonged to an "inferior cast". Our interpreter was probably son to an ex alumni from the colonial "school for the sons of chiefs ".

*

In order to incorporate clans and tribes into the French colonial order and the new Nation-to-be, based on the values of the Republic, the colonial administration did not want to rely only on the works of the missionaries. (The conversion of Muslim tribesman into Christian Republicans was a dream the colonial administration did not believe in very much.)

So, the colonial administration invented the "School for the sons of the chiefs". The Chiefs of tribes and clans were invited - more so, obliged - to send to these schools at least two of their sons, preferably the oldest, to be taught the moral values, the mechanism and laws of a Nation-State, the fatherland and the Republic, resumed in "Liberty, Equality and Fraternity". That was the idea. In some countries more to the South into the rain forest, the system worked quite well, but in the Muslim Sahel zone it did not. The chiefs of the Islamic tribes simply did not send their sons to the colonial school but the sons of their slaves or inferior casts instead.

Result: The first Africans with modern instruction and on whose shoulders laid the task of building modern states, are not sons of chiefs, or chiefs-to-be, but sons of families of an inferior social status. The tribal traditional structures remained untouched and blood pure. The dominating casts lost influence in the administrative and political construction of the Muslim countries in which they did not, or very little, participate, but their tribal power stayed intact. This is how the social-political structure of these countries is difficult to define: nobody knows where the power is. Tribal structures stay as the foundation of society, which explains that every normal internal conflict in the "modern democratic" country becomes rapidly a tribal war. This, of course, does not facilitate "good government" in African states. Later, I'll get to know ministers and secretaries in high positions who owed obedience and submission to their drivers, because in the tribe they were superior. The case of one ministry - I believe it was mining and natural resources- staffed from minister to gardener all coming from the same tribe, is outspoken. Questioned about this strange conception of public administration the minister told me:"One day I have to go back to the tribe". Exercising power in the central government is a theatre play to be acted so as to bring as much wellbeing to one's tribe as possible. The real, permanent power resides in the tribe and not in the government.

*

I had all the problems in the world to prevent Jack from jumping out of the jeep as long as the interpreter did not come back with the authorization and the invitation to a conversation. In a general way, the Americans know little about "etiquette" and proper behavior, this does not bother me, on the contrary, but here this could have damaging consequences. Americans are efficient, not good mannered, and little respectful of what they consider as useless. Eventually, the interpreter came back with the Moor carrying a gun, they stopped in the shadow of an acacia a few yards from us. I grabbed a sugar cone from one of our carton boxes and a small bag of tea, since Jack was already out of the cabin. Going to an encounter with a Sahelian tribesman without a present is like going to a Christmas party without a gift for the hostess. We passed the traditional fifteen minutes of greetings and introductions, while Jack showed signs of increased impatience. I gave the presents to the interpreter who gave them to the Moor, who started to thank me for another good while. All this was going on in three dimensions: The Moor talked to the interpreter, who translated to me and I gave it to Jack in English, who besides this registered all on his tape recorder. When we got close to half an hour of ceremonials, Jack could not hold it any more:
- For God's sake how many cattle has he?
If there is one thing you cannot ask a Sahelian herdsman, it is: "How many cattle, sheep, goats, donkeys, camels and horses do you own?"

218

This question is totally forbidden for two reasons: One is related to the colonial administration raising taxes on cattle. Since that time, the cattle are hidden, as probably this man's cattle were hidden in the nearby bushes. Two: Not all the animals he is herding belong to him. It's customary that for a protection and security matter, cattle are dispersed into the herds of family members. In a herd of, let's say, one hundred animals maybe only twenty belong to him, the remaining eighty are from the herds of his brothers, uncles, father and including his wife's family.

- Jack, you can't ask that!

He looked straight at me:

- I want to know how many heads this man has and how many he has lost because of the drought. Is it simple enough?

I thought too that it was that simple, but it is not.

- Okay, okay I'll ask him.

Putting myself face to face with the interpreter, so Jack could not see my face, I started moving my eyes and making grimaces while I talked fast so that Jack could not understand, because I had started to suspect that he knew more French that he was showing me.

- Look Yusuf, the American wants to know how many cattle this man has and how many he has lost because of the drought. I know that this is going to offend your brother and that his anger is going to fall on you, so explain him to say anything that comes to his mind, just to make the American happy.

I repeated this twice. I knew he got it from the first time but that he couldn't believe that I was asking him to lie. The drivers, the peul interpreter and the cook sitting in the shadow in Yusuf's back close by started to hide their mouths in their hands so as not to show they were laughing.

The dialogue between the two Moors lasted for a while. Finally Yusuf came back.

- Listen Boss, he says that he has only three cows left, providing blood and a little milk for his small children, he has six goats left and all his camels died. He says that he lost one thousand and forty four heads half of which were cattle and the other half goats. He says that he has not eaten for three days and that his wife lost a baby the day before yesterday.

When they exaggerate they do exaggerate. Maybe from all this only the last phrase was the truth, and even that I doubted. I translated all this to Jack's microphone, having a couple of times to turn back to Yusuf to check the numbers which he had already forgotten, giving me others. Jack was pleased and showed it with a large smile.

The meeting was closed with a round of handshaking. The Moor stayed a long time with both his hands holding Jack's, in sign of utmost respect, meaning that Jack's hand was so heavy, powerful and noble that he needed his two hands to hold it. At the same time, he murmured a thousand blessings. He did the same with me, I thought that he was never going to let go my hand. The rest of the team he did not even look at. Yusuf stayed for a while saying goodbye to the Moor after which the man left with his presents to where he came from. Which meant that his family and his herd were over there some place and that he wasn't going anywhere, as I had suspected since the beginning.

Here in the middle of nowhere from the Malian Sahel zone, not far from the Mauritanian border, was played a play of a Brooklyn Theater or the Comedia del Arte, as you like. Who are these stupid high-placed foreign aid civil servants who send other stupid men, asking stupid questions to Moor herdsmen not stupid at all?

Because of the position of the sun, a white gray glimmer in the gray dusty sky, Jack ordered to set up camp, consisting of a two room tent, a table and two chairs. With the apparition of Venus- the first star, indicating that the herdsmen were allowed to go back to the village- and the yellow shadows of the wood fire, we enjoyed a Johnny Walker on the rocks (yes sir, one of the jeeps carried a small bar refrigerator plugged to the battery) around the table dressed with a white tablecloth. Wrapped in a cloud of good smelling rice with meatballs and pieces of tomatoes and ketchup, we listened to good old jazz from New Orleans, Louis Armstrong and gospel by Ella Fitzgerald. Working with the American tax payers' money has its advantages. We reedited this play a dozen times before we got to Nara.

Thinking of it today, thirty years later, it is possible that even up to now, sometimes, in the camps of the Mauritanian nomads around Nara, the herdsmen or their children, are still laughing when someone tells the story of how their fathers mocked the "small white men" when they asked how many heads of cattle they had.

In Nara, the representation of the play had a variant. The main actor was not a Moor herdsman but the sub-prefect of Bambara origin, also son of an ex alumnus of the "school for sons of chiefs", maximum administrative authority of Nara and its territory. Of course much before our jeeps entered Nara he knew what it all was about.

We got lodging in the "administration camp", a three bedroom sort of primitive hotel for government agents passing through, which allowed us to wash something more but our hands and faces, with highly nitrated brownish water. Jack was obsessed with the water reserve; often he counted bottles and checked jerry cans. From the beginning, generously, he wanted to share our drinking water with the crew; they accepted, although I saw that it was just to be polite. Soon I found out that they washed their faces with the bottled water and drank from the jerry cans when they spread their carpets eastward to pray. I made them aware that the bottled water was for drinking and the can water for washing. On which the Peul interpreter who acted as the spokesman for all, replied:

- Boss, this bottled water has a bad taste.

No comments, because everything is relative: "De gustibus et coloribus no disputandum est" as the Romans already said.

The sub-prefect knew the whites well for having spent some time at the University of Rennes in France and rapidly integrated the rules of the game. Seated on a huge thick carpet around an impressive variety of dishes – which surprised me, Nara being close to a miserable place- we shared dinner with the cream of the social society of Nara; some civil servants, a couple of traders and four Moor and Peul dignitaries. The young Bambara painted us a dantesque hell. Up to the point that I feared that the sheep we were eating was the last one left in the whole region. Everybody told his story, which seemed to be a contest for the most dramatic screenplay. Meanwhile, I was trying to reach out to grasp a piece of boule- a sort of pudding made of sorghum flour in form of a half football – make a small ball of it, dip it in one of the many sauce bowls, taking on the way a piece of meat and getting it all into my mouth with an elegant movement of the wrist, without spilling it all over my shirt. I was in the middle of the crossfire of questions and answers flowing back and forth between Jack and the Sub-prefect. The only moment I had to expedite a maximum of small balls of sorghum with pieces of meat into my mouth was when one of the dignitaries told his story to the sub. I had no intention to let the night go using my mouth only for talking. Each time I turned to Jack to translate something they were saying, I saw his face, sleeves and shirt getting more and more decorated with pieces of sorghum, meat and greasy sauces. He confessed that this was the first time in his life he was eating with his hands. I presumed: apart from hamburgers and Kentucky fried chicken. After some time he gave up and kept smiling. Apparently he enjoyed the whole situation even if he was almost completely covered with sauce and sorghum, taking some pictures, which was of course very bad mannered.

The more the stomachs got filled, the calmer the conversation became to finally stop completely. All were convinced, including me, that we had done a great job to prepare for the rivers of American dollars that were going to flow into Nara. Three young girls came and presented to each of us small buckets of water to wash our hands and faces. Some washed also their feet which I neither did nor understand, considering that these extremities do not participate in the eating activity. Then, the girls brought cushions. Meanwhile stars had filled the sky with their entire splendor; I stretched out and lay on my back not to miss a second of it. The sub-prefect reached out for his enormous shortwave radio and we listened to the news bulletin of France-International which gave a good pause to my tongue. I don't remember what was in the news of the day but I got again a kick out of listening to the extensive report on   Parisian traffic jams. Isn't that delightful? Every time I remember it, I enjoy it more: stretched out on a thick carpet, looking at the Milky Way in Mali and listening to the story of how poor Parisians are stuck in the evening traffic on the Porte de Versailles, de Champerret or on the highway to Orleans? Deliciously surrealistic.

After the ceremonial of listening to the news, we passed on to the ceremony of tea. Yet there was little to translate, the conversation went on about the news and some matters of the sub-prefecture. Nobody talked anymore about cattle which had disappeared in the horrible drought. We got up when the sub decided that it was time for us to sleep, which of course could not take place before a long ceremony of handshaking and goodnight wishing was completed.

As I did every night, I hauled my camp bed into the open, the firmament is the most beautiful ceiling, besides Jack's heavy snoring is of little harmony.

Boubakar Sy had told me not to miss a visit to an animal reservation one of his friends was in charge of, about seven hours of jeep from Nara through open country in the direction of Timbuktu. Jack was an excellent navigator and we fell straight into the camp in the afternoon. I am telling you this because something strange happened. Boubakar's friend, his companion for seven years in the vet school in the Parisian suburbs, was very well read and a specialist of Marxism-Leninism. I'll never know if he was also a good vet, but about Marxism-Leninism he was definitively a specialist.

The only Leninist I will encounter in my whole life, including Isabel Monal and some of the Cuban intellectuals, who really had read the thirty two volumes of the complete works of Vladimir who had changed the world - politically, economically and socially speaking - and dominated the state of the world since I was born. All these books he kept in a metal trunk wrapped up in chains and locked.

Around a camp fire, wrapped in blankets - because Sahelian nights are fresh- keeping us awake with coffee and tea, we discussed the matter until the sky announced the inescapable new day. We both liked the chapters of "Left Wing Communism: an Infantile Disorder". We ventured into others, of which I only had a vague notion. He even had the works of Marx's son in law; "The Right to Laziness" or something like it. He postulated that the working class had the right to power. I was more inclined to defend parliamentarianism, having seen the working class in power in Cuba and what they are capable of. We did not agree much, but this is the most intellectual night of all my life. Tired of Vladimir Illich, I asked him some questions about his job.

- Are there many contraband hunters?
- Oh yes, many, they come from Mauritania in caravans.
- What do they look for?
- Everything, hides, ivory, elephant tails, they even buccaneer the meat.
- Do you go after them?
- Very little
- Why?
- Oh, there is always something lacking; gasoline, munitions and for other reasons too.
- What other reasons?
He took a deep breath and looking away from me answered:
- It happens to be that when they see us, they turn into wild animals, even into lions.

My mouth fell open, all by itself. Here was the most learned Marxist-Leninist I had ever met, telling me in all simplicity, that the illegal, contraband hunters from Mauritania turned themselves into wild beasts.

There are connections between the Marxist Leninist dialectics and African witchcraft that only Africans can understand.

Jack accepted the invitation to make a tour in the reservation to look at wild animals. This gave me the opportunity to sleep and do nothing all day long. Upon his return in the afternoon, he told me that the socio-economic data about the drought he had collected was enough, and that we would go to Mopti cross country to take from there the tarmac back to Bamako. That was not easy because we were on the wrong side of the river. Here is where our peul interpreter came in, this was his country. He resolved the problem getting the jeeps on a dozen of hollowed wooden canoes tied together. Crossing the river took us all day, all that time   Jack kept a very white face: he already saw his jeeps on the bottom of the river. But all went well. Finally, our teammates could drink all the river water they liked and bathe without sparing water.

Mopti is a busy place, many people, much dust, much noise, an immense market of everything but especially dried fish. The whole city smells of dried fish, a very penetrating odor that sticks to your clothes. Later on, I will come back to Mopti a few times to visit the close by Dogon country, a special tribe hanging around sharp cliffs, animists in an ocean of Muslims. Because of their particular way of living and culture they'll become a tourist attraction; also to visit Djenne which has the biggest and tallest mud built mosque in the world (that's what they say).

*

Sahelian Muslims are peaceful people, easygoing, good humored, and preoccupied to do good as they have learned from the few Koran verses they memorized. To them, Islam is good and tolerant. To them, it is unimaginable that a Muslim can wrap himself in dynamite and blow himself up just with the purpose of killing as many innocent people as possible in a cafeteria in Germany, or Israel, or Spain, or highjack airplanes to fly into buildings in New York with the sole purpose of killing - including Muslims, or decapitate civilians as do the followers of Bin Laden, or blow up a market place in Karachi. To them, all this is the behavior of fools but certainly not Muslims. They expect that on the entrance to Paradise nobody will be waiting for them to settle accounts for things they would have done which are not in conformity with the rules.

That these Muslims share the same values as the pilots of the planes that destroyed the twin towers or the train and subway killers of Madrid and London appears to me incredible. The first ones are afraid of the weight of sin: having cheated a companion, having slept with the wrong woman, having cursed or killed - by accident - a dog crossing the road and that will stand at the door of paradise to keep them from entering. The others imagine that they are expected in

Paradise with open arms, parties and eternal virgins of whom they can dispose as they please, just for having blown up the lives of innocent people. The same book justifies these two attitudes situated at the extreme opposite of the same humanity. One longs for sanity, the other achieves barbarity. Michel Onfray : " In no way I depreciate the believers in angels, the positive effects of prayer, the efficiency of rituals, the well doing of enchanting, the tears of the virgin, the resurrection of a crucified man, the power of mushrooms, the prayer mills, the virtues of the Gods, the value of animal sacrifices, or gods with elephant trunks. I don't depreciate anyone. But in all parts I realize how much man invents fables not to have to look into reality. Creation of the "after" worlds would not be that bad if it were not paid at a heavy price: ignoring and forgetting the only world that is real. When beliefs get annoyed with what is eminent; atheism reconsolidates with the earth, the other name for life".

*

In the meantime, Paule had made friends with an Italian woman married to a Malian writer-poet, from whom she had three children, two boys and a girl. In my opinion, Diabaté was not much of a writer or poet. He aligned good sounding words but with little sense. I believe in his efforts to resemble the French writers and poets of the nineteenth century, he had lost himself. Apart from this, he and his wife were very agreeable company. Diabaté is a name that indicates that he belonged to the Malinké tribe and inside this one, to the clan of the Griots.

Who are the Griots? They are many things: messengers – very important, the messengers: if you have to ask somebody something you send a messenger, so you don't have to listen to a negative answer and the respondent does not have to say no to you directly – musicians, story tellers, public shouters, buffoons and poets. Until recently, all their knowledge was orally transmitted, from the mouth of a Griot to the ear of a Griot. They are the memory of the tribe, the clans, the families, and their historians. All this makes that they are untouchable and enjoy privileges. In a culture where precedence is of primary importance, to know the story of everybody, his ancestors and the heroic deeds they accomplished (to which they can add or substract according to the generosity of the compensation they receive) all this gives power and imposes respect. Within the Malinké tribe, as in all other African tribes, before you are you, you are the descendent of somebody on whom your place in society and the respect all owe you depend. To all this, the Griots have the keys.

Who are the Malinkés? They are a peasant tribe, settled on both side of the Mali-Guinea border. They have a warriors and bloody history because they also were conquerors and founders of an empire, subjugating many tribes around them. They conquered the Dioula and Bambara Kingdoms, subjugated the Bozo, Dogon, and part of the fierce Peul tribes from Futa Yalon and Macina in Mali; also the Mossi and Diolaso kingdoms in Burkina and went as far as tickling the Ashanti empire in Ghana. They ventured into the forests of Ivory Coast and conquered all the tribes from Senegal to Liberia. They opposed fierce resistance to the French colonial conquest. Their emperor, Amory and his deeds are still glorified in all the songs of the Griots, for whom he constitutes the greatest source of inspiration. They can sit around a wood fire for a whole night, playing the Cora, and singing the glory of these times. The Cora is a sort of harp, mounted on a pumpkin with up to forty strings and is played with both hands.

Because of my sociological curiosity, the following Sunday after I came back from Mopti, we loaded everyone in our Mehari (a plastic jeep made by Citroen with a 2HP motor) and off we were to Kangaba, sacred capital of the Malinké on the Malian side (there are others on the Guinea side) on a very dusty red lateritic road. Two hours and something later we had Kangaba in sight and stopped to get as clean as possible: all of us were red, blacks and whites alike. I felt again as an explorer, discovering mysterious and different tribes and lives, as years before in Burkina Faso and Ivory Coast.

After cleaning up, as much as is decently feasible on the road side, we paid the obligatory visit to the sub prefect of Kangaba, a good looking young lieutenant, simpatico, a little formal, enthusiastic and much updated on the writings of my host. While we passed an hour saluting and in small talk, there was a party in preparation in the town quarters where the Diabaté Griots dwelled. When we walked down from the hill- of course the sub-prefecture headquarters were on a hill, according to colonial urban layout- an escort of women, dressed up in enormous boubous, richly decorated with gold or silver embroidery and crowned with enormous head scarves giving them a gigantic stature, were waiting for us. We were escorted to the Diabaté quarters by well over two dozen singing and hand clapping women and girls accompanied by several coras and marimbas. On all sides there were laughing happy faces.

The Griot quarters is made up of several compounds, each one consisting of several circular mud huts with palm leaf roofs. The Maya villages here in Yucatan have the same.

The main social activity is saluting and greeting, it took a long time before we finished the round of shaking hands and saying a few words in Malinké language, trying to stick to the etiquette, not very successfully I fear, judging by the big laughs we got from the crowd. It does not really matter, the Malinké have a saying that goes as follows "Children and foreigners have to be excused for everything, the poor things, they don't know"

Here is where I met my mythical mother and my two brothers for the first time, but that's a story for later.

Diabaté took me to visit the village where there was not much to see, except for a huge circular construction in the middle of a big square. They pompously call this structure the "Kaaba" – like the one in Mecca- or the "big hut". It is a structure like any other, except that it is bigger and especially for the mysteries that it is wrapped in. Nobody has a right to approach it, less to see what is inside, except the village chief and the oldest of the Griots. My guide told me that he knew what there was inside for having looked through a hole when a small boy. That was the reason why they had exiled him from the village. If he had told anyone what he had seen, he said, very likely they would have killed him. I figured that he was exaggerating. His exile to the capital, where he lived in the family of an uncle on his mother's side, had allowed him to go to school and later on to France. To resume: he owed his writer and poet career to his young boy's curiosity. Inside there were some wooden statues one of which was full height, and wooden and metal boxes. The other story of this sanctuary is that every year the young male children, in a supervised ceremony reconstruct and repair the walls. It consists of spreading mud mortar with their hands on the walls. He told me, but I did not quite believe him, that if the mortar of one of the boys does not stick to the hut walls, the boy is separated from the group and sent home with the recommendation:"talk to your mother". Supposedly he is not his father's son.

We went to salute the chief of the blacksmiths clan, friends and allies of the Griots. Blacksmiths are much respected and somewhat feared in all the tribes, since they dominate two powerful, mysterious elements: metal and fire. They make all the agricultural equipment but also arms, spearheads, arrow points and even the famous slave trade guns, nothing sophisticated but efficient. The Blacksmiths are a much exclusive clan: they only marry to sons and daughters from other

227

blacksmiths clans. It is very rare to find a non blacksmith descendant among the blacksmiths.

The afternoon was spent, lying on thick carpets, eating a lot and listening to stories and songs about the heroic deeds of Amory. I was surprised to see the great dexterity with which Paule sent the little balls of sorghum, wrapped in greasy sauce and meat, into her mouth without spilling any, it looked like she had been doing this all her life. I figured that we drank all the Coca Cola and beer available in Kangaba.

Each weekend, we'd return to the Diabaté dwelling in Kangaba, learning to live according to the Malinke style. I went hunting with them and even learned to play the balafon – a sort of marimba with different size calabashes – without much success. I helped them to hire a pair of oxen for their rice fields.

On one of these Saturdays I found a young man sitting Indian style next to the door of my hut. He looked kind of wild with his eyes sticking out of their holes and the eyeballs looking up to the top of the tree behind me. He also had   Rasta style hair hanging in long braids to his shoulders. Up to then I had not seen any rastas in Africa. He did not respond my greetings which is very, very rude in Malinké country.
- Who's he? I asked Djibril who took me aside.
- He comes from Kayes and he is sick.
- He rather looks a little crazy no?
- His father sent him to France to work and send money back but they had to bring him back soon: he lost his spirits and got crazy.
I do understand that for a young man, passing brutally from the peasants short shovel in Kayes to the Parisian metro, could be disorienting.
- He is here to be healed.
- You heal him?
- I and all of us, he'll stay here until he gets his spirits back.
So, I learned that among the many things they do, the Griots are also the tribes' psychiatrists.

Years later, guiding one of our SOTERA associates from Chad, down the Champs Elysee Avenue in Paris, realizing that I was short on cash, I got some from a cash dispenser. Back in Chad I found out that the guy had been telling all over the place what a great magician I was, having got money out of a wall. Cultural shocks exist and some are hard to overcome.

I learned some of the social rules which I found very clever and enchanting. As for example: The avoiding of the mother in law. Since your mother in law has given you the best thing in life, your wife, by definition she is your friend. To avoid that this friendship gets hurt you don't speak to her, don't look at her, when you meet her in the street you cross to the other side; if you have something to say to your mother in law you tell your wife who'll tell her, etc…Who does not have a problem with his mother in law? Here is a way to fix it.

The other thing I liked very much was the way relations between generations were regulated. The relations between father and son are very arbitrary, very rough, and very strict. The father is feared. He is the one with the right to kick, slam, punish, repress, throw stones, and shout. On the contrary, the relations between grandfather and grandson are very soft, they are accomplices and joke together, they are pals who like each other. Since your grandfather is the father of your father, things got to be balanced and looked after so that there is no excess and harmony reigns in the family.

Luckily several spoke understandable French and when not, we made do with signs and mimics which always gave us an occasion to laugh. I discovered that within the village hierarchy, very strictly organized and strictly ruled between the different clans and trades in a vertical way, there was one with another pattern, completely horizontal and egalitarian: the "fraternity of hunters". On the condition to accept the long apprenticeship period, the grades and internal hierarchy, everyman from any clan could become a member of the fraternity and accede to the very envied status of "Hunter". It is also a semi-secret organization in regard to its hierarchy and teachings, based as much on technical knowledge as on a very intimate relationship with nature and what we would call witchcraft.

One night I asked my friend Djibril – a Griot but also a "great hunter"- to introduce me to the fraternity. He replied that he'd give me an answer on my next visit.

When I was not in Kangaba on the weekends, we made – Paule and I – long trips into the Sahel zone just for the pleasure of discovering villages, towns and other people who were not like us, to sleep in the open, and to hunt (closer to scaring birds than killing). Coming back from one of these escapes one Sunday afternoon, the house guard, a gentleman of a very respectable age, veteran from the anti-Nazi and Algeria wars, like most of the people living in our neighborhood (which was named Quinzanbougou: all the veterans from the French colonial

army who had served the Republic for fifteen years received a concession to build their houses. From there the name: "the fifteen years neighborhood"). So, the house-guard came up to me and without properly greeting me, he almost shouted:
- She slept, Boss.
He had never talked to me like that.
- Who slept with whom, Abdurrahman?
- She did, the black girl who lives with you.
I understood that it was about Béatrice, he went on:
- Three nights, three nights, Boss.
As I did not react much, at least not as much as he expected, he started to explain with a lot of details how "the negro girl" had received a man, maybe but not sure her boyfriend. Anyway, he was from the same Mossi tribe and from an "Office du Niger" village.

The following day, looking at Beatrice consciously studying her shoes, I knew that it was true. I did not mention the matter, which by sundown I already had forgotten. C´est la vie.

In Kangaba, I got welcomed with laughter and good humor. Yes, the council of the hunters had agreed to initiate me to the fraternity as an apprentice. But before that could happen I had to be part of a Malinké family. The adoption ceremony took place that very same evening and was very brief.

Djibril took me to his mother's house. She stopped milling sorghum in her wooden mortar, making flour. A thing that even at her great age, she still did with great energy, trying to control the bouncing of her breasts. When I talk about advanced age you have to consider that for the Malinkés this is around forty. She had a slightly bent slim body with a smiling face and eyes that said that she had well acquainted with life and that she was not easy to kid.

We entered and sat down on a straw woven carpet. On one side my friend Djibril and his mother who had covered her chest with a blouse, behind them, a cloud of small children, her grandchildren and my future nephews. I sat in front of her. Djibril talked to her in a low voice and looking at the carpet in sign of utmost respect. At a signal from Djibril, I handed three pieces of colored printed textiles and an envelope with money which Djibril started to count into his mother's hands, who looked very pleased. Once the money hidden under her dress, she grabbed from under her blouse her very flat and long left breast. Holding it with both hands she tended it to me. On my knees I crawled towards her and mimed as if was sucking it. We did the same with her right breast. They smelled awful, of sweat and sour milk.

Having sucked the same breasts made me a brother of Djibril and a member of the whole Diabaté family. That's how I became Yusuf, member of the griot clan and of the fierce tribe of the Malinké in West Africa. I was in my late twenties.

To check that all this was according to the rules and that my entrance in the society of men of the tribe pleased the ancestors, I had to spend the night in the sacred wood where the spirits of the ancestors dwelled, and all the past people of Kangaba from as far as memory reaches. I put my carpet under a tree and hung the mosquito net on the branches. Regardless of the fact that I had installed myself according to the rules of the art, I spent the night chasing mosquitoes and other flying and crawling creatures that the ancestors had maliciously helped enter under the mosquito net. The sky was black without stars or moon, I managed to sleep on and off between two mosquito chasings.

In the morning Djibril came for me with a calabash of water with which he filled up his mouth and spat it in my face in a fine sprinkle. He did that four times turning me to the four corners of the world, while he murmured what I believe must have been spells, asking the ancestors to be good to me until my time will come when I myself will become a spirit in the sacred wood.

I had already seen, and would see it again later, how the santeros in Havana spit in the same way into the faces of the receivers of some blessing or something else. However, in Havana the santeros spit with Rum.

I was relieved and happy to see that the ceremonial and the exams ended with this. At one moment I was afraid that they would ask me to show them my nude body and see my intact penis. Discovering that I was not circumcised – all the Malinkés are - the whole process would have come to an end. I could accept almost everything to become an initiate Malinké hunter to satisfy my curiosity, except getting circumcised.

After all this Djibril, as a great hunter, hung several amulets around my neck; they were supposed to protect me from al sorts of things: the evil eye, snake bites, the claws and teeth of lions, being struck by lightning (I thought of Saint Donatus in the church of Heur) toothache, the claws of scorpions and a lot more. They were small envelopes of fine, smelly goatskin leather, and supposedly containing verses from the Holy Koran with all these powers.

What was left of the day, I spent resting and sleeping. One night in the sacred wood does tire you. The family banquet that followed is to be remembered. I did not know what I was eating, all the meat was from big game and very tasty, same thing for the vegetables of which I hardly recognized one, I just remember that there was no salad nor tomatoes and that everything tasted fantastic. Drinks were from all kinds of roots, leaves and herbs, some fermented. While eating, we listened to the very long litany of my genealogical tree and the one of the Diabaté griots of whom, from now on and forever, I will be part.

I have to tell you that all the genealogical trees that are sung by the Griots start with the prophet Mhuammad, nothing less. Of course, they are going to give you the noblest heredity possible. What makes them so long is not only the litany of names but the stories of the deeds that each one accomplished. These deeds can go from having killed a lion or having fallen into a well; having single handed conquered a village or saved the mother in law of being eaten by a wild beast. It is of course a great honor to listen to your genealogical tree that only is told from the mouth of a Griot to the ears of a Griot.

During the banquet, a great number of young girls paid much attention to me, smiling and dispatching sensual looks. I responded with a thousand thanks. Because, it is certain that good manners impose that one treats a queen as if she were a servant and a servant as if she were a queen.

I don't know at what level of my genealogical tree they were when, little by little, I felt that I was raising, better said that I started to float, and got wrapped in a cloud that changed the form of things. Hallucinations started to invade my brains with images from the sea, waves that broke on a coast of red colored rocks. Clearly I saw people walking on floating cages, grabbing fish with their bare hands. Nude white women moved in very suggestive and erotic ways, kissing and caressing while they smiled at me. At one moment I saw myself crossing a canyon, crawling on four legs on a metal ladder. Another moment I stood as a captain, with captain's cap and long beard, maneuvering a sailboat. Once, I was dressed in tuxedo holding by the shoulders a white man, waving to a black man, also dressed in a tuxedo. These men turned out to be my sons. The things I have seen during this hallucination turned out to become real. Years later in Theoule, the sea was rough, the rocks red and the floating cages became our fish farm. I took a pillow and squeezed it strongly in my arms, I was aware of hands caressing carefully my head. Before losing completely consciousness I said goodnight to everybody, which in Malinké country is done with the beautiful formula: "May you rest well and that tomorrow we all wake up one by one", meaning that if we wake up all at the same time, the village is on fire.

The powers of the hunters are great and their infusions efficient.

The teachings of a Malinké hunter are not only about tracking and killing wild animals, learning their behavior and ways. It is much more than that; it is learning to dominate the spirits, incarnated in all sorts of things, plants, animals and magic. Learning how to properly handle a gun from the slave trade to avoid that when you fire it, it explodes in your face, is the least difficult. To know how much powder and which bullet you put in the barrel, how to efficiently compact it, how to fix the firestone in the horn, select the bullet in function of the animal you are aiming at, all this is not of another world and can be learned. But to establish a relationship, a dialogue, an exchange with the spirits and the ghosts that constantly live by your side, that's another thing. Managing to attain that level is the superior degree of a hunter. All this is taught through in a million stories and metaphors.

My initiation banquet as apprentice hunter of the Mandingue or Malinké tribe and son of the Diabatés left me without a penny but happy.

When a great hunter dies, better let's say a great magician in Merlin's style, his burial is celebrated weeks after, because his spirit has to get used to go around without a body and also to give the living from the surroundings a chance to be there, prepare the feast and the election of his replacement. This is really a competition of magic among the aspirants to the status of "great hunter". That's how I ended up in strange nights assemblies, heavily charged with mystery and unusual situations. Like, for example: One night it rained mangoes, without having a mango tree around. I read something about hypnosis and collective neurosis, but these mangoes really fell on my head, hurt my skull and I ate them. Another night, I witnessed a parade of wild animals in a space there was no way they could have entered it. The objective was that the chief of the village selected one to be served as dinner. I know it was not possible but I witnessed the killing, the cutting up with all the blood running and I too, ate my small piece of deer.

I better stop here, because one of the oaths of the hunters is not to tell stories of this kind to strangers. After all, I never got any farther than apprentice with barely the right to hunt feathered creatures and shut up. They hunted big game. One night, Djibril recommended me not to take part, things were getting strong, and there would be black magic: dangerous. What I had witnessed was something like baby milk.

233

The Hedonist

In these days my brother hunters instructed me about plants, herbs, leaves and roots which all have something to cure or to hallucinate.

*

My brothers,
Ika kené wa, somogow dew ka kené ?
Many, many moons have gone by. It is possible that my brother Djibril and the Malinkés who knew me, are living in the sacred wood, because that's the way life is in Mali: short. I hope they are having fun, playing tricks on the living, hiding their things, making the water of the well come up and wet them. I hope you could buy the tractor that you wanted so badly to cultivate tobacco as you all wanted to do. Because the earth is less low, seen from a tractor, than seen from a short daba daba.
I want you to know, the living and the dead the same, that in all parts where I have dwelled in life, I always had thoughts for you. Your faces, smiles and laughter still accompany me and sometimes, when I am alone, I sing the sacred melodies and dance the sacred steps you taught me and which are agreeable to our mother earth.
Salaam, my brothers
Yusuf Diabaté

*

For a few weeks Beatrice had not been well, on and off. She was not ill, but not well either. Vomiting, depressed, even her skin changed color; from dark black she turned dark grey. One night after a vomiting crisis, I looked her straight in the eyes, asking her to tell me what was going on. She started weeping and crying, this kind of crying that translates desperation, fear and inconsolable anguish. Little by little, she started to tell it all, shaking and drying up her tears with the towel I gave her. The story is this one: She was pregnant and d not returns to the village, from which the author also was. The latter did not want to marry her. In these catholic villages, a single mother is a disgrace for all the family, the clan and the tribe. She'll be banned or reduced to the state of slavery for the rest of her life. On the other hand, she dared not ask for assistance for abortion, because the Pope in Rome prohibits abortion. What she was doing in fact was trying to abort without having to notice it, provoking an accident or a surprise, taking herbs or boiled roots, let herself fall, jump, all things she had heard about so that abortion would look like an accident. In fact, she was

234

poisoning herself. When she finished and kept looking at her bare feet, which all of a sudden I noticed were very big, there was nothing left of the proud girl I had seen before.

I turned the story around in my head and this is what I came up with:

- Look Beatrice, if you cannot have your baby because your family will doom you and throw you out, and if you cannot abort because it is a sin and you want to remain a good catholic, I propose that you have your baby and that you give it to me.

There followed a long moment of heavy silence. Both of us quickly tried to think of future implications. Finally she stuttered:

-You take him? How?

To my understanding there was only one solution.

- We adopt him.

I was surprised by my own simplicity.

- And when you go back to France, what then?

- We take him with us.

I felt somewhat trapped in my own story, Paule was sleeping a few meters away and I hadn't even talked it over with her. Little by little Beatrice's face recovered serenity. I even thought that I noticed a smile. I know that the dream of many African mothers is to have a daughter or a son in Europe, studying, making a career and sending money to sustain her, once old age points his nose.

-And what do I do?

I could not make the engagement to take her along with us.

- We will pay you a pension for your schooling until you become a teacher. If we can, we'll pay you a trip to Europe to visit us.

By now she was totally calm, her eyes had dried up and she looked at me with an immense gratitude in her eyes.

This is how the future of Mister Hervé, Sekou Goffings was sealed. Today a Master of Arts of the Royal Academy of Performing Arts in Manchester and also from the School of acting in Glasgow, a good man, very good baritone, talented actor and magnificent artistic dancer, with a heart that big that it does not fit in a cathedral. Pride of his mothers Paule and Beatrice, and of his brother Sebastian of whom in a certain way he is co-genitor. But that I'll explain later.

*

Last night was a marvelous night, just because of a conversation with Mariana, the daughter of our friend Marisela (civil servant here in the walled and sleepy city of Campeche) the key person for the reason why you are able to have the pleasure – here I am presumptuous- to read this.

Few times there are conversations which are worth struggling a whole year just to be part of it, it is of the utmost rarity that a conversation like that takes place in Campeche. Let me tell you that Campeche, since last year, is also called "San Francisco de Campeche" for the simple reason that one local congresswoman, who surely has a mysticism problem, proposed this name change. Considering that there is a religious connotation to it, nobody dared oppose a such profound law making. One more time the Republic and the free state of Campeche put down their pants and the motion was adopted unanimously. Knowing that; the name "Campeche" is a contraction of "Ah Kim Pech", which in Maya language (40% of the population of the state) stands for "territory of snakes and ticks". Once translated, the whole name gives "San Francisco of snakes and ticks". Nobody noticed. Devotion produces blindness.

In this small community, where a few families control and dominate every aspect of local life, as in any other part in the world where there are small towns, everything is family related. They swear by the family name, live in the close circles of families, pass every weekend with the family, get corrupt in the family circle, drain the public budget into the family, do business in family and always marry in the same family circles. In reality, they don't like each other at all: they spy, envy, even hate each other, but all is dressed in the coat of Christian respectability. In such a way that those who don't have families are excluded from public, social and economic life whatever their value is. All this results, sociologically speaking, in a very closed, very conservative, very boring and backward society, while we, the "without Campeche family", are floating elements and by the force of things we have to meet some day.

Let's go back to Mariana, who fortunately does not belong to a Campeche family but lives here with her mother, two brothers and an uncle, my good friend Angel. They came from Mexico city, many years ago, meaning that they are "naturally" more awake, open minded, cultured and read than the average campechano who got his social position from his "family". At least, they don't belong to the people who were born in the Guadalupe neighborhood and died in the San Roman neighborhood and between the two lived some years in the Santa Ana neighborhood, which would have been the most outstanding adventure of their lives.

It happens that Marianna in her nineteenth year, having exhausted everything that a place like Campeche has to offer, went to study chemistry and physics at Jalapa University – capital of the state of Veracruz. (One of the very few Mexican universities that deserve to be mentioned on the list of Latin American Universities). She was spending her last days of Christmas break, and preoccupied by a term paper she had to give, first thing, once back at the University. She was desperate for she did not have any idea where or how to start. The subject: "The connection between philosophy and the dark material", nothing less. There followed a conversation so intelligent and fascinating that I want to tell you, because to me it was a ray of light among the thousand and one miseries of daily life.

Soon, we got to the key point: does science give birth to philosophy or is it philosophy that creates science? (If you have never given it a thought, this is the moment to repair that negligence).

*

What is creationist science? – The one that proclaims that God created all things in six days, some five thousand years ago, that he made everything and that everything is in the Bible. For them, philosophy is what the religious concept of the world proclaims, the dominant one being the Roman Catholic and apostolic church. We made a pass to the origin of philosophy, to what Onfray calls "the animalry of philosophy ". Remember that the ancient philosophers built their reasoning and questioning on precise observations of nature and to begin with, about themselves. The questioning of sexual impulses and the orgasmic joy, love, feelings, discovering of atoms and the materialistic theory (all is made of material including the soul) are at the origin of philosophy but also the observation of animal behavior: The monogamous elephant, the masturbating fish, the gregarious bee, the ever single porcupine, the thousands of tales, legends and stories – sometimes very flavored, sometimes horrendous- constituted the prime material for their reflections and thoughts. For example: Pasiphae fell in love with a steer of divine origin, up to the point that she asked the clever Dedale to build a false mechanical cow in which she could lay in to receive the divine semen. Ulysses's seamen, seduced by the sirens' sensual songs and whose dried bones were found in the fields the morning after. Tiresias, the man who separated two snakes coupling and therefore got punished by the Gods to become a woman for seven autumns. Coming back from his experience he told Zeus – who was very interested to know about this- that the pleasure of a woman is seven times superior to that of man. (That the Master of Gods in the Greek mythology wanted to know about this kind of question, makes him more simpatico to me than the dark looking God Father we have to cope with in the Christian mythology).

All these tales and stories that turn around nature – radically animal- are the elements around which philosophical thinking was constructed. Homer, Diodore, Lucrece, Epicure and especially Diogenes, enemies of Plato, are more to live than to study. The monogamous elephant and the gregarious bee - ideals of Platon- compete with the pig of Epicure, the masturbating fish and the single porcupine, to prove, promote, impose philosophical theories that try to define the nature of things and happiness. These theories come from scientific knowledge and not from "believing".

From the confrontations of these two lines of thinking: the Pythagoras-Platonic-monotheist-Christian philosophy will come out victorious. Not because this option is more just, acceptable or better, but because the Plato thoughts got powerful political and military support from Constantine, the Roman Emperor, who imposed them as a state religion, as I told before.

What does the philosophy converted into dogmatic behavior postulate? "Yes to science, on the condition that it fits the doctrine", giving all the power to those who pretend to talk in the name of God and send the concept of individual thinking to the garbage can of human history.

In all this time that the dogma dominated without sharing power, science - in the best of cases - became underground, if it did not come to a complete stop: Reality, logic and progress made a pause that lasted for fifteen hundred years in benefit of the ascetic victorious ideal.

Centuries after the Plato-Paul-Constantine victory, the natural impulse for understanding and progress made that science recovered some cards with the fall of the ridiculous pair: Doctrine makes science. The human impulse for the search of truth and progress is so strong that no bonfire, persecution, torture, lies, wars and other manifestations of love for the fellow human beings, can stop it forever. Erasmus, Bruno, Copernicus, Galileo, Montaigne, Spinoza and thousands more, obliged the adepts of the dogma to give way.

Today we are again in the configuration when science, giving the impulse for philosophy, values, liberty and individual thinking, has a chance.

Mariana enchanted me, she gives me a look at a generation I don't know very much about, in contrast with the surrounding youngsters I use to cross in the walled town of   Campeche. I don't know what came out of this exchange, I never saw her term paper but I heard that she got a good grade.

By Jove: youth is beautiful when it decides not to be old before age.

*

I believe it is right to tell at once the story of the birth of Hervé. Beatrice came to the term of her pregnancy. Of course, this always happens at night. I took her with the plastic two horse powered jeep to the central hospital of Bamako. What I saw there was a horror movie. Two nurses trying to attend two dozens of women having babies. They were all over the place, even on the stairway. No way I wanted my son to get born that way. We got back to the plastic two horses and headed for "point G" hospital, where French medics and nurses attended the whites, the diplomats, the powerful and the well-off, in an acceptable hygienic environment. The problem was that "Point G" is on the top of Koulouba, several miles out of town and only reachable by a sinuous, steeply climbing road. Working its way to the top, after the bend along the zoo, the two horses decided to stop.

Beatrice started to whine, holding her enormous belly with her two hands and her eyeballs upturning. I laid her on the back platform and was blowing into the carburetor when I heard the first angry sound: he sure didn't like to come into this world. It must have been around three in the morning, no stars and not a cat on this road. I was surprised with the ease this all happened. Beatrice was made to have babies. When I was busy with the cordon wondering what to do with it and with what to cut it, salvation came from a nurse who was going to take her shift at the hospital and in no time fixed it all. It was the first day of October of 1972.

This was not the most difficult. The matter of your coming along got complicated three days later when we wanted to take you home and therefore had to certify your existence. The civil servant in charge must have had problems with his wife that very morning; he was in a killing mood and refused to give you legal existence. He, seated behind his desk, his head bent towards his register, not giving us a look; the four of us, Beatrice with Herve, wrapped in a bundle with just his face showing, in her arms, Paule and me standing in front.
He -Mother?

Me-Beatrice Sawadogo
He took the identity papers without looking up, copied them very carefully and very slowly.
He-Father?
Me-Unknown.
He pushed his chair backwards, looked at me down and up and over again
He-I cannot write that.
Me-Sure you can
I knew a little bit about Malian laws which are much the same as the French. Where else could they come from?
He-No!
Me-Yes!
He- No, because it's a boy.....
Me-Yes you can, I know the law!
He- I know it too, I need an identification of a man.
At that point we were shouting, I with my hands on his table and my face just centimeters away from his. He was very ugly with many deep scares in his face.
Me-Any man?
He-Any, if you give me your passport I write you down as the father.
I consulted Paule with my eyes. After all, if he put me down as father I won't have to adopt? Isn't that so? I pulled my Belgian passport from my pocket and threw it on the table. Slowly the scar faced man examined it and wrote me up as the father. That's how I became your official father. The thing seemed to have come to a happy end, but no.

Two months later, upon Paule's insistence, I wanted to write you in my passport as my legitimate son. The honorary Consul of the king of Belgium in Bamako was a Lebanese shopkeeper, specialized in women's dresses and underwear. In his shop window was displayed the King's and Queen's official photo – Baudouin the first of Belgium and Fabiola de Mora y de Aragon – among negligees, transparent dresses and daring underwear. A tall, slim, grey haired, very friendly man, who certainly must have a different opinion of the subjects of his majesty from what I was showing, received me smiling but he did not invite me to sit. He examined the documents and with a deep voice told me:
- I cannot register your son as a Belgian subject.
- Why not?
I felt immediately that problems were cooking
- You are married to Beatrice Sawadogo?

- No, to Paule Englebert, a Belgian subject too.
- That's why I cannot proceed; the Belgian law does not permit to recognize children of a married man from another woman. It is called "from another bed".
Politely I thanked the consul and left the store.
Well, son, if you are not going to be Belgian, you are going to be a citizen from the Malian Republic. The day after, I presented myself in the offices of civilian affairs with the intention to give you a nationality. But here too, they did not want to recognize you as an official human being, saying: "If you are Belgian, your son is Belgian". The vicious circle was complete, and my blood was boiling.

For more than ten years we did not encounter a solution. This only came when I became a French citizen, because in France yes, the law permits for a man to recognize up to three "children from another bed". (Who knows why three and not four or ten?).

Having an illegitimate descendent did not prevent us from crossing Mali from one end to the other: Segou capital of the Bambaras, and Djenné where we met an Italian architect; Fabrizio Carola who was fascinated with the huge mud, straw and wood structure of the Mosque with an over twenty meters high tower. Fabrizio headed a project to build a covered market in Mopti. The Djenne mosque fascinated him to the point that he wanted to build the Mopti market in the same traditional cheap material; a proposal for which the government almost threw him out of the country. They wanted cement and zinc that cost three times as much and will heat twice as much. The concept of "development" and its stereotypes anchored in the brains of civil servants only can feed back what there is in these brains, and that is not very much.

In Mopti, where I was known (who knows why?) they gave me a baby elephant whose mother had been killed. I didn't know what to do with the animal and gave it to the children of Fabrizio, they were enchanted. Not many kids have a baby elephant as a pet. I also met in Mopti the French expert Michel Levante, who was gathering facts to work out a general five year development plan for the country. Michel is from the second generation of Russian immigrants and besides that his father's fled from communism; he was nevertheless a convinced Marxist-Leninist. We had interesting conversation. Michel will become an important factor in my life because he will connect me to the SEDES my future employer in Chad and with Annie, his sister in law

241

with whom I'll fall in love. But that's another story for later. The development plan of Mali never saw a beginning of realization.

We visited the Dogon country several times. The Dogons: a particular tribe, still practicing their pre-Islamic beliefs. For the account of the ministry of livestock of which my friend Boubakar became a cabinet member, I accompanied different field missions of all nationalities and aspects. In one of those, I participated in the crossing of the Niger River of the Fulani herds. Thousands of zebus jump into the river all together at a signal. The event takes place once a year, when the herds are coming back south from their nomad wandering north of the river. To prevent anybody from taking advantage when crossing and having the primacy of entering new pastures, the Fulani organize a massive crossing the same day.

In Timbuktu, the mythical very ancient scholastic center of Islamic penetration in these parts of Africa, I witnessed how the very devote and obedient dignitaries from the religion of the Prophet hide themselves to drink whisky camouflaged in small tea glasses. Also in Timbuktu, I passed one of the scary moments in my life. Already seated in the DC3 plane, which carried a silver inscription with its year of construction: 1938, the pilot asked us to leave the plane because one of the engines did not want to start. Walking back to the palm roof, hardly sustained by four crooked wooden poles, acting as airport, from where we watched the mechanic put up a ladder under one of the motors, open the belly of it and start to hammer and work it with a screwdriver. Half an hour later we were invited to board again. Passing the mechanic with his ladder on his shoulder, I asked if it was going to work? On what he replied:
- With God's will!

With the Songhais and Tuaregs in Gao, much further up the river from Timbuktu almost at the Niger border, I learned to dance seated, moving shoulders and head, in the midst of a very nice smelling incense cloud, in a perfect sensual atmosphere surrounded by women who threw such seductive looks that it would have awoken a dead elephant.

Bamako to Saint Louis, in Senegal, is a three days train trip, which I made in company of two Australian backpack girls. In any part of the world you meet Australian backpackers. They explained that they

242

work two jobs for several years and then take off for the world trip for as long as their money lasts. I liked that. This train stops five times a day wherever it is, to allow the machinist, his assistance and the passengers to pray towards Mecca, and of course also in all the dwellings and villages along the railroad, plus whenever there are cows or any other wild animals sleeping on the rails. One night, I had to assure the Australian girls that everything was all right when we saw the assistant machinist walking in front of the train over the bridge of the river Senegal, with a petrol lamp, to check if it was alright for the train to cross it.

I spent a couple of days in a Bozo village - Bozos are a fishermen tribe - on the river Niger. They do the same thing with their canoes that the Fulani do with their livestock: hide them. In colonial times they had to pay taxes on every canoe and they have a memory. Bozos are the only people in the world I know who don´t bother about mosquito bites, which is absolutely a must if you want to live as a Bozo fisherman.

Little by little, the project Paule was working for came to an end. Just for once I have to admit that this was an intelligent project, which is very unusual coming out of a United Nations Organization. It had been conceived in the brains of a Congolese poet, Mister Tchicaya U'tamsi, the son to a former Congolese congressman in the French parliament in colonial times. It consisted of a postgraduate program in Science and Mathematics in which, instead of sending African students to Europe – 80 % never came back – they brought the teachers to Africa for short but intensive studying programs. It worked.
It gave us an occasion to meet scientist and intellectuals of high level from all over the world: Indian mathematicians; Yugoslav engineers; Brazilian professors of science and many more. I got kicks out of their intelligent conversation and pleasant behavior. Having met these people was a first class gift.

What had to happen, happened: Paule, a professional woman, United Nations civil servant in New York, Paris, Cuba and Mali, after living together for years without ever bothering about having children, because we did not need to procreate to realize ourselves in life, got pregnant one year after Hervé entered our lives. I say so, because there is a relationship between cause and effect.

The Hedonist

Slowly, we started saying goodbye to Bamako, its market place of Sudanese architecture, its smells of all kinds of spices, dried fish, buccaneered meat and burning wood in which the whole city got wrapped up. The train station and its trains that rarely managed to climb the hill outside the town at the first try, allowing the whole city to see the train back up again to the station to disconnect one or two wagons, and try again crossing the city at full speed to get enough power to climb the hill. Its variety of people coming from all the tribes the country was composed of, all being Malians; they nevertheless live in separate neighborhoods, where tribal hierarchy, customs and behavior are strictly reproduced. My friends: Jaques Letelier an authentic Trotskyite and his wife Mary, an authentic gringa from Indiana. Kamatchek, an authentic Touareg, future chief of his clan and independent freedom fighter. Jean Courtelier, a French restaurateur who kept a pig as a pet, named Sekou Touré, after the president of Guinea from where he had been expelled, Father Paul, who in the end almost could have been a Meslier, keeper of Beatrice. Bamako: a picturesque city with strong and convinced people, like all those who live close to the desert.

My brothers Diabaté and my fellows from the hunters fraternity of Kangaba, gave me a three days feast of which I am not going to give details, too emotional, too strange, too much of everything.

To say goodbye to my friend Boubacar Sy, we had agreed for a lunch in his house, which meant that one afternoon we stretched out on a thick carpet in his garden in the shade of a mango tree- mango trees give the densest shade from all Malian trees. Bouba Sy lived in an old colonial mansion the garden of which looked more like a park, even if the keeping of the park had ended with the latest French colonial civil servant who occupied the place. What was left is a huge mansion with a columned terrace, screaming for a paint layer and a grey dusty space all around it. Spending money in watering such a lawn is not in the Malian environmental culture. We ate pieces of chicken and meat floating in a red spicy sauce, almost in complete silence. Once the meal over, we stretched comfortably on the carpet and the cushions to dedicate ourselves to the tea ceremonial. The noble Fulani dignitary, who was my host, was dressed in white pants and a white shirt with gold embroidery around the neck and the sleeves.
Getting close to me, he confided:
- Do you know that I am going to have a son from Miriam?

Miriam, a tall young woman equally from Peul descent to which we have to add a couple of years in the French university of Rennes, studying I don't know what, was Bouba's mistress.

- No, I don't know, congratulations.

This became delicate, because Bouba was married to Marianna, a French sociologist he had brought from Paris and who, of course, was tall and blond. Many times we had interesting conversations about the different tribal customs in Mali, she sounded like a very intelligent and well read person, pleasant to talk to and above all driven by an enormous desire to make her mixed marriage work. I tried to get my thoughts together blowing on my hot tea.

- What does Marianna say about that?

He did not look at me either but concentrated on sipping his tea.

- Marianna is having a bad time, she spends her days quarreling with my sister.

- With your sister? The one who's the mistress of the minister?

It was a public secret that his sister was the lover of Captain Ouedai, the very feared and brutal minister of the interior who handled his problems with his pistols which hung from his hips in the purest John Wayne style.

- Yes - he did not seem to be bothered by my direct speech, a mode we had been using since we knew each other - Marianna does not accept her place in this family.

- And what is exactly Marianne's family position?

- You know that in our customs, the wife of the brother is servant to his mother and his senior sister, and that they have the right to use or take her personal belongings including her clothes.

Yes, I knew of some of these customs and a lot of bizarre things more.

- It does not surprise you that Marianna, a sociologist from the Sorbonne, has some problems to accept this social status in your family, does it? Don't you think that you are pushing a little far?

- I do understand, but that's the way it is, she has to accept.

This was said very firmly.

- Are you going to marry Miriam?

- Of course, she is having my son!

- So you are going to be polygamous.

- Yes I think so. After all, polygamy is much too good to be left in exclusivity to illiterate Negroes and stupid Arabs.

We laughed. I knew that polygamy was useful and could create harmony in a household; things usually were that way when it was the first wife who selected the second or the third one. It is a way of sharing the work: cleaning, washing, cooking, collecting fire wood or water and even raising children and having company when the husband is away. Things usually get complicated when it is the husband who brings along his second spouse and get dramatic when the two women quarrel or start hating each other. In that case, all that is left to the poor husband is to lodge his second wife in another neighborhood and start traveling from house to house every other night, without skipping one, in which case he'd be getting into more problems.

- You know Marianna is going back to Paris?
- Yes, it is quite logical, I'd thought of it.
- Too bad, she is a fine person, very intelligent and well read.
- True. But you see, I cannot escape - or go on living isolated from my family, from the ways and customs of the people I still belong to, in spite of my education.

No, I didn't see it that way. But looking at my friend in his traditional garments, being served by young girls, lying on his carpet in the shade of a mango tree, sipping or rather slurping mint tea, I started to understand. Here was my beloved friend with his seven years of studies in Paris, westernized as nobody else, living with a white blond woman, in the process of being recuperated by traditions and ways of living of tribal society, and changing his soul. I had seen this coming: months ago he had asked for my hunting rifle so he and his father could shoot at the moon as soon as it appeared on the breaking of Ramadan. Another time, he had taken me to the market with the Mehari jeep, to buy two sheep that should be killed ritually for the Muslim feast of Aid el Kibir, because those who kill a sheep in this day can sit on it when they ride into heaven.

- Bouba, you are going to end up as a traditional Muslim, I hope you'll not go as far as to excise your daughters to come.

He laughed, but I knew that he had already thought of it and was taking an option on reintegrating traditional Mali. From his sister on, who was making life look like hell for his white wife; his father and mother, and even the tribe's elders, all had gone together to recuperate their son, recently appointed Director General of the Malian Cotton Company, a state within the state of Mali.

For what was left of the afternoon, we stayed remembering souvenirs and anecdotes: about the young Peul he had once appointed to feed our oxen at the feedlot we created and who refused to do so since, according to him, "these animals are big enough" - and hundreds more of stories of the same kind.

The vet Boubacar Sy, Director General of the Malian Cotton Company died eighteen years later in a car accident. He left three widows and seven children and was very respected and loved in his community. So I was told.

CHAPTER VI
PARÍS- N´DJAMENA

Regardless of the lack of official existence of Hervé who already was over a year old, our return to Europe passed without mayor incidents. The UNESCO, provider of the soup and the meat, appreciating Paule's work, reintegrated her in their bureaucracy. To return to the Latin Quarter in Paris, the Maspero bookshop- which will close in a short time because the owner Maspero had too long closed his eyes on the hundreds of people who stole books – sipping coffee at the Deux Magots or Café de Flore (I have to say that in these times it was still affordable, today only millionaires can afford to sip coffee in these joints), all this was very agreeable. Somebody said- I don't remember who - that: "to appreciate a city you have to leave it". This is true.

*

The banker and President of France, Pompidou, had died and the country was governed by a sort of aristocrat - claiming to descend from Lafayette – Giscard d´Estaing. Belonging to the centre-right, he made reforms and governed in such a progressive way that no leftist government ever had dreamed of. Traditionally, French politics are that way: if you want socialist reforms, you vote for the right. If you want a more conservative government, you vote for the left. The first ones want to prove that they too have a social sensibility and the latter want to prove that they know how to govern a capitalist state.   He was also an accordionist, which he called the piano of the poor. Much talk was going on about the construction of a United Europe.

Marie-Chantal, reassured that I was not going to steal our son Jan, accepted to have coffees and dinners. All this was very pleasant and civilized.

Paule´s belly became very respectable and we moved to Waterloo (Belgium) to allow her mother to participate in the birth of her first consanguineous grandson. For ten years I had not really walked on Belgian soil. It was not in the least moving and I found the Belgians boring as death itself. They talked about cars, houses, country homes, money, food and sex. Yes, they fucked a lot, the sexual liberation and Woman's Lib, inherited from May 1968, had passed through there.

I investigated about Hervé´s official existence but found out that not much could be done besides a procedure that could last for years. A lawyer explained to me that this was the way the Catholic Church, still very influent, protected the society from the disorder that would result of men sewing bastards all over the country. Also, that these were laws to protect heritages and which probably would disappear with the uniformity of European laws. It indeed happened years later but who can wait for a law to be labeled, voted and enforced? I was afraid that I would die before that happened.

Living with my in-laws became an interesting psychological experience. Sometimes they did not talk for days. Paule´s father had a hearing problem: words only reached him when he turned on his hearing device which he carried under his jacket and made you the favor to turn it on only when it pleased him to listen to you. So, you could be talking and talking to him, just to find out that his device was turned off. In the middle of a conversation he would make a discreet movement to his chest and turn it off, keeping nodding his head as if he understood you perfectly well and to encourage you to keep talking. I believe that he was a man with a great interior life, since he only frequented himself. Her mother, very nice and agreeable at some moments could the following moment paint the expression of a police officer or an army sergeant on her face. But altogether they were pleasant, quiet people.

Paule´s belly became enormous. I liked to caress it and feel Sebastian boxing and playing football inside. He already wanted to swallow life and fix the world, and still does. I felt good about not being born in an African tribe, where from the first signs of pregnancy the future mother leaves her husband's house and goes to live with her family for the whole period of pregnancy and even months later, leaving her husband managing his life as he can. This is one of the many reasons which justify polygamy: not wasting time in the reproductive mechanism. Also, having as much male descent as possible is the only way of getting social security once time has come that one cannot work the earth anymore with a short daba daba: your children will provide for you.

It is not feasible to caress your wife's belly all day long, so I went to explore Brussels and specially its cafés. Cafés are a social institution in Belgium, always decorated with good taste, comfortable chairs and benches, often leathered or oak walls, paintings, pictures and huge mirrors. The café is the second, sometimes the first, home to many Belgians. If the tables have some character of privacy, the long bar with its high stools is socially speaking "open country" where everybody talks to everybody about everything. People you have never seen in your life offer you a beer just because destiny put you next to them, pleased not to drink alone, which always is sad. They tell you all about their life. You learn things about their wife and relatives that, of course, they would never tell in front of them. You can also learn about their political opinions, about the government, the police. Of course these opinions are very rarely positive. Most of them are convinced that when the people have a nice opinion about their government they are fooled. For most of the Belgians being happy with the government is the beginning of decadence. This explains in a certain way, how this country lives at regular periods for months without a government. When after, never a short time, your stomach is full of beer, your lungs full of smoke, your brains starting to float in your skull and your bank of memories full of confidences, you say goodbye to your pals with a firm handshake or a kiss. You know that you will probably never see them again. A society with such solid institutions can't go wrong.

Screaming loud and red as a tomato – of anger? - Sebastian Aurélien Goffings joined the Homo sapiens species. This happened on the territory of the Brussels suburbs called Uccle. Yet we were four, a typical European family except for the variety of skin color. The danger of the agrarian bee was pointing. Paternal and social responsibility pushes towards that.

*

The Hedonist

The agrarian bee, blindly submitted and programmed to satisfy natural necessities (the type of behavior that is predetermined by the circulation of the universe and the solar orientation of flowers), obeys and reacts to the most insignificant movement, the smallest changes. Everything she does is subordinated to the order and the law of the cosmos: she eats little, flies to the calices of flowers, produces wax, builds the beehive at the millimeter, taking into account the ventilation, precise up to the fraction of a degree, making honey, managing pollen, calculating the density of light and more.

All this comes from an ancestral, genetic inscription in the living material. The bee is the most excellent example of blind obedience to universal laws of nature. It is not surprising that for many philosophers (who are interested in human relations, the politics of submission of the individual) have a fascinated devotion for the bee. The organization of the community, the pragmatic and efficient management of space, the banishment of all individual particularities are the patterns on which were built the Egyptian monarchies, the Roman Empire, Greek democracy, the medieval kingdoms, modern republics, political organizations, the tribe and the family.

The bee obeys the natural program that predetermines her behavior. She has no choice whatsoever, neither for her birth as a queen or a laborer, neither for the way she dies- violent or exhausted- nor for her sexuality- active or chaste. She is submitted to the law. She does not exist, she just obeys. Do we have to be surprised that all the philosophers who proclaim the domination and the cult of collectivity just love the bee? Pythagoras, Plato, Aristotle, Xenophon, the holy writings, Clemente from Alexandria, Augustine and the fathers of the holy church: all celebrate the communitarian qualities of this insect, metaphorically political. Any animal or human that does not think but abdicates renounces and is ignorant, is easier to govern and to dominate.

Tireless workers: dedicated, caste, virtuous, pure, prolific and sedentary, truthful and disciplined, viscerally obedient and slightly stupid, the bees are cited by the Christians as examples to follow, as to how man should live.

Where is the beehive which demands renouncing to the essentials that constitute a male individuality and a female subjectivity? Where can the machine be witnessed, transforming particular energies into a collective project? In the micro-family!

The family is built when a third element comes to integrate it; she – the family- is the absolute triumph of nature, the partnership between man and animals and goes beyond the couple to erase the

250

individual in benefit of the status and functions of: father – mother-child.

The western family is constructed around the central prehistoric axis of the phallus that obliges: heterosexuality, monogamy, fidelity and reproduction. Outside this concept of the couple male-female, all is considered disorder and is discredited. All other expressions of sexuality are proscribed and considered unnatural: homosexuality, polygamy, polyandry, incest, pedophilia, exhibitionism, fetishism, voyeurism, and also: masturbation, celibacy, libertinage, voluntary sterility. All of these are considered non-productive forms of sexuality. Where is the rule? In the beehive! Fortunately things are not anymore exactly like that, but this is very recent and only true for a minority.

In our civilization, Pythagoras and Plato are the ones who perfection it. For these killers of pleasure and desire, the model of society has to reproduce the order and harmony that reigns in heaven. They even go as far as to recognize that the male authority and domination was given to him by divinity. The male reigns in his family the way God reigns in heaven. Admitting that paternal authority proceeds from God, the decisions of the spouse are equivalent to the divine laws of the ideal world where the other father establishes the rules: God. Asserting that when a woman submits her own will to the will of her spouse, she realizes the will of God was a very daring and successful trick. Pythagoras wanted the celestial order to reign on earth. All he got was to legitimize masculine domination over the female by form of tyranny.

Oh no, I hope you did not consider this as old stuff and that things have radically changed. The inspectors "of marriage affairs" in Plato's laws and the obliged sexual service in Aristotle's "Politics", dispose nowadays of unexpected prolongations, reformulated in terms of ideological pressures, the dictatorship of "what are the others going to say", fiscal pressures, the Sunday sermons of all kinds of preachers, the glorification of the "family" in the mouth of all the politicians, whatever their party or ideological tendency.

Actually, the desire for eternity anchored in the stomach of all the fans of "the family" translates an existential anguish, incapacity to admit their own end and consequently the will to project them into eternity by the procreation of a descendant. To leave a trace as a justification of the family is a poor reason, a ridiculous argument, "nothingness" will triumph over everything, including these incredible pretensions of taking an insurance, a security on eternity by way of "the family" comedy. The family as a device to produce individual eternity, how about that?

On the contrary, the compromise of two individuals within marriage (of monstrous nature if one thinks it over), renouncing to their specific and particular qualities in order to accede to a social function, is paid for in symbolic money of social recognition. The couple with children unmistakably contains the same animal forces the herds, tribes and the beehive are based upon.

*

Coming down the steps of the hospital in Uccle, I carrying Hervé and Paule Sebastian, these thought were not mine yet. At that time, I had never dedicated much thought to searching the essence of things, the history and the background of the rules we live by. However, today I know that it is better, that life is easier, when one knows and understands, just because understanding and knowing open choices.

We'll probably never know the real reasons why we did it, but we decided to make a pause in our traveling and establish ourselves in an almost abandoned village in the Ardennes region. Bagimont is the name of the place, close to Bouillon and the French border. A low mountains region covered mainly with pine woods. We rented a house on the outskirts of the village which counted two dozen houses and a church, all made in local grey stone. As grey as is the sky of this region for about three hundred days a year, even the twenty five people living in that place looked grey.

Close by, the village of Bouillon and the majestic castle of Godefroy de Bouillon – who in the first crusades crowned himself King of Jerusalem- built as and eagles' nest on top of a rock dominating a pretty valley with a river, was the main attraction. Visiting the place we immediately understood why Godefroy- a name that stands for God's friend or God fearing - preferred to immigrate and live in Palestine: the two meters thick walls permanently dripping with water. This place was inhabitable.

*

Excuse me, I am kidding: This Noble Count of Bouillon; descendant of King Dagobert (the last of the Franc Merovingian kings who founded Paris and was assassinated by the Vatican), also got mixed with the Mary Magdalena descendants, - Mary of Magdala: of the house of Benjamin, came to seek refuge for herself and her followers in France, after the crucifixion of her husband, better known as Jesus Christ, where she gave birth to the descendant of the crucified rebel and whom she raised here. The master of Bouillon was rather anxious to recuperate the proofs of his blood connection to Christ and charged his Templar knights to find these proofs. When he climbed to the throne of Jerusalem in a certain way he was recuperating his rights. Some historians also pretend that he founded the Priorato of Sion, a fraternity the reason of existence of which is to protect the proofs and the descendants of the crucified Nazarene. Of course, for centuries nobody in the Vatican liked that.

This version of the facts is as good as: and even more solid than any other.

*

Here, close to Bouillon, in a social and spiritual desert, I wrote a very bad book of which Paule has kept one single copy. A leftist essay on revolutionary social theories, incoherent, naïve, dreaming, unrealistic - inspired by the theories of an Italian female writer, Machiocchi, I believe she was named. After a few months I knew for sure that a hermit monk's life was not my cup of tea. More and more frequently I went to Paris to look for a job, leaving Paule alone in the Ardennes woods with two small kids. Up until now I am not very proud of that period but that's the way it was. Contemplative village dwelling is definitively not for us. I felt a lot better roaming the Latin Quarter, reading in Maspero's bookshop, smelling smog in a metropolis. Finally, we all returned to Paris and Paule to UNESCO, while I kept the children between two job interviews. We lived in the seventeenth arrondissement, middle class and full of kindergartens.

Thanks to Mister Levante from Mopti, I got recruited in a third world development agency – that's how these parts of the world were called in those times. Today, they use many other more "politically correct" names but it all means the same thing. The agency was part of the "Caisse des Dépôts" a very powerful financial government organization, money provider of many big state owned strategic enterprises and administrative entities of the French government. The "Caisse des dépôts" makes the French stock market laugh or cry. The SEDES agency was close to the National Assembly and the Seine River, just off the boulevard Saint-Germain. Inside the agency there reigned a soft leftist, generous atmosphere, but believing that underdevelopment of the ex-colonies was all the fault of the colonizing power, which resulted in a guilty feeling hanging around in all the offices. Most of my colleagues, very cultured and well-read people, believing in the rightness of what they were doing and of their convictions, were floating in unreal perceptions. Later on I will call them "the caviar left".

The project I was going to work on and lead, was in its preparation phase and consisted of nothing less than dressing a complete inventory, qualitative and quantitative, of everything with four legs – except cats, dogs- in the Republic of Chad, just south of the Sahara desert in my beloved Sahel region. The European Community was financing this census.

As you'll already know by now, the governments of the Sahel countries had understood that the monies they were getting from the rich were proportional to the horrendous, dramatic pictures they were able to sell to the world. The picture in vogue at that moment was that of the drought which brought starvation to the herds and misery to their people. The content of their dramatic reports had reached the point that, mathematically, there was not a single goat, sheep, donkey, camel or cow left in the whole Sahel from the Atlantic coast to the Indian Ocean. Somebody in Brussels got aware of this absurdity of sending money to help out on the drought herds that already had died off three times. The industry of "asking, claiming and demanding" – still very flourishing in Mexico today - was functioning at full regime. The idea of my project was simply to gather data to adjust development aid to reality. The project was supposed to last 18 months. Long days and not a few nights I passed studying sociological reports, statistics, searching for documentation: ethnological, political, economic and everything related to Chad and its people. Slowly, the country entered my brain and stomach.

*

As Don Juan said: "I have an irresistible tendency to give into the things I like:"my nomad libido" – you already know – awoke seeing, admiring and desiring, everyday, one of the most beautiful females of the SEDES. We looked at each other, we liked what we saw and heard, we felt desire, we made love and we loved; life is that simple. At least when desire and feelings are not being used as merchandise put on the counter. It is totally impossible that an intense erotic relationship – to say it that way – does not spill over in the dominium of: affection, caring, loving, liking and appreciating. Soon we were lovers. This was not difficult; Annie is of very agreeable company, pleasant, with a great sense of humor, intelligent and affectionate. This situation, in our civilization, creates difficulties; a world of lies and cheating, hypocrisy and drama. All things that I don't like as I did not like to leave a loved person, at midnight, to run into the deserted streets of Paris to catch the last subway, just to wake somebody an hour later and start telling lies that nobody believed anyway. Neither Annie whom I left, neither Paule whom I woke up, neither me running in the night, were satisfied with this situation. So we agreed, without many words, in fact none, that I would sleep in Annie's bed if there I was. One day, what had to happen; happened. Both women met, liked each other and became friends. Then came the nights when I stayed home babysitting, while Annie and Paule went to the movies or any other event. My married life was moving into some sort of soft polygamy – in which I will be passing the rest of my life, so far. This happened naturally without words or theories. Thanks to the enormous luck I have of having met, and pleased to, two people of exceptional grandeur.

*

Have you ever noticed that a company of three makes you more careful of how and what you are saying or doing? How a conversation of three is more interesting and lively? How much more attention you pay to your partners when you are three than when you are only two and always are looking at the same nose in the middle of the same face? The man, who ever says that he has not dreamed, wished, fantasized about living in harmony with the women he loves instead of living like a hiding thief, is a liar. Polygamy desired and freely accepted is nothing of the other world and much too pleasant and enriching to be left as the exclusive right of illiterate Muslims, as said my friend Boubacar. Contrary to the Islamic institution of polygamy – based on female submission to male barbarism – ours is a sweet agreement based on love and friendship. Of course it is only possible with people who have learned to live with themselves and already constructed their personalities and values; people who don't look for comfort and security under someone else's skin; people who understand that desire is not a matter of harm, fault or curse, as has been said for at least fifty centuries, but an opportunity of infinite pleasures of body and mind; a song of life. This takes years to conquer and very few people ever will succeed, maybe we are talking about a two percent or less. Nietzsche: "Loving a sole being is barbarian, because it is practiced to the exclusion of all the rest of human beings". Who can oppose that? It is mathematic.

According to fundamental beliefs, misogyny surges with the creation of the world and a male who got bored. The first book of Genesis tells the origin of light, universe, water, animals, plants etc and, "The Male" – superior mammal- who walked around in a paradise among wild animals and juicy fruit trees, all created to please him. In a place like this, you cannot encounter death, suffering nor sickness, and of course neither a female. The male got bored, and suffered from loneliness. God, who for this reason is not that perfect, offered him the female. Already by the order of appearance of the female on the stage, she is a supplement, in fact a "walking rib" very little independent. But that's not all: misogyny starts with the definition of what is bad, personified by the female - sin, fault, pleasure, guilt and disobedience. To be chased from Paradise is the entire responsibility of the female, taking along forever the totality of humanity towards the absolute wrong. Really, this is not an insignificant thing, is it?

Who opposes misogyny? The Hedonist libertine does. How?
A Siberian legend tells us that two porcupines were in a frozen dessert. Not to die frozen, they decide to heat each other with their body, but getting too close they prick each other and getting away from each other, they freeze. Excessively close to each other or too far away: the risks are the same: loneliness or saturation. Situations will decide the same distance to be kept in which there is neither suffering from too much closeness, nor the cruel absence of the other. (M. Onfray)

In the field of love relations, this excludes equally forced celibacy and the suffocating ties of the fusion couple. It refuses forced chastity and also the permanent love dwarfing, as it refuses the condemnation of the priest to sexual abstinence or masturbation and the unconcerned behavior of the classic libertine. The right distance can be obtained by way of language: the verb, signals worked out by two or more lucid actors, informed and decided to make their acts coherent with their desires. Nothing forces the promise of fidelity in a couple if you don't have intentions of fidelity. There are fidelities more important and transcendental in a partnership than a promise of sexual exclusivity and sentimental monopole.

The libertine I am talking about, never will contract compromises above what he can hold, he does not promise what he cannot keep. He does not put himself in compromises with eternal goals, he does not show paradises he does not believe in, he does not lie to obtain depreciable success, he does not give a mortgage on the future, does not sign blank checks on his own future and less on someone else's. The libertine does not compromise his liberty; he does not talk about monopolistic and exclusive sentiments and body rights. The Hedonist libertine does what one day he promised: give and take pleasure and to accept that the contract is broken in the moment that one of the parties does not find it satisfactory anymore.

The Hedonist contract is exclusively made of the refusal of suffering:"Only man has the power to transform sexuality into eroticism and to turn carnal violence into the elegance of bodies" (M.Onfray).

The drama of considering the monogamous couple as the only possible sexual relation already appears in the ancient Greek theatre. Just look around you, where aggressive, dramatic divorces are prospering; painful separations often wrapped up in home violence and sexual misery if not miserable sex. It is necessary - for the sake of public health and the pursuit of happiness – to throw out the "love laws" and the obligatory pattern of the fusion couple.

Finally, let's establish the differences between the things that our civilization hides from us: pleasure and love; sexuality and procreation, sentiments and cohabitation, fidelity and exclusivity, monogamy and physical monopoly. Because: yes we can make use of our body without being "in love", love without an obligation of cohabitation and without demanding the exclusive rights over another body and soul.

In these times, when our family took in a new element, just before the Chadian adventure, I did not know all this in a reasoned way. I felt it, lived it by instinct. The word "Hedonist", I discovered only twenty years later (I regret it very much). Things can be lived and exist without being named. Naming brings in more clarity, that's all.

*

Leaning over three kilometers on the western shore of the Chari River – which has that particularity of not running towards the sea but inland towards Lake Chad - N'djamena is one more colonial city that the colonial armies sprayed all along West Africa, south of the Sahara desert. Starting with Saint-Louis in Senegal and ending on the Sudanese border where the English colonial troops won the race of colonial conquest over the French. As it does not have a hill to dominate from, the residential, administrative and troop barracks

257

together with the airport are all concentrated in the north of the city, along the Chari River, starting with the cathedral and ending with the slaughterhouse and the Farcha neighborhood. For more details, please see: Ouagadougou, Bamako or any other place of colonial Sahelian origin.

The animal census had to be based on ethnographic maps, administrative reports and the last human census conducted by the French colonial administration. Since then nobody had done another. There are eighty-four ethnic groups in Chad, with a dozen outstanding ones. Each one speaks its own language and has its particular customs and traditions. As to the ones dedicated to cattle, they roam in three fourths of the country, from the south of the Sahara desert to Sarh – old name: Fort Archambault after the name of the commander of the colonial conquering army. In this most southern region the cattle herdsmen have a brief contact with the peasants during the dry season. In the wet season, the south is kingdom of the tsetse fly, preventing cattle from dwelling there. The southern region, in ancient times, was nevertheless often raided by the nomads in search of slaves, for themselves or to sell. Today, thanks to the Pax colonial, peasant families and cattle herders are connected to each other by agreements of mutual interest. For example: In exchange of a couple of millet bags, the nomads will station their herd for a determined time on the peasants' fields, fertilizing them! As already explained, a difficult factor in organizing a valid census is the fact that the herds have several owners. The head of the "tent" or family- let's call them family but this can be very extensive- for sanitary reasons disperses his herd among his kin or friends. Almost all the cattle owners are transhumant and can be divided into "big" and "small" according to the distance they cover. This can go from around 900 kilometers (one way) to just 100 for the "small" ones.

A transhumant tribe has a harbor, a village or a dwelling of origin and travels on a very precisely defined route. Under no circumstances do they go where they please, neither with the number of cattle that occurs to them, or whenever they choose. A transhumant family from a determined tribe has a right to transit with so many heads towards a defined region, at a determined period of the lunar calendar and can stay there for so much time on such and such water wells. The first to enter a pasture zone, after the first rains, has of course the advantage. This order of moving changes each year and is agreed upon in clan or tribal meetings, after very heavy discussions and disputes.

The colonial reports are full of stories of how the "Méharistes" – a colonial police corps mounted on camels – had to run all over the country from well to well, from camp to camp, to settle disputes and enforce the law. These disputes almost always ended in bloodshed, which is only understandable if considering that the matter- water- is deadly serious and often is a question of life or death. I read that in cases of homicide, the cases came before a French judge who fixed "the price of death" to be paid in cattle heads and "servants", the other word for slaves.

The only nomads who move wherever and how they like in search of good pasture and enough water are the Borroros - the only Fulani clan out of dozens, to refuse Islam - already mentioned.

The main Chadian transhumant tribe as to distances covered, heads of cattle owned and "tents" are the Misseries who have their roots in the East of the country up to the Sudanese border. To complicate a little more: There are two brother-tribes of Misseries: The red ones and the black ones. The legend says that two brothers coming from Arabia long before Islam established in Chad and are the ancestors of these two tribes. But that's the legend. Since the conquest by Islam, all tribes and everybody want to be of Arabian descent.

With the Arabs from the Batha region in the center of the country, the Goranes to the West and North together with the Fulanis make up the bulk of great transhumant tribes. Add the Kanembou in the extreme West, on the Niger border, and the Kouri from Lake Chad and we have four fifths of the cattle of the country.

To start with, I organized training lessons for the censors to become the head of the eight censor teams that will roam the country. The rest will be recruited and formed locally, region per region and tribe per tribe according to the languages spoken. Our operation base will be the veterinary laboratory of Farcha, a huge domain with several houses and buildings serving as permanent vet training, research, laboratory, and museum. In colonial times, Farcha was the Mecca of French veterinary services for the whole of West Africa.

When I entered his office to pay my obligatory protocol visit, the head of the Farcha vet station was not alone. He introduced me to Doctor Dragesic, a man who had reached the age when grey hair gives way to no hair. Very slim, that kind of figure that comes close to dry. I had already heard about his rather extravagant and folkloric reputation. Very smiling, he shook my hand firmly and kept it for a long time. When I started wondering when I would get my fingers back he freed them with a loud laugh.

The office was of ministerial type with in a corner four heavy leather armchairs looking like they had reached the end of their presentable period. All the walls, from floor to ceiling, were covered with glass fronted bookshelves in which at first sight was stocked everything that the French veterinary surgeons had seen, investigated and cured over the whole colonial period; a treasure packed in leather covers and gold numbers showing the year of activity. Three big ceiling ventilators tried to freshen the air and big heavy curtains made the place bathe in half light.

Briefly, I explained why the SEDES was paying me with the money from the European Community. When I finished, the director moved a small bell and invited us to the armchairs. Almost immediately, a tall servant wearing a white jacket, white trousers and white gloves, but barefooted, entered through a lateral door I had not noticed.

- Mamadou, whisky for three.

The impeccable white jacket disappeared to reappear seconds later, with a silver plate which sustained a bottle of Walking Johnny black label, three glasses, a bucket with ice and a bottle of water. The colonials always have their whisky with water. The supreme chief of all this, Doctor Chevalier, pulled out his pipe, the signal to get my Blond Gauloise out of my pocket. Dragesic to end the introductions told me that he was of Yugoslav origin – what I had figured by his accent and specially his name.

- I, Mister Goffings, left Yugoslavia in a Russian tank, but which was moving to the West!

We all laughed, even Chevalier although I was sure that he had heard that story many times. It was more the way it was said than the story told that made us laugh.

Blowing a few clouds from his pipe, immediately filling up the place with a smooth, very sweet smell.- he smoked Amsterdamer that I too once had tried, before quitting the pipe for cigarettes, easier to carry and handle, Chevalier continued.

- With Doctor Dragesic, who is the chief of the veterinary post of Bongor, we were just talking about the vaccination campaign against the pest that has to be organized soon. We have some reports of small outbreaks of the disease in different places.

I had no idea that there was still pest in the country. According to FAO reports the disease had been eradicated a long time ago. On animal diseases I knew little, but that sounded serious.

- There is pest in the country?

Chevalier let escape a big blue cloud of Amsterdamer

- Yes, as you know, it is not dangerous for man, even the meat of sick animals can be eaten but it is very contagious among animals. If we don't act quickly it can be catastrophic for the herds.

Of course I didn't have a clue, but all the same shook my head as if it were all familiar to me. Chevalier talked professionally and after having blown to the ceiling the most beautiful blue cloud ever seen, kept talking.

- The cold chain to keep the vaccines at temperature almost disappeared completely. We have solicited the French government and they are sending eighty four petrol refrigerators; in fact they are already on their way.

Up to here everything seemed normal. I already had experienced that fifteen years of independence had finished with the equipment and the infrastructure of the Sahelian countries. I still did not see the point but in the back of my brain a dim light started to glow. After another cloud of Amsterdamer blown to the ventilators, Chevalier continued.

- Even the majority of the veterinary technicians have abandoned their posts; they have not been paid for over one year.

Dragesic showed impatience to enter the conversation. Turning to me he said:

- Mister Goffings, the veterinary colonial service got killed and do you know by whom?

- No, doctor, I don't know

- By three elements: The independence, the white woman and the air conditioner.

I was surprised. If I understood the first one, I did not get the two others. Noticing my surprise, he followed up after taking a sip from his whisky.

- The air conditioner softened the vets. Once the air conditioners in place, the vets were not anymore what they were before and the coming of the white woman to this country finished the job: they did not accept that their spouses absent themselves for months, running after the asses of the cows with vaccines.

We all laughed, but it was not untrue. The colonial vet, in charge of enormous territories, organized vaccination, curing and assistance campaigns roaming the country from nomad camp to nomad camp, from station to station, with a small caravan of camels and a goat herd. These caravans were composed of: his assistants, his cook, and the goat herders. These goats served for food but also for the fabrication of the antidote vaccine. A goat liver, buried and coming to

261

a certain degree of rotting decomposition is an excellent vaccine against the bacteria of the pest. These tours started with the first rains of the rainy season and finished with the beginning of the dry season.

I heard about extravagant vets who apart from their usual caravan took four more camels along charged with wooden cages full of earth in which they planted a vegetable garden to grow salads, tomatoes and other greens. Scurvy is not only a danger for sailors but also for the sailors of the desert.

Dragesic, with at least thirty years of colonial veterinary service, had been one of them. As some more, of whom I'll tell the stories, he belonged to these people who just could not return back to the mother country after dwelling in Africa for almost a lifetime, this was home to them. After "the independences" many of them got recycled in development agencies, established by the French government with their ex colonies. Many fell into something you can call "gone native", but nobody can put in doubt, and less so the herdsmen; that they are dedicated men, extremely reliable and exceptionally competent.

After the brief intervention of Dragesic, Chevalier spoke again. At this point we were enveloped in a blue cloud of tobacco smelling like caramels.

- There is a possibility that we can help each other if we combine the vaccination campaign with your census, what do you think?

I turned it rapidly around my brain, already a little bit cloudy with three walking Johnnies. The weak point of my census was how to approach the herdsmen. I had not come up with a response yet. It is nice to walk into a nomad camp with a sugar cone and some bags of tea and tell the chief that you are coming to count his herd. This will not work. But if you can add to the tea, that you have vaccines against the pest, that you came to vaccine his animals free of charge, things look quite different. They will get out the dancing girls and won't mind that you count - counting goes with vaccination- and ask some questions about the cows age and what became of the calves, how many died, and how many were kept or sold. Making a census with vaccines, looked immediately like a park walk and would make the census 90% more accurate.

- It appears to me, Doctors, that this is not only feasible but highly recommended. I am at your service.

Chevalier slowly took his pipe out of his mouth, smiled and said:

- Welcome to Chad.

A little ceremonially we stood up, lifted our glasses and made a toast to the success of our two projects: the national herd census and the national vaccination campaign.

This combination would give us complete access to all the veterinary posts in the country, their staff and tremendously valid information about local tribes and their behavior. I felt a lot better.

The following hours we talked about a thousand and one things in a very civilized way. Dragesic is a phenomenal optimist, exuberant and humorous. Not a few times I had to hold my stomach that was hurting from laughing so much.

Later, I would have occasions to visit him in his beautiful rat hole in Bongor, I'll tell you all about it. There was only one kind of people that he could not stand, who put him in a dark and mad mood: the Swiss. He hated profoundly the Swiss and very often made it known. The Helvetians to him were exploiters of the miseries of the European peoples in the war against the Germans. Not a single Swiss found grace in his eyes.

- To the country of crazy vets! added Dragesic. I, for my part, had problems keeping straight on my feet, the whiskies, the caramel clouds, the heat; were getting the best of me. While them, thirty years older, stayed straight as light poles.

My main problem, how to approach the tribes, just came to be resolved. Yet I was not going to be like Jack in Mali, who walked into the camps saying: "Good morning, I just drop in to count your cattle", with the result that the Malian cattlemen are still laughing. Mine would be: "Good morning. I came to vaccinate your cattle and it is free". They were going to receive us with songs of praise, slaughter sheep and goats, give us chicken, traditional dancing and for years will say good things about us. As head of a cattle census I was feeling a lot better.

The General Director of livestock in Chad was Touade, another vet coming from Maisons Alfort (France) after seven years of studying, one of which as a rural vet in the center of the country. He knew a lot more about France than I did. We were of the same age, became friends and buddies from our very first encounter. He belonged to the Sara tribe, the most powerful tribe in the agricultural south of Chad. Related to the President of the country, the also Sara General Malloum, who became President after a military coup, with the agreement of the all-powerful French chief of African Affairs: Monsieur Jacques Foccard. This man was charged by de Gaulle with decolonization of the French African colonies, this converted him into the President of the African Presidents. This was not difficult: he gave the African regimes a semblance of functioning, paying everything with the French taxpayer's money, from the military up to the teachers, including the complete civil service, the doctors and the nurses and their gasoline tickets.

The previous president of Chad, also a Sara, was Tombalbaye who got crazy and finished with the little cohesion existing between the animist-Christian tribes from the South and the Muslim cattle dwellers in the North by imposing on all his civil servants, including the Muslims, the initiation rites practiced in his tribe. He called it "Africanization" of public service and institutions. It mainly consisted of spending weeks in the bush to be initiated, instructed and humiliated by shamans and elderly Saras. Tombalbaye also renamed the towns to give them Sara names. Fort Archambault became Sarh in the south and N'djamena (meaning "The tree under which we rest") instead of Fort Lamy, by the name of the commander of colonial troops who founded the place. This latter name of course isn't very appropriate either, but it had the advantage of being neutral in a highly diversified tribal context, while the former is not.

This process of course did not please at all either to the Muslim part of the country, or to the ex colonial power that was paying for it. Tombalbaye was ousted by a military coup in which he lost his life. But the deed was done: the Muslim tribes refused the africanization Tombalbaye's style, and isolated themselves from the central government. The disintegration of the modern Nation-State, inherited from colonization – in Chad it only had lasted for eighty four years- accelerated and its prerogatives were recuperated by the tribal powers.

The difficulty of governing African countries has its origin in the stupidities committed by the first post-colonial elites. Everything returned to the sieve of the tribes. Elections degenerate into tribal bloody war, the latest cases are Kenya and Nigeria. I bet you that it is not going to be the last ones of the long list of barbarianism with which the tribes demonstrate their inability to build modern democratic nations.

Touade was married to a Princess of the old kingdom of Dahomey (today Benin) on the Guinean Gulf coast, he met in Paris in his student years: Geraldine looked, walked, behaved, talked like a Parisian. But for the moment she is Touade's wife and also Secretary to Malloum. Many times I asked myself what she was doing in this dusty, dirty town. An issue of course I never talked about with Touadé. Our trio, as the three musketeers, soon became four, with the joining of one of the couple's friends: Kasser, also ex-Parisian student but this time with a specialty as agricultural engineer. Kasser belongs to one of the Batha Arab tribes, up north. The three of them had been very familiar with all the African-Caribbean hangouts and night clubs in Paris. I wondered why an Arab from Batha became an agricultural engineer (there is no agriculture in the Batha region) while a Sara from the south became a vet (there are no cows in the south.) But that's the way it was among many other strange things. Later on, I understood that I could never understand the strange ways of African development when I discovered a huge and complete meat industry in Sarh (deep south) complete with: refrigerated slaughterhouse, huge cold and deep freeze storages, a hide factory, a canned meat factory, even a shoes factory (I already said that there are no cows in the south). About at the same time I discovered a peanuts oil factory in Abeche in the midst of the cattle region with almost no agriculture!

The story of these white elephants is simple: Tombalbaye is from Sarh, the Sara capital; therefore the meat industry complex – a gift from Germany and UNDP, (United Nations Development Program) is in Sarh. When the chiefs of the cattle tribes heard about this, they were not happy and complained. So the next factory (it just happened to be a peanut oil complex, gift from the Italian government) went to the town of Abeche up north to the Sudan border (where of course there are no peanuts plantations). Full stop. So, the country ended up with a meat industry in peanut country and a peanut oil factory in cattle country. That's the way the countries were governed in the first decades of independence. The French vets still joke about how the first thousand animals were sent to Sarh for the inaugural ceremony, a six hundred kilometer walk. Half of them died on the road and the other half arrived with just the skin over the bones. This was done in the rainy season, while Zebu cattle do not withstand mud, humidity and even less the deadly Tsetse fly. The day after the inauguration, the meat industry complex in Sarh was closed to never reopen again. The latest try to make this industry operational was still going on when I got to Chad. This consisted of building relay stations every twenty kilometers, all along the cattle trail to Sarh. These stations were made of a huge cement floor, a well and a vaccination corridor. This time it was the European Community that was paying. Once it all was done – for how many millions? – The developers discovered that cattle do not like to be parked on a cement floor heated by a tropical sun. Soon these cement plates turned into dance floors and parade grounds for all civic and patriotic events and as such were very useful. Never the idea of sending cattle down that trail became reality. No herdsmen risked their animals in that region.

However, we should not forget that the French vets also have their white elephants. The French government was persuaded to build a new cattle market on the outside of the capital. It was a good idea and prevented hundreds of heads of cattle every morning to race through the center of town to reach the cattle market, located on the edge of the big market place in the town center. The thing is that the French built the new market in the dry season. Only to find out that in the rainy season the market stood beneath half a meter of water.

That is the way that the development monies were spent and probably still are. To finish, let me tell you how, driving for hours on a muddy road in the south, approaching a village, all of a sudden we touched a five kilometers long, four lane cement road with public light poles. We had reached the village- merely three dozen huts- where Tombalbaye was born and where he had built a mansion he visited twice a year. Damsou told me that he had also asked for a jet plane runway, which he had no time to get.

African extravagancies? Or human stupidities? The governments of these times were like children who had received toys too big for them.

As my counterpart, Touadé assigned a veterinary technician by the name of Damsou; a soft man, in his thirties, a little overweighed and short, good humored, competent and with great common sense. He spoke Fulani and half a dozen of other languages and belonged to a small tribe established on the Chadian-Cameroon border. He was born in the town where the French Africans fought heavily the German Africans, in World War One (1914 to 1918). Fighting was heavy and bloody and lasted long after the peace was signed in Europe since nobody had heard of the German capitulation until months later when the English colonial Indian lancers presented themselves on the battlefield and informed the belligerents that Great Britain had recuperated the ex German colony.

For the following eleven years Damsou will be my companion, friend, accomplice, confident, ambassador, critic and teacher of tribal ethics. Many awkward situations in which I have a tendency of putting in myself, without him would have ended in catastrophes.

Finally, two months after my arrival in Chad, at the beginning of the rainy season, with us leaving N'djamena, the National Livestock Census started for real. Eight Land Rovers, carrying everything that was needed to run, for months, after the cow's asses of the Sahelian nomads of central and western Chad, made up the caravan and I was in charge.

Like on that occasion when I started my brief career as wood man and "tracer" in Ivory Coast, I felt again like Stanley looking for Livingstone.

The refrigerators of the veterinary stations were full of vaccines which shared the space with beers and Coca Cola. In many villages the petrol-refrigerator of the vet post was the only place, for many kilometers around, where a fresh beer could be found. Chevalier and Touadé had done their part.

Ati, capital of the Batha prefecture looks like two peas in a pod like Dori in Burkina Faso, maybe a little bigger and with two particularities. One: on the edge of the town stands a colonial military fort in the purest Sudanese style. It is a huge, imposing structure and could have come out of a Hollywood movie. The latest tenants were a section of the French Foreign Legion and a section of Meharists, the very imposing desert police. The second particularity of Ati is that it has a riverbed running through it. I have to say a riverbed, because it contains water only in the wet season, for eight months out of the year it is as dry as a laundry dryer. The river Batha runs from east to west; from the Sudanese border to Lake Batha in the middle of Chad. All the Chadian rivers turn their back to the sea and run inland. When the Batha runs, it runs like a mountain stream of about thirty meters wide and three deep. It is a very important landmark for the herder's transhumant system when they go north and when they come back south. Crossing the Batha is a strictly regulated affair. Going north, it indicates that the northern pastures, rich in minerals, are ready to receive about three million heads of cattle and that times of abundance have come. Milk flows in streams, the animals give birth, families and clans who have not seen each other in the dry season, meet and feast for marriages, to conclude new alliances, to harvest wild sorghum, to sow a few fields of sorghum left to the care of the elders and the small children who cannot keep up with the transhumant pace: they will be harvested upon their return. In the Sahel the rainy season has a perfume of Paradise!

I have to specify that for the Sahelian herdsmen, whatever tribe they belong to, livestock is not only a matter of survival, it is also, and maybe above all, a way to affirm one's social status in the clan. Isn't that so for all cattle people in the world? This implies that the economical exploitation of the herds is not the determining factor. They'll keep animals that should not be there and have nothing to do with a rational exploitation of the herds, taking into account the few natural resources the Sahel offers. The sentiments that exist between the herders and their animals are very strong. Selling an animal is like cutting off a part of their body.

Doctor Meyer, originally from the Southwest of France, was the chief of the vet station in Ati. He was not a relic of the French colonial veterinary service but a young graduate of Toulouse. Married to a beautiful woman of Gorane or maybe Zaghawa origin, I don't remember, but for sure she belonged to one of the few clans who did not practice on their young girls the amputation of the clitoris. (Later I will tell you how one night, I watched one of these barbarian ceremonies practiced on a seven year old girl). Meyer had three children, two boys and a girl, brown skinned and swimming pool blue eyed, with curled hair going towards blond. It is true that genetic mixing gives the most astonishing results.

With Meyer's assistance and knowledge, the Batha census was a piece of cake. We sent the word that we were vaccinating against the pest and the vets' post filled up with cattle from hundreds of kilometers all around. After some days of trying the system and forming the censors, I went with Damsou and three Land Rovers to install the Abeche and Biltine teams. Abeche, the most eastern town of Chad, and the last one before the Sudanese border. You may have heard or even seen Abeche in a report on the Darfour drama, since it is in Abeche that the Darfour refugee camps are.

I left one team in Ati in the keeping of Meyer and went with two teams in search of the clans and herds which had escaped and were moving north, spreading all over the pastures between Batha and the Sahara desert. Before starting this roaming I made a quick trip to N'djamena and back to welcome Annie who had not found a better idea than to come and spend her vacations counting cows between Batha and the Sahara.

Don't think that our census was just counting legs and dividing by four. The SEDES experts had invented a complete program of research which enabled to trace the productive history, evaluate the sanitary and death tolls, and predict the future productivity of the national herds. From each vaccinated herd several animals were selected and profoundly investigated: Age? Place of birth? How many calves? What happened to the calves? How many died? Of what? How many sold? Castrated? Where were they sold and for how much? Etc... All this done over the whole country should give a pretty precise idea of present and future wealth of the Republic of Chad.

Parisian, regardless of being born in Tunis, the adaptation capacity of Annie surprised me. After twenty-four hours one would have sworn that she had lived her whole life in a nomad camp just south of the Sahara desert. We taught her to ride camels and horses. I have no idea how, but she communicated and got along fine with the Misserie women and girls. Sleeping in a shack made of two poles and a woven straw carpet, isolating herself in the bush at night to satisfy natural needs, drinking sour milk and eating sorghum crepes, not washing, all that seemed natural for this usually Saint-Laurent dressed, high heeled, Parisian woman. She accepted everything with good humor and laughing as if she were living a good joke.

I don't remember where we were, but one early morning, before the dark eastern horizon became less dark, the interpreter woke us up with the news that, close to the camp, gazelle traces had been found and that a hunting party was getting organized. Less than half an hour later we were mounted on two camels in company of two more, four herders on horses and a bunch of dogs en route towards the glimpse of soft blue light of the eastern sky. I carried the only gun wondering how they hunt deer with spears and swords. In the end it turned out to be an exhausting pursuit. We followed the traces for hours until finally with the sun high above we saw the gazelles for the first time. They were Thompsons, with fine small horns, brown skin, with the characteristic black stripe on their back from neck to tail, looking at us. I got them in the line of the visor but with no heart to kill such beautiful animals I shot quite wide. They started running and jumping. The four horsemen started a pursuit, wildly galloping and shouting. We followed them as fast as the camels would take us. It took not much time before we caught up with the horsemen who had dismounted and surrounded two gazelles: I thought there had been four or five. When we got to them they had killed the animals that were exhausted, unable to move, with their lances. I did not feel very proud: this was not a particularly heroic way of hunting. It did not prevent us from eating it with taste that night in the camp with the girls singing and dancing. They did laugh at the fact that I had missed my shot. C´est la vie.

We moved to the north, leaving the Misserie country and into Toubou and Zaghawa territories. Here, the cattle were camel herds. Reception was correct and polite but not very friendly. The kidnapping (was it really one?) of Madame Claustre was about to end. You don't remember? A French female ethnologist was studying something in Faya Largeau- the desert capital and largest Oasis of the Tibesti mountain chain – when she was kidnapped by the Zaghawa rebel head Hissein Habré. It came out that the ethnologist and Hissein Habré (I'll tell you more about him) had known each other at the Sorbonne in Paris. It was never to be known whether this kidnapping was a political one or a romantic one. However things got a dramatic outcome when the French negotiator -an army captain- sent to negotiate her liberation, got assassinated by the rebels.

At that time Goukouni Ouedai, chief of a Toubou clan and Hissein Habré, a Zaghawa, joined forces to make up a rebellion against the central government in N'djamena. Later on, once they'll be the masters of Chad in Ndjamena they will fight each other furiously for ultimate power.

The head of a Toubou camp, veteran of the Meharist desert police, told us his story: As a young man he was sent by his father into the desert- with one water calabash – to find the lost camel he was supposed to herd and had lost. Keeping camels is somewhat hazardous. They just tie up the front feet and let it jump around the country searching its food. To get it back, days later, you just have to follow the tracks. After having roamed for weeks, he eventually found his camel in the herd of the Meharists' camels of the French army. The commander of the camp, who bought the camel from the thieves, agreed to give him back his camel in exchange of three months of work, washing his clothes and watering the palm trees of the camp. Some years later he went back to Faya to claim part of the dates of the palm trees he had watered, because desert law stipulates that the fruits of the palm trees belong to those who have watered them. Since nobody paid attention to him, he stayed, became a Meharist himself and learned some French.

Among the cultural values of the desert tribe there is one very peculiar: A youngster, to become a man and have some success with the girls of his tribe, has to have robbed at least one camel or having been put in jail for some time. On the matter of different moral values, here we have something.

Back to Ati with a metal trunk full of census documents, we found out that the European population of the place had tripled. A couple of young Belgian medics from *Médecins sans Frontières* had spread their straw carpet in the hospital which had not seen a doctor for a decade. Enthusiastic, very nice, dedicated to what they were doing, they reminded me that there was another world outside the Batha region and the livestock census. A world that still counted with generous young people who believe that humanitarianism is not only words.

270

The third evening we paid them a visit with two bottles of fresh beer. They were very nervous and told us that their very first day they had to do surgery cutting the leg of an elder with gangrene. This was the first time in their lives they made surgery. It had come out all right. What else could they have done? Before we left Ati, surgery had become a common practice to them. Great people, Greetings to them all.

One night we got into a strange conversation with three venerable elders, who asked very respectfully for an audience. We spread the carpet, borrowed from Meyer, and got ready for something I'll remember all my life. All were grey haired, which in Africa stands for a signal of wisdom, and were wearing their feast boubous richly embroidered with gold and silver thread; they even spoke very understandable French. Through the introductions I learned that two of them were veterans since they proudly stated their military grades. I was in the presence of one sergeant and a corporal, the third one was chief of a Misserie clan. We too looked swelling: Annie was wearing a red blouse and black trousers, on her breasts hung many colored shells held with a black string. I stood in my eternal blue jeans and eternal Sahara shirt but ironed and clean. After the ceremonial of introductions, we looked at each other for a while and sank on the cushions. A quarter moon and some stars were playing hide and seek with black clouds. The sergeant cleared his throat, the signal that he was going to speak.
- Doctor.
In these parts, when you have a white skin and you have something to do with livestock of course you are a "Doctor". He repeated:
- Doctor, when is Independence going to go away?
This was said with a grave ceremonial tone, slowly and well articulated. I looked at Annie who looked at me with the same blank eyes that I must have. Never had I dared to think that one day someone was going to ask me that question.
- Sergeant Mamadou – that was his name- you are asking me when Independence is going to finish?
- Yes Doctor, we'd like to know when Independence is going to finish?
- Sergeant why do you want Independence to end?
I called him sergeant out of respect and also because I saw that he liked it. Many are called Mamadou, none "Sergeant Mamadou".
A grave silence followed, even the grasshoppers that were making a fiesta in the nearby pasture to tell us that it was going to rain, got silent as if the whole world wanted to listen to this conversation.

271

- Doctor, before when there was the colony, everything was good, now everything is bad, marching on the head, and looking like shit.
- Tell me sergeant why everything was good in colonial times?
I thought this was close to the biggest absurdity that ever had passed my big ears. The other listeners got animated and came closer.
- In these times, Doctor, there were teachers in the schools and blackboards in the classrooms and chalk to write on the blackboards. Nowadays when the next teacher comes, the last one left five months ago; there is no blackboard and no chalk.
The civilian on his left side interrupted:
- For seven years there has not been a real school, with books and notebooks.
Mamadou cut him off:
-The hospital has not seen a doctor for more than ten years. No medicine, the Sara assistant nurse who stayed is no good, he has killed many people and is drunk all day long.
I fell from a big surprise into a bigger one. Mamadou went on:
- Before, there was a French judge who came every two weeks to speak the justice equal for all. Today all the justice is according to family's reputation and money, nobody is happy with this.
Then the corporal joined in and, after having made a large movement with his right arm to put part of his boubou on his shoulder, made his point.
- Before there was an airplane coming here twice a week and the road was maintained by the prisoners of the judge and with a tractor; there was electricity in the administrative quarter. Now everything turned to shit.
Mamadou again:
- Before, every Sunday the French Prefect assisted at the horse races. Today there are no more horse races.
Faraway thunder was rolling, The sky had become ink black as if it wanted to participate in the nostalgia of these old men, regretting old times of colonialism.
What could I say? They followed up with a long list of complaints, sometimes in French but out of plain excitement mostly in Arab. The civilian held his tea glass with his feet to liberate his hands and give more weight to his speech.
- The colony was good; things were in their right place and worked. The Independence is shit.
This seemed to be the final verdict. Never in my whole life had I dared to imagine that colonized people were going to sing the glory of colonialism. Within my dialectical scheme this was exclusively

reserved to the colonialists. These three old men were shattering all my patterns, all my references, and burdening my conscience.

I looked at Annie who looked at me like saying " I told you so", Her youth in Tunis, told to me as a marvelous fairytale, coincided with the glorification of "la coloniale" just as I came to hear here in the Sahel outskirts. I turned to her and asked to go for a bottle of whisky.

Their discussion went on, in form of monologues recounting stories and deeds of the marvelous times when the French administrated them with laws to be respected, laws made five thousand kilometers to the North in the white men's country who just happened to pass an abortion law very respectful of women's liberties; of the marvels of education which taught that all are born equal in rights and that their ancestors were the Gallic tribes.

Years later I read some documents of the colonial archives and discovered that in the case of the Sahelian colonies the accounts were very bad. The colonial adventure in these parts had cost a lot of money to the French taxpayer. Why did they do it, if there was nothing to be gained? This did not correspond to the average vision of: colonialism equals plundering, as it was the case in Latin America plundered by the Spanish crown. There is nothing to be plundered between the eastern border of Senegal and the western border of Sudan, besides having raised some troops who heroically fought in European wars, the survivors of which were deploring   that colonization had come to an end. What else? Why did they do it?

A short explanation can be given considering that the irrational romanticism of the European powers valued "land" as the source of political power (which it is not anymore) even if this "land" was made of mainly sand dunes.

What was happening to the Nation-State when the Nation is made up of a conglomerate of tribes who kill each other for a well, access to a pasture, an election, and religious beliefs, or simply because the tribe next door is hated for old reasons nobody quite remembers? What the hell were the colonizing countries looking for in countries like Chad, or Niger, Burkina, Mali and others?

Annie came back with the whisky bottle which I gave to the sergeant. With a big smile he filled up the tea glasses. I cleared my throat to signify that I was going to speak.

- Gentlemen, I believe that Independence is here to stay.

They did not weep but their faces told me that they did not like that at all. Looking down Mamadou with a low voice said:

- That's what we are afraid of.

A dog started barking not far away.

- And you? Sergeant Mamadou, filling the glasses looked up again.
- What about us?
- You brought vaccines for the livestock and are not charging. The white medics have come back to the hospital. Doctor Meyer also has come back.
- Right, so what?
I did not see what he was aiming at. After a long moment charged with silence:
- We thought that the Independence had finished.
I could not keep from laughing. They were taking us for the Messias who had brought back colonialism.
- This is not the way it is Sergeant.
- Then what is it?
I could not give a course on the mechanisms of post-colonialism, neither on neo-colonialism, about Independence supposedly wanted by all the peoples, about how the National governments were stealing the monies and giving nothing to them in return; about the French who thought they were acquitting themselves of the bad conscience of having been a colonial power. Etc…
- The Chadians wanted independence and de Gaulle gave it to them.
That was all I could think of. Hearing the name of de Gaulle, the "Great Charles" as they called him, provoked big eyes and smiling faces. I thought that they were going to stand, salute and sing the Marseillaise. Fortunately, they did not and held on to their whisky tea glasses.
- I saw him, said the caporal
This was a nice diversion and got me out of something I did not see the outcome of.
- Oh yes, where?
- Here in Massaguet.
It is a small village with a big cattle market, at the crossing of the roads from N'djamena going north to Moussoro and Algeria and east to Sudan. The caporal pursued:
- I was a soldier with Leclerc.
This could well be so. Weeks later we would sleep in a village where we were saluted by a huge mulatto woman, who pretended that she was de Gaulle's daughter, who supposedly had passed the night here with her mother. I did not believe her but it is true that she was the right age, that she was a mulatto and huge like her supposed progenitor.
- I was in Tobruq and in Monte Cassino, went on sergeant Mamadou emptying his fourth cup.

- Tell us sergeant.

Definitively, I was out of my Messiah's role. The moods were getting light and pleasant. Tobruq, on the Libyan-Egyptian border, is the place of a famous battle fought by the allies against the Nazis and Italian fascists commanded by Rommel. After this, in very crude terms he chained on with the Monte Casino slaughtering, a monastery on top of a mountain, controlling the southern access to Rome. For the Nazis, to lose Monte Cassino was to lose Italy, so they opposed a fanatical resistance to the allies who fought in open fields, moving uphill. The battle lasted for days and weeks, on both sides it became savage and ended up with body fighting with bayonets. Sergeant Mamadou confirmed all this.

We finished the bottle. Annie had fallen asleep, the petrol lamps, one by one dimed their soft light. Close, from the east, thunder was rumbling and lightning flashing. The last thing I saw from these three strange nostalgic souls of colonial times, was their slightly curbed backs very insecurely disappearing into the night.

The next day, Damsou showed up having left a census team in Abeche and another in Biltine. There was lack of vaccines; he brought two cases of perfectly classified documents. Almost 80 % of the Misserie families who were on our list had been counted. We decided, with two teams, to open the eastern part of the country opening two camps: one in Moussoro in the Barh el Ghazal, Gorane territory, and another in Bol on the slopes of Lake Chad. From these camps they also had to cover the Kanembou kingdom territory. Needless to specify that the "Barh el Ghazal" (river of the deer), had not seen any water for hundreds of years. I even supposed, since it runs north-south, that the last time it was wet was when the Sahara was a tropical rain forest. But I guess that's an exaggeration. When I saw it, the "Barh el Ghazal" was just a stone bed, sometimes fifty meters wide.

It happens that the Kanembou are governed by an authentic king, vassal to the king of Sokoto in Nigeria. So, I had to make a protocol visit to his majesty. Seen from the distance, Mao is a town escaped from the Bible; it could have been Jericho in the year 3,000 before Christ. Walls made of mud and straw, with only two entrances, square houses of two floors above which sprung several mosque towers and the still higher towers of the king's palace. Here we were not walking in the Bible for environmental or architectonic reasons but also for social and political ones. This was, in all ways, equal to any

275

dusty, sundried, dirty town of the Bible, donkeys, dogs and humans included. This is the real stuff of Jesus's country.

Entering the palace compound, under a huge arch, I noticed to the left a garage with fully automatic opening doors, with a shining Range Rover and a black Mercedes Benz, latest model. The Range Rover, yes I do understand, but the Mercedes? Of course anybody displays his social status as he pleases, and for the King of the miserable Kanembou people, that was to have a Mercedes Benz sitting in his garage with an automatic door, in the middle of the desert. There was not one road hundreds of kilometers around a Mercedes could be driven on.

The bastard of king made us wait for two full hours, sweating big drops in a waiting room, carpeted from floor to ceiling, with two standing ventilators that were not working. This was the way he wanted to show me who was the king? Of course it was out of the question to bring along a woman to this date: Mister King is a fanatic Muslim. So Annie had stayed behind at the veterinary post. I did not like at all the way we were treated, after all we were going to vaccinate his cattle and the herds of his court for free.

The same night we left Mao, politely declining the king's invitation to stay in one of the dependencies of his palace. I preferred to spend the night under the open sky than in a suffocating palace, having to make conversation with an obese pig, with grease hanging in pockets under his small vicious eyes. Damsou told me that he had over seventy spouses. The image that stayed was that of the black shining Mercedes and of the spear and dagger equipped guards.

On the shores of Lake Chad we discovered a race of cattle unique in the world and never seen before. The particularity is that instead of horns they wear globes on their heads: some measure more than half a meter in diameter. These globes are made of fibers which enclose small air compartments, that's why they are very light and of great floatability. They are called the "Kuri" of Lake Chad. These horns are the result of an evolution process running back for hundreds of thousands years and are due to the fact that these animals pass almost all their lives in the lake, only coming out of the water to graze for a few hours a day. The balloons on their head serve as floaters: once in the water you only see their nostrils. Lake Chad is the kingdom of mister mosquito: from the beginning of the afternoon they invade the shores in such quantity and opaque clouds that you cannot see farther than a few meters thus obliging every living mammal to seek shelter in the water, under a mosquito net or, as the people do around here who don't have the money to buy a net, stand or sleep wrapped in a cloud of smoke coming from a wood fire with green leaves.

If Darwin, for some reason or another, hadn't gone to the Galapagos isles but had come to Lake Chad instead, he would have built his evolution theory on the Kuri cows and not on the Galapagos turtles. For sure, the small transhumant herds with their Zebu cows and normal horns will never come close to the lake which is dangerous for the animals, and so preserved a certain genetic purity of the Kuri herds.

For the last days of Annie's vacations we decided to install the first census team of the southern region in Bongor and start the intermediate zone between the northern transhumance and the southern peasant region and of course headquarters of Doctor Dragesic.

Even if Bongor is not that far from N'djamena, the roads at the end of the rain season look more like freshly plowed fields than a transit device. So we got there at nightfall. Bongor is very extended with circular houses, with mud walls and palm leave roofs, all together it looks very much like Kangaba in Mali. It lays on the right bank of the river Logone which unites with the Chari in N'djamena. All along, these two rivers are home to many hippopotamus families including two in the center of N'djamena. Here in Bongor, the Logone is also the Chad - Cameroon border, as is the Chari in N'djamena.

After having left the team in their dwellings, as night had fallen Annie and I went looking in the dark for Dragesic's headquarters. These were easy to find, at the outskirts of town, in the form of a majestic alley bordered by dozens of huge flowering flamboyant trees which, after a hundred meters, gave way to a circular plaza in which a trailer could move around. Never, in my whole life I'll see again such a beautiful, long and flowered driveway as the one leading to the veterinarian station in Bongor. Coming into the plaza, appeared all of a sudden in the lights of the jeep, a huge metal cage made up of mosquito net with, in the middle of it, a petrol lamp and seated on a chair, completely naked, playing the accordion: Doctor Dragesic. Turning off the lights and the motor, a keen melancholic accordion melody filled the plaza. We just kept quiet and did not move. For twenty minutes we listened to Slavic songs of which I only recognized: Sunset in Moscow and the Volga boatmen. The doctor was a good accordion player.

The Hedonist

*

On my first exploration trip with Damsou to Moussoro, I already had experienced another extravagancy of this type. I was told that in one of the dwellings, a French ex- legionnaire had installed him with four wives, many children and a very well kept vegetable garden. We made a side trip to salute him, because desert ethics require that if you pass at less than fifty kilometers from a white man's house you have to go and say hello. If you don't comply with that rule, for as long as you live they will never talk to you anymore - and one never knows, one day maybe you'll need some help in the desert. Mister Legionnaire was not at home, but a boy told us that he was: "off to Paris as he did every Sunday" and raising his arm showed a vague direction saying "Over there"... We followed a path for a couple of kilometers and fell head upon a DC3 fuselage which apparently had made an emergency landing there maybe decades ago. One wing was missing. In the pilot seat sat the legionnaire, with his women behind and a bunch of kids sticking their heads out of the small square windows. We watched the "flight and landing". I presume that's what we did, since nobody came out of the plane to greet us. Finally, the legionnaire extracted him from the cockpit, dressed up in his full parade uniform, very impressive with a long white cape, high white cap and four bars of decorations on his chest. Coming to us standing beside our jeep, he gave us an impeccable military salute with palms outside, shook my hand very tight and said with the greatest natural tone of the world:
- We went to fly over Paris with the family. The Arch of Triumph, the Eiffel tower, the Ministry of War, the Concorde and the Invalides.
Something told me that I'd better play along:
- How was the weather?
- Excellent: not a cloud in the sky. Over Orleans we had a few air holes, nothing worth talking about.
We climbed into the jeep and drove back. For the rest of the conversation and behavior, the legionnaire was perfectly normal, even intelligent, funny and good mannered.

*

Dragesic put his instrument carefully on the floor, wrapped a towel around his waist and came out of the cage heading towards us.

278

He saluted warmly, but by the red of his eyes I saw that he had wept. Nostalgia is a very heavy burden to carry.

At first, you don't see the house: you just see an enormous bougainvillea of different colors towards which we started advancing. Dragesic's house was completely covered by a bougainvillea.

The reception of Dragesic's wife was grandiose. She was what one can call a "Norman wardrobe", huge and massive and even if neither I nor Dragesic can be called small, she was a full head taller than us. She had abundant long blond hair falling on her shoulders and bright blue eyes. Without complex, Dragesic told us that he had encountered his wife in the advertisements of the "Chasseur Français" i.e. the French Hunter, a monthly magazine specialized in hunting tips and matrimonial ads for rural isolated bachelors. While his wife went to prepare "some snacks, because we dine lightly" the doctor took us on a house tour. On the back, the house had a large terrace, overlooking a garden finishing at the Logone river shore, from where hippopotamus noises were heard. The whole premises were well illuminated by an electric plant hidden somewhere in the dark and hardly heard. My attention was caught by a bed standing on wheels and four poles from which hung a mosquito net that stood on the terrace. Looking closer, there were also several cement blocks hanging from ropes. Seeing that I was intrigued, Dragesic laid on the bed, pulled a rope and the bed started to move, riding into the house through a double door. Incredible, the guy had invented a mobile bed by way of a system of weights and counter weights. He laughed much at our surprise saying that sometimes they liked to sleep outside and if by accident it rained, the bed just moved into the house with them on it.

The "snacks" and "light dinner" of Madame Dragesic turned out to be a feast with: pheasant pâtés, pork head jelly and foie gras for the entrees. Then: rabbit, ratatouille, pieces of beef cooked in red wine, chicken with mint and herbs, homemade bread. Later on: tartlets *flambé au Grand Marnier*, floating island, coffee and cognac. During the meal they did not close their mouths for a second; they talked and talked each in turn between two mouthfuls of food. It must be that occasions to talk were few. They owned an apartment close to the Champs Elysees in Paris. When in Paris, the doctor used to take great pleasure sitting on a café terrace on the Champs to admire women and girls in miniskirts walking by, of whom he gave picturesque and funny descriptions. Occasionally, she would interrupt him with a dry "Dragi that's enough" with the effect that we changed the subject just to come back in a few minutes later to   the legs, the bottoms and the breasts of Parisian women and tourists of whom he made exact descriptions of their dressing, walking and looking according to their nationality.

When the moment came that, after a day of jeep riding, we could not take any more eating, drinking, laughing and talking, Dragesic got up and taking, in a casual way, some magazines from a low table, handed them over to me saying "something to read" he showed us to our room wishing us a good night.

Once on the large bed, I remembered the magazines. On top of the pile there was" Catholic Life" under it, "The French Hunter" and then "Vogue", "Playboy" and "Hustler".

Why did this selection surprise me? Some rare intuition surged in my brain, but what? Hustler was very suggestive with pages and pages of oral sex, lesbians caressing and kissing, full mouthed and tongue whirling. These are some of the things that, even full of food and tired provoke a reaction. Almost in an automatic way I started caressing the body beside me, who responded with enthusiasm. However, something was holding me back, preventing me to freely express myself, but what? After a few minutes I knew it, I felt being observed. We had heard how Dragesic and his wife had talked in the room next to ours, how they had gone to bed. Automatically, I started to examine the opposite wall, turning on the side with one hand sustaining my head and with the other caressing the legs, belly, hips and shoulders next to me. I got concentrated on two small black spots that were not in harmony with the wallpaper, they were of the size of a pencil. The Dragesics were spying on us. I got up and in my Adam outfit went to turn off the light. It was not going to be the Doctor Dragesic who was going to spoil a love night, even if this had to happen in the dark and in silence, which is very difficult.

All the white people traveling from N'djamena to the south passed in the bed I was lying on: civil servants, missionaries, nuns, teachers, engineers etc... We laughed at the perverse pleasure of this special couple spying on missionaries and nuns discovering the Playboy review under Catholic Life and masturbating with Hustler. In the morning I looked it over, yes there were two pencil-sized holes in the wall.

Not minding, Annie decided to pass her last days of vacation with the Dragesics, which enchanted them. In the morning I had a date with the census team in the veterinarian station. Annie stayed with Dragesic's wife. At my recommendation to take care not to be raped, she laughed and said that maybe she'd like it.

To my surprise, I found a herd of about a hundred heads ready to enter the vaccination corridors, with vet technicians with white blouses and surgical masks over their faces. Asking what this was about, a vet nurse told me that every time someone from the veterinary services came to Bongor the Doctor made up this show. He also told me that the animals ready to get vaccinated had their butts like a strainer for having been vaccinated so much.

The livestock of this region is in majority domestic, oxes pulling plows or wagons, a few cows and fewer calves. Camels had disappeared from the flock, so had horses. On the contrary, sheep and goats were abundant. All this made the census easy.

*

Bongor is not anymore an exclusive Islamic territory, even if here and there some mosque towers barely bypass the roofs. The majority of the people here are Christians from the American churches, Catholics and even more often animists. This can be noticed in the ambience and the faces of the people. As said an old friend "Where Islam disappears, merriment appears." One feels better in this atmosphere, freer, looser, lighter, than in the heaviness of Muslim tribe camps where a book written in the years 600 (dictated by an angel to an illiterate camel driver, they say) decides and regulates the details of daily life, constantly under the vigilant, judging eye of the whole community.

Of course, the peaceful Sahelian tribesmen are not fully aware of the fundamental violent character of their religion. They just expect to go to Paradise and that there will be nobody at the door to prevent them from going in, even if that somebody is a dog he involuntarily killed in a traffic accident. They will refuse to admit that Muslims can steal planes and crash them into buildings with the only objective to kill as many people (including Muslims) as possible. However, it is not because of the passivity of the Sahelian tribesmen that we can deny the extreme violence written in the two hundred and fifty verses, justifying killing anyone who does not believe in the Islamic story. This would be like denying the extermination of the American Indians by their Very Catholic Majesties the Kings of Spain, because of the writings of Father De las Casas, who tried to convince their majesties that the American Indians were some sort of Negroes and therefore, almost human: the tree that hides the forest.

The history of Islam is a story that denies history. This generates a society completely closed, denying the dynamics of evolution, putting history beyond time. Applying the Koran concepts is converting society and the world into a nomad camp, unchanging, unmovable. This is the extreme opposite of a democracy which lives from movement, dialectics, dialogue, reason and diplomacy, tolerance, abolition of censure, combat against tyrants, abolition of state religions, freedom of expression, adoption of equal rights, the will of happiness here and now etc... Islam is at the opposite of all this, it lives and proclaims immobility, irrationality and death.

At the age of conquering the space, of global information in real time all over the planet, of the codification of the human genome under the goat hides tents the center of the universe is the family. It is not the national community, less the human community but the head of the family and his many children who are the only skyline, the center of the universe. This authority stems from Allah, of course, but through the father and the husband, personification of God under the goatskin tent. All action is lived under the suspicious eye of the community who judge of the conformity of individual behaviour in the smallest details. The father but also the older brothers, the uncles and the other males of the family reign over the life of the females.

There are two hundred fifty verses of the Koran that legitimate the holy war against the "non believers". These are enough to drown the few verses inviting to tolerance, respect of the others, equality, liberty. The life of the prophet testifies this barbarism: punitive expeditions, crimes, assassinations, thousands passed by the sword. These pages are enough to legitimate for every Muslim to kill the "non believers". As the Jews, the believers in Islam proclaim to be "God's elected people". Unfortunately for us, two "elected peoples" is one too many. Believing that God himself established a hierarchy among mankind – first come the Muslims, than the Christians because they too are "people of the book", then come the Jews, because they are monotheists, and then what is left, put on the bottom as "non believers" among whom the polytheist, the philosophers and of course the atheists – this justifies killing a lot of people and if not killing them to despise them in a most barbarian way.

Inside the community, hierarchy is heavily enforced: the men dominate the females, the mullahs the believers, the devoted believers the weak believers, the elderly the younger. This phallocratic organization is fundamentally incompatible with modern society. "Muslims are not fraternal: brother to the fellow believer, yes, but not to anybody else who do not count for anything and are despised " (M.Onfray).

This logic of dividing all humanity into: included and excluded was implicated as soon as the 11th century when the Caliph from Baghdad imposed on the Jews, the Christians and the Zoroastrians to show distinctive signs (a yellow star or a yellow turban or scarf). Theoretically, Islam shows itself as a tolerant religion. Don't believe it. To have the right to live in an Islamist country one had to pay a special tax, to show distinctive signs and respect special rules such as not having the right to possess a horse (in a time when horses permitted to exist, move, work). You could walk in the street but had no right to pass a Muslim. Of course, having arms was strictly forbidden (this put you at the mercy of any bandit). These rules were abandoned in the year 1839 by the Turkish Empire but still persist in the heads and minds.

Islam, as all the theocracies, functions backwards: they live of immobility, of irrationality; they are the most dangerous enemies of democracies of all times.

All the intellectuals of all the western democratic nations got it wrong when Ayatollah Khomeini came to power in Iran in 1978 and established a theocracy with eighty thousand Mullahs, inaugurating a real Islamic fascism, very consequent and in conformity with the writings of the Koran. All theocracies - and specially the Muslim - aspire to bring to an end the separation of private beliefs and public organization. Religion – a matter of one with oneself – wants to conquer the totality of what life is made of. There is no room in a theocracy for a direct, secret, personal, mystic relation of one with his God, but a chain of command directed by the poltical chiefs and related to the government. At this point; religion ceases to be a personal matter to become a matter of State. The State at the service of an idea: an idea of the family, the work, the school, the military barracks, the hospital, the press, sexuality, the stadium, culture etc....All this at the service of the dominant ideology.

How to ensure the totalitarian use of the sacred writings? Simply just pretend that you possess the only legitimate way to interpret them. Muslim theocracy is the maximum possible cohesion in the matter of religion. It contradicts all the philosophical and social progress made since the 16th century : condemnation of superstition, abolishment of censure, fighting tyranny, the end of state religion, freedom of speech and thought, the adoption of equal rights, the will of a social wellbeing here and now, the reign of reason, all clearly denied all along the Koran verses.

The Hedonist

The Muslim collectivity imposes the sacrifice of singularity to the benefit of the collectivity. Enclosing everything into the global political corpus, justifies the sacrifice and the martyrdom of an individual. All this allows the follower to disappear as an individual and operates a transmutation in the mystical community in a sublime way, for eternity. This is the theory that makes the "human bombs" with their explosive belts. It is not the fault of humanity that our contemporary Muslims are on the fascist side and not on the religious, cultural tolerant side of history as were their fellow believers who conquered and administrated for eight centuries the country of the vandals (Andalusia) bringing along a tolerant and harmonious way of living with Christians and Jews. It is the responsibility of the Islam community that the Mullahs from Iran, the Taliban and Al Qaeda do not look at all as the Caliphs of Andalusia who governed with tolerance, peaceful cohabitation, science and progress. (We have to note that this tendency could have taken Islam on a completely other road, but it was wiped out by the very catholic kings of Spain, especially Isabel, who oriented Spain into the black ages of the Inquisition.)

As M. Onfray says: "Whether we like it or not, the XXI century opens with a merciless battle between different gangs: on one side the Judeo-Christian civilization - brutally capitalist, mercantile, consumerist, nihilist, harsh with the weak and weak with the strong, fascinated by money source of all powers, generator of marginalization, poverty and misery for a good part of the human community, in one word the triumph of the merchants. The communist variety finally came out not to be very different. In the opposite corner: the Islamic world - brutally intolerant, violent, and devout, conqueror, fascist. Both sides proclaim that they are on God's side. Which side to choose? Do we have to choose? Caress the arrogance of one to fight the Barbary of the other? Staying on the side is impossible, with the risk to lose part of the human conscience". To be franc, having lived on both sides I prefer the first option. There is more future and change possibilities in movement than in immobility. There is no future in Islamic theocracies.

The Sahelian Muslim herdsmen, live, think and die exactly the same way their ancestors did, in times when a camel herder by the name of Muhammad circulated in the Arabian Peninsula. In Sudan and Somalia lovers are still stoned to death and in Palestine (Gaza) we witnessed how 450 around 25 years old men got collectively married to 450 seven years old female children, because the prophet Muhammad also got married to a 6 years old child and, according to Jomeini the spiritual leader of Iran, a father who gives his child to marry at such an early age goes straight into heaven. Also in the same Islamic Republic of Iran, one of their holy men proclaims that the students who manifested their discontent with their government should be murdered: "All those who oppose to the Islamic government are enemies of Islam and should be killed". If you want to know more about daily Muslim immobility just turn on the tv, the radio or read a newspaper.

*

In the last four months of the cattle census I went all over the huge country as far north as Koro-Toro on the road to Faya. There, I noticed that something bad was cooking for the central government. The rebellion of the northern tribes, around the axis Toubou-Zaghawa was not folklore anymore, but got to be an efficient military organization armed and sustained by Colonel Khadafi, master of Libya. There were all kinds of armaments all over the place and many dozens of new Toyota jeeps too. "War Taxes" were being raised in places as far south as Moussoro, Ati, Mao and the Lake. They did not bother me, after all I was vaccinating their meager livestock, but they did not hide either. My skin color still did impose some respect but Damsou was feeling very uncomfortable, they thought he was a Sara from the tribe of the President they were fighting. I sent him back to N'djamena and I stayed alone with the local team to finish the census and the vaccination campaign.

In all this whirling around the country I passed a few times through the capital for food and money. A couple of times I was lucky to accompany the "Payer" of the French Embassy, also running all over the country every trimester, to pay the war veterans' pensions. He provoked many vocations. Every boy encountered and asked what he wanted to be in life, invariably answered "war veteran". I have to say that a big part of the circulating money in the towns and villages originated in the veterans pensions. The "payer's" caravan was made up of: one jeep full of soldiers, waving their guns, another one with the payer and his secretary and another with more soldiers waving guns. Then followed a truck or two, loaded with everything you can possibly dream of that is sold in African villages from soap to plows. After this, one or two trucks of "Gala" the local beer and at the end, sometimes kilometers behind, a herd of young bulls – to become oxes - pushed by young Peul herdsmen.

I sent three big trunks full of census documents to the experts of the SEDES so they could have some fun over there. My employee's contract would finish with three months of studying these and writing up the final document.

A couple of days before leaving, around the eternal whisky-ice-water, around the pool of the hotel "La Tchadienne", Touade, the administrator of every mammal on four legs in the country, with a nostalgic voice started:

- Now you know more than anybody about our livestock.

This was possible because civil servants and politicians usually don't know very much. He took a long sip of his drink as if wanting to wash away something in his throat.

- It could be. As a matter of fact, I think you are right.

We kept silent; the night was fresh and pleasant. Some tourists were splashing water in the pool. A few yards away, one table was occupied by officers of the Foreign Legion.

I did not know how to continue this conversation.

- What do you suggest?

He took another big swallow of the brown-yellowish mixture which sometimes makes me think of horse's piss, the ice cubes tinkling against the glass, which is a pleasant sound. Putting down his glass he looked straight at me:

- That you stay and help us make something out of all this.

"All this" was: around five million heads of cattle; over nine million sheep and goats; also: two hundred thousand camels and seventy thousand horses. This was the result of the livestock census we were finishing. Compared to the Chadian population; every living soul would have a cow and two goats. We were pretty far from the extinction of the national herd by effects of the drought which was feared by the European Community developers.

Another time he raised his glass

- How many do we have?

I took a drink to give me time to think.

- There are more cattle than people.

- Yes, but they don't vote.

This was a joke since during the fifteen years of Independence nobody had ever voted in the Republic of Chad. Touadé leaned back laughing at his own joke which made the legionnaires look in our direction. I thought I had to say something.

- If you think that only one third of the population is dedicated to raising livestock you have four cows and eight sheep and goats per head, women and children included.
He looked at me surprised.
- That's a lot!
- In any case, much more than the Argentineans who built their development on cattle and got rich.
From the garden of the French ambassador's residence neighboring the Tchadienne, we heard the pop-pop of tennis balls meeting rackets.
After a deep sigh, Touade followed up:
- What can we do?
- There are many things that can be done with such a huge amount of potential wealth. Anyway, it is just not right, nor acceptable, that people live in misery with this on their hands. Here you have to set your imagination going.
A woman in the swimming pool, to my left, had looked in our direction several times. She wore a black bikini showing generous breasts. Even if this had not escaped from Touade, he went on:
- We are like donkeys charged with bulks of water, dying from thirst.
- Something like that. That is a good metaphor.
- Have any precise ideas?
I called the waiter and ordered a beer. Yes I had some ideas.
- Yes I do.
Touade moved to the edge of his chair, lighted up a cigarette, I did the same.
During twenty minutes I explained an idea that was traveling in my brains since I had seen the first Chadian herds, encouraged by my companion's expression, who did not lose a second of it. The Chadian herdsmen possessing a real treasure were living in misery because they knew nothing about commerce and the real value of the millions of legs they were walking around the Sahel zone. At the end of the rain season they have to sell off part of their herds because they fear that the animals are not going to survive the dry season when pastures and water are scarce and thus submitted to heavy competition from their fellows and kin. Every excess of heads is a matter of dispute and struggle – often bloody – so they sell off part of the herd to the intermediaries at very low prices because everyone is doing the same thing at the same time. The majority of these buyers are Nigerians who take the cattle walking in huge herds as far as the big cities on the shores of the Gulf of Guinea: Douala, Lagos, Cotonou, Accra and Abidjan, all big consumers of cattle meat. This is

one thing. On the other hand, in spite of being a cattle country, in the dry season meat prices raise sky high, preventing ninety percent of the people from having access to meat products.

The idea I laid out was a regulation mechanism. The creation of a regulation authority in form of a mixed - private and State owned - company. In this latter, the private shareholders would dispose of a legal export quota and pay for a sanitation certificate before crossing the Chari River into Cameroun. With that money, at least one of the three enormous stock ranches that existed previously and were presently abandoned by the colonial companies that had worked along more or less the same scheme could be reactivated. At this moment, the ranches were state owned. These ranches would act as price regulators, buying up livestock at the end of the rainy season and injecting them into the market in the dry season. A fast calculation had shown that the company could pay the herdsmen as much as three times the price that actually the Nigerian intermediaries were paying, including, a nice profit margin. Part of the cattle guarded in these stock ranches would go for export while the other part would go to serving a chain of popular butcher shops in the city quarters, making meat available in the dry season at a very reasonable price.

After this, I had a dry throat and ordered another Gala. Touade let himself fall in the back of the chair, looking at me smiling.
- That is what we have to do he said looking at something way above my head. I laughed and said:
- Do it!
- No, no: you are going to do this!
Here things were getting more serious.
- How I am going to do this? This is your country, your people.
- Sure, but it looks better to me if we would do this together.
One hour later, the young woman having disappeared, not without giving me a most beautiful smile, the SOTERA company ("Societé Tchadienne d'Exploitation des Ressources Animales") was created in our heads. A mixed company, private-state owned, for the good of the Chadian people. Our enthusiasm was that of children on a Christmas morning. As Touade was insisting and insisting, I agreed to delay my departure for a couple of days.
When I finally got on the UTA jet plane, we had planned the formal creation of the company: its constitution, registration, the incorporation of major cattle traders and the liberation by the government of one domain for stocking the cattle had to be completed before I'd come back to Chad. How soon? That depended on how fast they could handle all this.

EPILOGUE TO BOOK 1

My dear friends (maybe after having navigated together through three hundred and some pages, we can call each other, with what I consider, is the most beautiful word of our vocabulary), here I close the first book. I hope you keep enjoying it and thinking about things and circumstances that have brought us together- you and I. Things from which nobody escapes even if it does not look that way and we pretend they do not exist.

On my side, telling the story and dialoguing with you made me enthusiastic to the point that I just decided to add another book and, if you wish so, go together over the years that we still have ahead.

What is going to follow is the end of the Chadian story which is going to last eleven years and a brief but significant incursion on the Congo River and forest, the return to Europe and the apprenticeship as fish farmer, my present trade. A second Cuban period and the establishment in Mexico where I keep learning to write in this wooden cabin on the shores of the Mexican Gulf you already know. All this wrapped up in a spiritual road I would like to keep walking with you.

I hope to meet you soon again and in the meantime: Good luck with your life.

The Hedonist

J-P Goffings

The Hedonist

Made in the USA
Charleston, SC
06 March 2011